SOCIAL PROBLEMS
AND
SOCIAL POLICY:
The American Experience

THE
National Purity Congress

ITS PAPERS, ADDRESSES, PORTRAITS

EDITED BY
AARON M. POWELL

ARNO PRESS

A New York Times Company

New York — 1976

Editorial Supervision: SHEILA MEHLMAN

———◆———

Reprint Edition 1976 by Arno Press Inc.

Reprinted from a copy in the Princeton University Library

SOCIAL PROBLEMS AND SOCIAL POLICY: The American Experience
ISBN for complete set: 0-405-07474-3
See last pages of this volume for titles.

Manufactured in the United States of America

———◆———

Library of Congress Cataloging in Publication Data

National Purity Congress, 1st, Baltimore, 1895.
   The National Purity Congress.

   (Social problems and social policy--the American
experience)
   Reprint of the ed. published by the American Purity
Alliance, New York.
   1. Prostitution--United States--Congresses.
2. United States--Moral conditions--Congresses.
I. Powell, Aaron Macy, 1832-1899. II. American Purity
Alliance. III. Series.
HQ103.N27 1895a   301.41'7973   75-17238
ISBN 0-405-07507-3

THE
National Purity Congress,

ITS PAPERS, ADDRESSES, PORTRAITS.

AN ILLUSTRATED RECORD OF THE PAPERS AND ADDRESSES OF
THE FIRST NATIONAL PURITY CONGRESS, HELD UNDER
THE AUSPICES OF THE AMERICAN PURITY ALLI-
ANCE, IN THE PARK AVENUE FRIENDS'
MEETING HOUSE, BALTIMORE, OCTO-
BER 14, 15 AND 16, 1895.

———————

EDITED BY
AARON M. POWELL,
PRESIDENT OF THE AMERICAN PURITY ALLIANCE.

———————

NEW YORK:
THE AMERICAN PURITY ALLIANCE
UNITED CHARITIES BUILDING,
1896.

Caulon Press, 20 Vesey Street, New York.

FRIENDS' MEETING HOUSE, PARK AVENUE, BALTIMORE.

Dedication.

To our beloved

Daughter,

IN THE LIFE BEYOND, THE MEMORY OF WHOSE LOVELY CHILDHOOD HAS BEEN A CONTINUAL INSPIRATION DURING YEARS OF EFFORT TO SECURE IMPROVED SOCIAL CONDITIONS AND MORE ADEQUATE PROTECTION FOR EXPOSED YOUNG GIRLS, THE DAUGHTERS OF OTHERS, AND TO PROMOTE AN EQUAL STANDARD OF MORALITY FOR BOTH MEN AND WOMEN, THIS VOLUME IS AFFECTIONATELY DEDICATED.

JOSEPHINE E. BUTLER.

PREFACE.

The Purity movement, vital in importance as involving the welfare of the individual, of the home and of the nation, has hitherto received but a minimum of consideration. In the old world the cruel and unjust system of State Regulation of Vice has long existed. The INTERNATIONAL FEDERATION FOR THE ABOLITION OF STATE REGULATION OF VICE, of which JOSEPHINE E. BUTLER is the gifted pioneer and leader, is laboring effectively for its destruction. It has advocates in America. It was to oppose the introduction of that odious system of legalized vice that the NEW YORK COMMITTEE FOR THE PREVENTION OF STATE REGULATION OF VICE was organized in 1876. Its first president was the honored and beloved ABBY HOPPER GIBBONS. Last year the organization was enlarged, and incorporated, under the name of the AMERICAN PURITY ALLIANCE. The National Purity Congress, held under its auspices, was its first appeal to the general public. The response, both on the part of writers and speakers, and in the great audiences in attendance throughout the seven sessions of the Congress, was most encouraging and grateful.

This volume is a record of the papers and addresses of the Congress, which, it is believed, will do much to extend and perpetuate its usefulness, and to interpret and emphasize to the larger public the urgent need and the fundamental importance, in its various aspects, of the Purity Reform.

vi

THE NATIONAL PURITY CONGRESS.

The papers and addresses are presented by the editor essentially as contributed by their authors. The general aim and purpose of all is the same. It is, however, to be distinctly understood that each writer and speaker is responsible only for his or her own paper or address.

The volume includes a rare galaxy of portraits of representative, philanthropic men and women, of America and of Europe, which will be of exceptional interest to its readers in any and every clime.

The book is sent forth upon its humane mission in the confident hope and faith that it will do much to awaken public sympathy with, and interest in, the work of rescuing the perishing; of the better protection of the young of both sexes; the repression of vice, the abolition and prevention of its regulation by the State, and to promote a high, equal standad of morals for both men and women.

AARON M. POWELL.

TABLE OF CONTENTS.

LIST OF PORTRAITS.

xi

MRS. ABBY HOPPER GIBBONS.
EIGHTEEN YEARS PRESIDENT OF THE NEW YORK
COMMITTEE FOR THE PREVENTION OF
STATE REGULATION OF VICE.

CALL FOR THE CONGRESS.

NATIONAL PURITY CONGRESS.

A NATIONAL PURITY CONGRESS, under the auspices of the AMERICAN PURITY ALLIANCE, will be held in the city of Baltimore, Md., on Monday, Tuesday and Wednesday, October 14, 15 and 16, 1895. The spacious Park Avenue Friends' Meeting House has been kindly offered, and accepted, for the sessions of the Congress. The opening session will be held on Monday evening, October 14, with morning, afternoon and evening sessions on the following two days. The definite programme of papers and addresses will be completed and announced later. It will include some of the most gifted and eminent writers and speakers of our own, and of other countries.

This National Purity Congress is invited, by the American Purity Alliance, because the time seems fully to have arrived to give more thoughtful, intelligent and general consideration to the profoundly important social problems involved in the Purity movement. The continued existence of licensed and State regulated vice in European countries,—a system of practical slavery for a victim class of women, and of untold degradation for men—is, with the increased volume of foreign travel, a standing menace to Purity in America. In the city of New York an incorporated organization, created for the purpose, prepared a bill for introduction in the New York Legislature, during its late session, to license and legalize vice in certain districts of the city. A kindred unsuccessful effort to license vice in Boston was made in the late session of the Massachusetts Legislature. The Legislature of Missouri, during its late session passed an act, subsequently vetoed by the Governor, delegating to the police and municipal officials of St. Louis and other cities of that State, authority to designate districts within which houses of ill-repute might be permitted legally to exist. There obtains also in many American cities municipal taxation and toleration, in effect, amounting to municipal and police regulation of vice. Prostitution thus organized, based upon the sensual demands of immoral men, gives rise to a cruel traffic in dependent women and exposed young girls, and gross outrages upon women, and mysterious disappearances of young girls have become ominously frequent. The need is urgent for increased restraint for the evil disposed of both sexes; for a more effective inculcation of the obligation of chastity, and the maintenance of an equal standard of morality for both men and women. The papers and addresses of the Congress will cover various phases of the question,—rescue, prevention, educational, legal and religious.

All Social Purity, White Cross, Moral Education, and Woman's Christian Temperance Union organiza tion; all churches and other religious bodies, and philanthropic associations, in sympathy with the objects of the Congress, are invited to send five, or more, representatives, and to forward the names and addresses of such representatives to the Recording Secretary of the American Purity Alliance, Mrs. NAOMI LAWTON DAVIS, United Charities Building, New York, by or before October 1st. Special railway and hotel rates, for all who may attend the Congress as representatives or fraternal visitors, it is expected will be arranged in due season and announced in a later circular. Sundry local arrangements in behalf of the Congress, which will be announced later, are being made by the Baltimore Committee.

Under the direction of the Baltimore Committee, October 13 will be observed as "Purity Sunday," with

addresses and sermons by a considerable number of the
Congress speakers, and pastors, on the subject of social
purity, in various churches of Baltimore.

Address all communications pertaining to the Congress, except those relating to representatives, to the
President of the American Purity Alliance, United
Charities Building, Fourth Ave. and Twenty-Second
street, New York.

AARON M. POWELL, *President.*

NAOMI LAWTON DAVIS, *Recording Secretary.*

BALTIMORE HONORARY COMMITTEE.

Rev. F. W. CLAMPETT, Mr. SUMMERFIELD BALDWIN, Mr. W. H.
MORRIS, Mr. JOSHUA LEVERING, Mr. P. C. WILLIAMS, Mr. ELI M.
LAMB, Mr. JNO. B. CARY, Mrs. ALICE C. ROBINSON, Mrs. PAULINE
W. HOLME, Mrs. M. GREEN, Rev. WM. E. BARTLETT, Dr. BERNARD
C. STEINER, Prof. H. B. ADAMS, Mr. W. H. G. BELT, Mr. EDWIN
HIGGINS, Dr. HOWARD A. KELLY, Dr. O. EDWARD JANNEY, Mr.
G. W. CORNER, Jr., Rev. C. C. CLEVER.

AARON M. POWELL.

The National Purity Congress.

THE FIRST SESSION.

THE PRESIDENT'S OPENING ADDRESS.

By Aaron M. Powell, of New York, President
American Purity Alliance.

We meet on this occasion in the First National Purity Congress held under the auspices of the American Purity Alliance. Our objects in convening this Congress are, the repression of vice, the prevention of its regulation by the State, the better protection of the young, the rescue of the fallen, to extend the White Cross work among men, and to proclaim the law of Purity as equally binding upon men and women.

Purity is fundamental in its importance to the individual, to the home and to the nation. There can be no true manhood, no true womanhood except as based upon the law of Purity. There can be no security for the home, there can be no home-life in its best sense, except as it is based upon the law of Purity. There can be no true prosperity, there can be no perpetuation of a nation except as its life is based upon the law of Purity. Impurity is destructive alike to the individual character, of the home, and of the nation. Of the need of such a Congress as is now assembled the prevalence and propagandism of impurity, at the present time, everywhere so conspicuous in our large centers of population, abundantly testifies.

In the Old World vice, in many countries, is regulated by the State; it is legalized as a trade ; it is a shocking system of practical slavery for dependent

I

women and girls who are made its victims. It gives rise to an unholy traffic in girlhood; it occasions untold degradation on the part of women ; it is a standing menace to the home; it abridges the liberty of all women in those countries. The relations between our own country and the Old World are now so intimate, the the steamers passing to and fro so quickly and constantly as an international ferriage, make it impossible for us in America to be indifferent to the social conditions which obtain in Europe. It is on this account of vital importance that we recognize the struggle which is now going forward under the auspices of the International Federation for the Abolition of State Regulation of Vice, that we do what we can to aid and encourage its work. Law itself is a great educator for good or for ill. When the State assumes to license and legalize vice it educates downward and debases the moral sentiments of its people by such legalization.

In America we do not have, nominally, State regulation of vice. We do have, most unfortunately, in all our larger cities, a great deal of tolerated vice. Here as in Europe dependent women and girls are greatly exposed to vicious influences. With extremely low, in many cases almost starvation wages, the woman's extremity becomes the vicious man's opportunity. In Omaha for a considerable period there has been a system of municipal regulation of vice in vogue tolerating houses of evil repute, imposing a fine ostensibly, amounting really to a tax, upon the proprietor, to be paid once a month with immunity from arrest. According to a statement some months ago made by the Mayor of Omaha in one of the journals of New York City, that tax, which has aggregated about $24,000 a year, has been appropriated to the support of the public schools, as though any use of such a fund, however good, could justify the municipality in entering thus into practical complicity and co-partnership with vice and crime. It is gratifying to note that efforts are in progress in

J. BIRKBECK NEVINS, M. D.

PRESIDENT INTERNATIONAL FEDERATION FOR THE ABOLITION
OF STATE REGULATION OF VICE.

Omaha which promise some degree of municipal reform, among other things that this vice regulation is likely to be abolished. In Cleveland, Ohio, a year or two ago, a system of municipal regulation and practical license for vice was inaugurated without the clear warrant of Law, by the Chief of Police of that city, but when the facts became known they awakened a storm of righteous indignation and the scheme was abolished. In the city of St. Louis, in 1870, was inaugurated the only avowedly license experiment America has ever had. It continued for a period of four years.

It is enough to say in this connection that, as might have been expected, it made bad matters worse, and when it finally was abolished by the Legislature of Missouri the last condition of the city was worse than the first. From time to time sundry efforts have been made to renew the license experiment there. Only last year a measure was adopted by the Legislature which, if it had not been vetoed, would again have made it possible, within certain specified districts, which the municipal authorities were by this measure authorized to fix, to again have in those limited districts legalized houses of ill-repute. The measure was recommended by ministers of St. Louis, with the approval of the police officials, in the hope that it might prove of a repressive and restrictive character, but fortunately for the good name of the State and the best welfare of its citizens, it was vetoed by the Governor, and though vice may continue to be tolerated it at least is without the warrant and sanction of Law. In New York City last year there was formed an organization, which was duly incorporated and which still exists, with the avowed purpose of securing the localization and license of houses of ill-repute within certain districts in that city. The bill was carefully drawn for this purpose and published in one of the daily journals, but with the protests which it called forth from the American Purity Alliance and other kindred organizations, it is said that no member of the Legislature could be found willing to take the responsibility of introducing it in that body, and it therefore failed to become a law. Even in the Massachusetts Legislature last year a licensing measure for the Puritan City of Boston was introduced and the Legislature urged to pass it, but it also failed to become a law. With these and other kindred illustrations which might be cited of the prevalence in this country of a regulation propagandism, it may be seen that we have here a vital interest for our own protection in the speedy abolition in all countries of the odious system of State sanctioned vice.

In another direction also may be seen an urgent need for the Purity movement which this Congress represents. It is in the so called Age of Consent Laws in the different States. The age at which young girls are deemed capable of controlling property is the age of majority: prior to that time the State intervenes for their legal protection in connection with their property interests. Not so with reference to their persons. In four States, Mississippi, North Carolina, South Carolina and Alabama the Age of Consent is fixed at the shocking low age of ten years. In four States, Kentucky, Virginia, Nevada and West Virginia, the age is fixed at twelve years. In three States, New Hampshire, Utah and Iowa, at thirteen years. In the State of Maryland, in Maine, in Vermont, in Indiana, in North Dakota, in Georgia, in Illinois and in California at fourteen years. In Nebraska and Texas the age limit is fifteen years. In New Jersey, in Massachusetts, in Michigan, Montana, South Dakota, Oregon, Rhode Island, Pennsylvania and the District of Columbia the age is sixteen years. In Tennessee sixteen years and one day. In Florida seventeen years. In New York, Kansas, Wyoming and Colorado eighteen years. In Delaware the original statute pertaining to the crime of rape is still unrepealed fixing the age at seven years, but the last Legislature passed an amended act which, practically, is designed to extend legal protection in that State to young girls to the limit of eighteen years. These so called Age of Consent statutes discriminate against girlhood and in favor of immoral men. They are, for the most part, a disgrace to the several States of this Union. Public attention has been directed widely to the subject through the combined efforts of the American Purity Alliance and other Purity and White Cross organizations, and especially by the Woman's Christian Temperance Unions, and the movement has latterly been powerfully reinforced by the *Arena* magazine, conducted by Mr. Flower, with the special aid in this direction of Mrs. Helen H. Gardener. But it should be made much more a matter of concern in those States wherein the age is still ten, twelve, thirteen, fourteen, fifteen and sixteen years. The figures which I quote are such as have been recently furnished me, officially, by the Secretaries of State in the several States. They may not be, as in some cases I have found they were not, strictly accurate, but for the most part they undoubtedly represent the present actual condition of the Age of Consent Laws of our country. It is a matter which women and high-minded men everywhere should take to heart and do all possible to secure a speedy reformation and amendment of these laws.

Another object which this Congress it is hoped will do much to promote is greatly needed rescue work among the victims of vice. Rescue work for women, rescue work among fallen men as well as fallen women. Some of the speakers who will address the Congress during its' sessions are experts in this sphere of service, from whose experience it is hoped, shared here by others, a a new impetus will be given in this sphere of greatly needed Christian activity.

But even more important is preventive educational purity work among the young, and the older, which shall, ultimately, make rescue work no longer a necessity. The White Cross movement, which is especially for men, will therefore it is hoped also receive an especial impetus from this Congress, and that the interest in it may become still more extended. Its object, as defined by its pledge, is to teach its adherents first, to treat all women with respect and endeavor to protect them from wrong and degradation; second, to endeavor to put down all indecent language and coarse jests; third, to maintain the law of Purity as equally binding upon men and women; fourth, to endeavor to spread these principles among younger companions; fifth, to use every possible means to fulfil the command, "Keep thyself pure." In the higher education of men is the best possible safeguard for womanhood and girlhood.

It is to be hoped that one outcome of this Congress will be an increased emphasis upon the necessity for one moral standard for both sexes. It is in the double standard, one for men and another for women which has so long obtained in the public mind, that the schemes for State and Municipal regulation and the licensing of vice, and the unjust and immoral Age of Consent Laws, have their chief root and strength. The message, "Blessed are the pure in heart for they shall see God," is addressed alike to men and to women. It is hoped and expected that this Congress will do much to awaken interest on the part of the now largely indifferent public to the importance of these fundamental truths.

LETTER FROM REV. DR. W. N. McVICKAR.

Rev. Dr. W. N. McVickar, President of the Philadelphia Social Purity Alliance, who had hoped to be present and give an address at the opening session, sent the following letter, which was read by the President:

Minneapolis, Minn., October 12th, 1895.

My Dear Mr. Powell:

It is a matter of great regret to me that my duties at the General Convention of our Church, to which I am a delegate, prevent my being present at the National Purity Congress in Baltimore. I had hoped to have been at it and to have been privileged with a part in its deliberations. As it is, I can only send it my sincerest wishes for its success in the great work in which it is engaged. May God prosper it.

Yours faithfully,

W N. McVickar.

ADDRESSES OF WELCOME.

By Hon. Joshua Levering, President Baltimore Y.M.C.A.

It affords me great pleasure on behalf of my fellow citizens to welcome you to our City, our homes and our hearts. Baltimore, famed the world over as the "City of Monuments," is none the less famous for its hospitality and its doors are ever opened wide to all who are worthy of being its guests. Here you will find educational, charitable, reformatory and religious institutions standing with open doors bidding you welcome and inviting an inspection of the great work being done along lines similar to that which has called you together, namely, the effort to uplift and bless humanity.

I consider it, however, a special privilege as the representative of Baltimore's sturdy citizenship to welcome you to our City as those who are engaged in a heroic effort for the suppression of an evil which is the source of so much misery and suffering to a common humanity, and which, like its twin-evil, intemperance, will, if not soon suppressed, lead to the degeneracy and final destruction of very many of our fellow beings.

The purity question is one of great absorbing interest, equalled only by the legalized liquor traffic, and like it, occupying at the present time the mind and attention of humanitarians all over our country and in all lands. Impurity and intemperance go hand in hand in producing so many of the evils which are cursing mankind in general. One is greatly dependent upon the other, and without the one the other would be largely shorn of its power of evil. They are both equally the enemy of the home, and the fact that one has been legalized is leading to the plausible, though

9

erroneous, conclusion on the part of many, that restriction of the evils of the other can only be secured through some form of legalization. I therefore the more heartily welcome you as those who entertain no such pernicious views; but, on the contrary, believe that where an evil exists the only proper treatment for it is its complete overthrow. Furthermore, if I understand the purposes of your organization, you have already learned the truth that an evil can only be overcome by attacking it at its root or source of life, and as the source of this evil is very generally believed to be found in ignorance, you make bold to advocate the necessity of laying aside that false modesty which has been to a large extent the prolific cause of much of the evil, of educating the public mind and especially parents and guardians of the young, that, if they will have their children grow up with pure minds and healthy bodies, they must instruct them in those divine principles which underlie this whole matter so that if they would perpetuate the nation, and have it consist of a pure and noble humanity, they themselves must be pure.

To accomplish this such an organization as yours is absolutely necessary, so that through its efforts the minds and hearts of the people can be reached by the printed page, by lectures, by conferences, etc.

I therefore assure you of a hearty welcome on the part of every true Baltimorean and in their behalf bid you an earnest and sincere "God speed" in your noble mission and labor of love.

By Mrs. ALICE C. ROBINSON.

Mrs. Alice C. Robinson, President of the Baltimore Woman's Christian Temperance Union, followed Mr. Levering. She said in part :

"I feel proud that I live in the city that first sees this Congress. It is an honor conferred upon Baltimore, which I know those who live here can truly appreciate.

HON. JOSHUA LEVERING.

PRESIDENT BALTIMORE Y. M. C. A.

There are many dark caves and many lives that have to be touched and many avenues that have to be opened. Rescue seems to be the first work, many of us know, and we now are going forward with glorious results The purity of the cradle is our first thought. The father and mother, too, must receive our attention. Neither parent must be overlooked in our work of education.

"There is a great work that has been done in the many Christian societies in our midst, but now we must seek special means to carry through the cause of purity. We must go into legislative halls, and secure the services of great men and women and carry God's work on. Those who have come from a distance we welcome to Baltimore especially, and may the work be blessed as our earnestness is shown."

MRS. ALICE C. ROBINSON.
PRESIDENT BALTIMORE W. C. T. U.

RESPONSIVE ADDRESSES.

By Rev. W. T. Sabine, D. D.

It is a pleasant duty which has been put upon me Mr. President by the Committee in Charge, of responding to these kindly addresses in behalf of this great body of friends and delegates gathered here from all parts, the North, the South, the East, the West, of our broad land.

It augurs well for the generosity and heartiness of our reception that we are assembled in this great hall and under the hospitable roof of a body famed for simplicity and kindliness, the *Society of Friends.*

The tone of the invitation, the place and this crowded assembly make it impossible for us to doubt the cordiality of our welcome.

We are already assured that what has been said of the hospitality of Baltimore and the interest now felt in our meeting is every word of it true.

We already see that every thing has been done that could be done to secure our comfort and give effectiveness to our gathering. It was my good fortune, Mr. President, to arrive in this city some forty-eight hours ago—and so I am qualified to speak from a personal experience of the generous provisions and attentions of Baltimore hospitality which many of my fellow delegates do not yet possess, and I can assure them that judging by my own taste of it they will not be disappointed.

The story is told of some visitors to the Isle of Shoals, that arriving upon the beach tired, hungry, and in need of refreshments they made their way to the rude hut of a fisherman which they saw at no great distance. Knocking at the door it was opened by a stalwart man dressed in his rough fisherman's garb—

14

"Walk in" he said "Walk in and make yourselves to hum, I aint got no manners! The gal's got the manners and she aint to hum!"

Well, as far as Baltimore is concerned, Mr. President, from what we now see and hear we are satisfied, the gal has got the manners and she *is* to hum.

But pleasantry aside, we are here not to be entertained and have a good time; we are here for downright earnest sober work. We are here trying to right a great wrong, meaning to fight a terrible evil which is threatening our country, our churches and our homes. Like the Apostle to the Gentiles we magnify our office, Mr. President, we are here in a great cause. There are other wrongs we are well aware bitter, terrible, deepseated, and with every wise effort to redress them we we are in fullest sympathy.

The wail of thousands crushed and oppressed,— many of them widows and orphans,—beneath the cruel heel of avarice and greed breaks on the air and enters into our hearts.

The cry of the Red-man, for long years, the victim of the grossest injustice and robbery on the part of his white brother and even of government officials, his sworn protectors; awakens a burning indignation in our souls.

The unspeakable woes of the drunkard's home and the curse of the drink traffic bring a pang to our hearts and sometimes tears to our eyes.

Fain would we sweep all these curses from our land.

But the evil this Congress gathers to consider is in some respects more vital, widespread and terrible in its devastations than any of these, certainly it is more insidious, more secretive, harder to get at, and more difficult for many reasons to drag out of its dark lurking places and hold up in its hideousness before the eyes of men.

Lieutenant Herndon in his Report on Explorations in the Valley of the Amazon presented to the Congress of the United States some forty years ago, tells of a strange weird cry which now and again breaks upon the ears of the traveller as he voyages up or down the waters of that mighty stream. It comes up from the depths of the dense dark forests which skirt the river shores. It sounds like a wail of agony, so plaintive, so penetrating, so full of an unspoken anguish that it thrills the listener with dread.

The Indians of the Amazon call it "the cry of a lost soul!"

It is the weird wild note of a bird in the forest depths.

Mr. President, we seem to hear to-night a far more bitter cry coming up from the depths of a lost sisterhood and brotherhood. A brotherhood and sisterhood lost to shame, lost to decency, lost to happiness, lost to morality, lost to itself, lost to every thing but God and Charity!

It is a kind of suppressed stifled moan, a horrible choking cry.

Those other cries are exceedingly great and bitter. They force themselves upon the ears of men.

But this cry even the best of men and women with the keenest ears for the wrongs of the oppressed and fallen seem hardly to have heard. Till now this most needed of reforms has been kept back and in the rear and out of sight.

Mr. President, it is time this cause came to the front and we are here to bring it to the front, and God helping us to the front it shall come.

We mean to speak in tones from this place which the nation shall hear and which we trust those charged with its highest physical, moral and spiritual interests shall be compelled to heed.

And now Sir it only remains for me concluding to reiterate our thanks to the Baltimore Committee. Sometimes I receive a letter asking a favor; the writer concluding with the words "Thanking you in advance. I remain very truly yours."

THE NATIONAL PURITY CONGRESS.

For all that we have in prospect and shall surely enjoy in the next two days of stimulus, encouragement, opportunity, information, "thanking you in advance, dear Baltimore friends, we beg to sign ourselves. Very truly and gratefully yours."

By Rev. Antoinette Brown Blackwell.

It is a pleasure to respond to the cordial welcome of our Baltimore friends, to feel that we are no longer strangers in this large assembly, your citizens and delegates from all parts of the country. Ten or eleven years ago, as a member of the Association for the Advancement of Women, I was among those to whom a Baltimore audience, sometimes as large as this one, gave a kindly hearing for several successive days upon subjects some of them hardly less unpopular than this we are now assembled to consider. I am glad to add my testimony to the abundant hospitality which has given me charming drives around your beautiful city with its extensive parks. I have even been taken over the Chesapeake, into the country, outside of the town limits, to the beautiful country which they say is one of the important feeders of your great city. So all parts of the world are in mutual dependence. As human beings we need not only physical, but mental and moral aid, support and co-operation.

Scientific men say that the common honey bee has between three and four thousand distinct fascets or little semi-independent sections for each of its marvelous compound eyes standing out on either side of its head in shining small hemispheres. Each fascet is a special mirror of an external object; thus an image of a single thing is repeated about seven thousand times at the same instant; yet no two of these images are exactly alike since the reflection falls upon each one from a slightly different angle. We know little about how these minute photographs, no two alike, can all be correlated into a single clear perception by the bee. The wonderful insect has some powers greater than our own; at least they belong to a class beyond our present comprehension.

But these combination eyes are a suggestive type of despondent humanity. The somewhat different outlook of many and various minds brought to bear upon any great question vastly broadens the comprehensive scope of the inquiry. In the multitudes of counselors there is wisdom; and we all see further in the light of another's vision than we could ever hope to do by ourselves alone. Co-operation is especially helpful in all practical work. This most difficult of all social problems has need of many friends in council.

A bee line is a straight line from the bee to the desired object; but I fear we shall find it impossible to closely copy our insect example. After flying spirally upward the bee flies almost unerringly, guided it is supposed by its associated eyesight. But the busy bee has also three simple eyes on the top of its head, and when some curious experimenter on insect nature paint ed over these single eyes and set the insect free, away from its hive, the poor thing circled round and round aimlessly instead of taking a direct line home. Many single eyes to every great purpose is indispensable to great achievement.

We all need united wisdom and earnestness; but if the public can begin to educate in the right direction, instruction and legislation by the better class will greatly check all forms of immorality.

Once more remembering the graceful hospitality with which we have been received here and elsewhere, I can only add my sincere hope and expectation that this first National Purity Congress may be eminently successful in awakening the public to the nature of the perils by which we are surrounded

HON. C. C. BONNEY.

THE NATIONAL PURITY CONGRESS.

LETTER FROM Hon. C. C. BONNEY.

Hon. C. C. Bonney, of Chicago, President of the World's Congress Auxiliary, who had hoped to be present and give an address at the opening session sent the following letter:

Chicago, September 28th, 1895.

Dear Mr. Powell:

I very much regret to say that I find my engagements will not allow me to attend the National Purity Congress to be opened in Baltimore on the 14th of next month. * * * I can only say, in a word, that Social Purity is indispensable to Political Purity; and that free institutions cannot endure without a high standard of Social Purity among the people. The lofty Puritan spirit to which we in America owe so much, was perhaps the most important factor in the formation of that free government on which the hopes, not only of America, but of the whole world so largely rest.

With renewed regrets, and as always with high respect and kind regards, Very sincerely yours,

Charles C. Bonney.

IMMORALITY OF THE REGULATION SYSTEM.

By Rev. Antoinette Brown Blackwell.

1. Regulation accepts and condones admitted wrong-doing. No one attempts to justify modern forms of vice on moral gronds. If law should not *Regulate* murder, arson or perjury, it has no justification for attempting to establish accepted limits and degrees of social degradation. No valid excuse can be framed for fostering gross wrong; for aiming to shield criminals or to whitewash their conduct by legal devices. The alcoholic traffic is licensed in most communities on the plea that moderate drinking is justifiable and should be protected; but no one attempts to plead the desirability of promiscuous vice. No ennobling social. relation needs a graded protection. Every form of legal sanction to the grossest of all crimes against humanity is an unparalleled infamy.

2. Regulation has proved inadequate to do what it professed to attempt. Investigation shows that it has nowhere lessened, that it has often increased the spread of disease. Carefully prepared statements made by eminent authorities after canvassing wide districts under the aegis of protection, prove that no amelioration results, but that demoralization rapidly widens its domain. So much might be expected. The futile dream of being saved from the immediate worst results of vice is not likely to prove a repressive influence. So obvious have such facts become, that regulation has been abolished where once established, as worse than useless; and wherever it is still maintained it is upheld both by immoral men and by the shameful greed of moneyed interests ready either to urge on the guilty or to betray the innocent for the thirty pieces of silver.

3. There is abundant evidence that attempted regulation tends directly to increase the depravity of the depraved. With the interposing great shield lifted to hide his sins from the world and to shelter his good name as in the hollow of the protective legal hand, the man is tempted into deeper dishonor. His easy conscience is quieted by the smooth devices of respectability high in authority; and while the system treats the woman with no slightest grain of personal consideration, it steadily tends to destroy the last remnants of her self-respect. What matter though it pares away all traces of a lost innocence! The womanhood which has bartered its standing at the family fireside and forfeited tenderness within the sanctities of the home, will receive but little more harm from the extra throwing of mud. The favored among them maintain their places only through the sufferance of capricious irresponsible individual favor. The common law knows nothing of their relations or their rights, it provides no legislation in their behalf; their safety depends on the opaqueness of their surroundings. Legal recognition of any kind should be gratefully accepted! Feet that have slipped yet a little lower down the dark incline can hardly be worse off in their hapless estate if shoved on and planted still more deeply in the surrounding slime! How can any added indignity greatly harm those whom respectability already forgets?

No wonder this most forlorn class in so called Christendom learns to manifest some almost diabolical traits. Legislation has no other recipe half so effective for the manufacture of all the crimes which arise from indignant despair and hopeless debasement.

4. Regulation deludes and deceives the weak of both sexes. Like Tetzell of old, professing to sell indulgencies and grant absolution for sin and shame, it plucks down unthought of condemnation on the heads of feeble folk too weak to stand alone. Legislation leads either upward or downward; it is everywhere an

REV. ANTOINETTE BROWN BLACKWELL.

education in the direction either of good or of evil, and regulation is but the digging of new and deeper pitfalls which it covers over with the green boughs of acceptance and apparent respectability. The unwary and the misguided become its more abundant victims.

5. By making it easier to lure the young to dishonor, the regulation system lays cruel snares and traps for their inexperienced feet. To district vice to special but open localities, means to stimulate juvenile curiosity and bravado. With the joint sanction of the law and the law makers, boyhood becomes the more readily demoralized often before it has yet learned right from wrong; and girlhood is the staple from which the down marching ranks are steadily recruited. Yet regulation takes no heed that the abhorrent profession is forever renewing itself from among the innocent children to whom life might offer some of the highest prizes of usefulness and happiness. It cares not that its deceiving half measures are but leaves and blossoms thrown into a devouring maelstrom with only the effect of covering up and partially disguising its deadliest aspects.

Authorized legalization has scarcely dared yet to lift its head in our own country; yet the police service has often pandered to vice and its claims, unrebuked,—if not liberally rewarded. Often they virtually execute an unwritten law which favors social depravity. Hypocrisy is a hateful word, but if regulation advocates are not self condemned for their perfidy, the bats and eyeless fishes of our great Mammoth Cave are no blinder than they. Their night-lanterns illumine only their own personal interests. The slippery places where the crowding young feet jostle each other along life's paths are thrown into a half shadow which becomes a perpetual allurement.

6. The whole system is based upon evident insincerity. The welfare of the commonwealth, the available plea for the hateful regulation which is claimed to be needful in order to check the spread of a wholly

needless leprosy! But sincerity would be compelled to establish an equitable all round law! It would plant a medical police at all the doors of all the licensed halls of vice, and would let neither man nor woman enter there until certified to be in conditions of sound health. Such measures, and such alone, would show some evidence of acting in good faith. But to single out the younger, smaller, poorer, fewer in numbers, who are calmly disfranchised and thus placed entirely at the mercy of legislation not for but against them, though they are at least not greater criminals than the richer, more prosperous, respectable men for whose benefit all regulation is made and provided—this is the sword of protection with its sharp edge turned the wrong way.

On the plea of the general good, official sanction invoked to send the already despoiled ones into the cruel wilderness of yet deeper social opprobrium!—compelling them to suffer for the sins of others as well as for their own. This is a paternalism to which heathendom never attained. Barbarism had no double standard either of morals or of remedies. Sheer savagery never laid one brutal hand heavily upon the woman, beating her into the dust while the other arm uplifted and upheld the man, seeking, despite his fall, to clothe him in honor and dignity.

7. Regulation is medieval legislation. So long as children inherited solely from the mother, vice was not held more blameworthy in one sex than in the other. The morals of the primitive people were little to boast of, yet their scales of justice were at least more evenly balanced; polyandry was not held in more disgrace than polygamy. It was only after it was decided to divide womankind into the sheep and the goats, and give men the privilege of associating with both, that the double standard of morals was erected and the device of seeking to protect fallen men at the sole expense of fallen women was invented. The earlier world was too simple hearted to have dreamed of a scheme so utterly unjust.

8. The regulation scheme is a shield manufactured and uplifted exclusively for men. It recognizes only their perils, needs, and wishes to be protected along a line of admitted debasement. It ignores the interests and rights of their women associates as completely as some vivisectionists ignore the sentient claims of the lower animals. If it were in earnest in its claim to furnish safeguards for innocent wives and children, it would deal directly with the men rather than with the women; it would require both men and women to take out licenses for prostitution and be able to show a clean bill of health or be placed in an hospital. Is it honest to forget that the evils to be stamped out in family life do not commonly originate in the female line? And if there were any intended provision made for the young, the needy, and the easily influenced for evil, the districted fallen women would be quarantined so conscientiously that these more helpless innocent classes would find them difficult if not impossible of access. Every form of evidence leads to the conclusion that the system re-members the interests of one class only—and that is the class of fallen men.

9. Regulation is organized flagrant injustice to fallen women and its one sided sanitary law-making is inexpressibly ignoble. They are assumed to have no remnant of modesty remaining; they are placed abso-lutely in the hands of men, often of most unscrupulous character—from whose decisions they have no appeal and against whose conduct they have no redress; they are practically enslaved and robbed of all personal rights, social or civil. A freeman's vote is needed by all women, but it is imperative first and foremost for the decent protection of this most wronged and pitiable class. The state of things as existing, whether author-ized by law or only by custom, does not merely forget the just claims of womanhood, it has not yet risen to the conception that such rights have any existence or need be taken into account. Such women have no rights

which either law or custom feel bound to respect. They have no claims except those of a money bought acceptance of the worst humiliation which is possible to even a degraded, weak humanity.

Suffrage to be withheld from all women for fear these outcasts will become voters, and may have some voice in the formulation and administration of justice! There is need to fear. In the face of the actual facts, one sided sanitary regulations become inexpressibly ignoble. They are grounded in the assumption that for a common sin, the woman shall forfeit everything; but, so far as law or manufactured opinion can help him, the man shall forfeit nothing. Manhood by no other legal act, has ever so fully proclaimed and illustrated its possible abjectness. It has never otherwise so stereo-typed its possible unmitigated selfishness, or so openly confessed to its own lingering brutality and unscru-pulousness.

The woman's point of view is so totally outside of all existing regulative systems, legal or illegal, that if the best women remained silent, and the stones did not cry out, the leaves on the trees would bleed with compassion over the dumb helplessness of fallen womanhood. Every silent green thing would droop and blacken because of unuttered sympathy. It is said that these women know nothing of their greatest wrongs? So much the more pitiable is their estate! Woe to all of us if we preach not the gospel of a whole humanity from the woman's stand-point! Woe to us if we remember not these bond-women as though we ourselves were bound with them.

10. Regulation menaces physical, mental and moral decay to the entire community. Unchecked, it will undermine and subvert any civilization which harbors it either openly or secretly. The only remedy is repression. The aroused conscience of both men and women must give the world an enlightened, just, and upright code of equal and unselfish morality. There is a befogged and near sighted moral vision as there is imperfect physical

eye-sight. Nothing but the blunted moral sense of a community could for a day tolerate the existence of a class set apart from all others to a special opprobrium from which no escape is provided or allowed. Think of perpetuating a veritable caste of pitiable women rarely spoken of among other women except in whispers and associated with by men only when they drop their identity to become anonymous. Could there exist social obloquy more unworthy, more humiliating, more distorted and inhuman?

Think that the daily bread and the social shame are the two values made to balance each other on the scales of modern justice! Is it any wonder that women at last are learning that work is honorable for them also? Is it strange that self-help, self-reliance, are taking the highest rank among feminine virtues? Is it incredible that women should assert that maternal functions are the full equivalent of paternal bread winning. The theory that the divinest tie which binds husband and wife is chiefly a moneyed bond must be consigned to the dark ages where it originated. Marriage no longer regarded as a masculine patronage and a feminine dependence, the only a little more detestable, irresponsible and miscellaneous patronage will become a hideous disgrace alike to male and female. Moral vice will become more disreputable than drunkenness. Considered as a disregard of anothers interests, it will seem baser and more craven than even murder itself. The time must come when the bribery of female virtue will be thought more vile than any other suborning of the human conscience. The time will come when money can no more be tolerated as the purchase of improper favor than it is now accepted as a bribe for the favor of Heaven. Then regulation, authorizing a money bought acceptance of debasing humiliation, will be scorned alike by regenerated manhood and womanhood. All legislation grounded upon a blended brutality, injustice and servility, is foredoomed as alien to the honor and dignity of rational beings.

The more helpless any class, especially if it be an enforced or an entailed helplessness, the more must every member of it become the special ward of every upright conscience. Plural marriage has been condemned in all civilized countries. It must continue under the legal ban of all civilizations. The modern intellect and the modern sentiment and conscience are not likely permanently to reestablish any form of outgrown barbarity.

Humanity is sure in time to regard the single marriage as an honorable equal, partnership. True affection, mutual respect and self-respect, alone can sanctify this life-long relation. Doubtless we shall not reach the perfectly ideal union until we have first evolved the ideal units; but while heredity transmits traits and tendencies from parents to children, the best units, the noblest individuals, are likely to originate through the most promising unions. Hence all legislation which tends even indirectly to detract from the personal or the social dignity of either men or women, or to tolerate anything in the morals of either which can wrong an exalted human nature, must be totally condemned and speedily amended.

The life-long union of marriage, alone can consecrate the fitting home for the reception of loving and beloved childhood. It is only in the unbroken home that the training of infancy and youth can be happily consummated and unstable character rounded into symmetrical maturity. Marriage alone can complete in husband and wife that unity in duality which leads on to the highest evolution of both. And marriage must be exclusive and permanent, because so only, in the most intimate, the most self-forgetting affections, at this noblest elevation, can the sensibility and the intellect broaden most worthily together through mutual stimulation. So only can all of the lawful impulses of a complex human nature best find a fitting nurture and adequate moral justification.

THE RELIGIOUS ASPECTS OF THE PURITY MOVEMENT.

By Rev. S. H. Virgin, D. D.

There is an evident infelicity in the statement of the topic upon which I am asked to speak during the closing moments of the first session of this most important Congress. The words that have already been spoken, the work that has been accomplished of which we have heard, the influences that have been generated and that are ceaselessly operative in regulating conduct as well as in controlling thought and forming purposes, emphatically declare that this Purity Movement is Religion itself, and that the topic might more accurately be formulated as the Purity Movement Aspects of Religion.

It is a truism to say that there is no religion where there is not purity of thought and life. Impurity is the death of religion. It shuts the eyes from seeing God, and seals the heart against any holy affections and buries out of reach all desires for spiritual associations. The so-called worship of heathen countries involving dissolute relations is a mockery of religion. You may as well seek water without hydrogen gas, diamonds without brilliance, snow without whiteness as religion without purity.

It is strange that in a so-called religious community there should be need of such efforts as we are constantly putting forth. When religion is enthroned this Alliance may dissolve, for the need of its existence will have passed away. Heaven permits the entry of "nothing that defileth."

It is a significant sign of the times that a man or woman may be thought to be religious and still be like

REV. S. H. VIRGIN, D. D.

31

mottled marble. Pious associations may for a time cover evil intentions and wicked practices. But the unmistakable evidences of corruption are more convincing than voluminous words of profession and the testimony of the ages, concerning the final issue of hidden sin, relieves us from the fear lest hypocrisy shall triumph.

If I speak of the aspects of this Purity Movement from the stand-point of Religion, that clear mountain top giving wide range to vision and a crystalline atmosphere in which to detect hidden things, I find:

1st. AN ASPECT OF ENCOURAGEMENT.

There is every ground of good cheer for what has been accomplished as well as for the forces enlisted in the work. This is seen

(*a*) In the rebuke of impurity in public men. There was a time when intellectual greatness, superb accomplishments in literature or art, grand service rendered to the State furnished an antidote to an immoral character. Evil was overlooked in the gratitude for contributions to the public good. But it is now well understood that no amount of good service can overcome the deleterious influence upon the rising generation of a low standard of personal life. A corrupt man sends the streams of his corruption through books and art studies, and his vile companionship is undesired by the decent world whether he be an Oscar Wilde in England or a Breckenridge in the United States. The public revolt is an evidence of progress in public sentiment. Genius is no longer synonymous with license.

(*b*) In the state of the public conscience respecting city corruption. The disclosure of the magnitude of the social evil, though a sad comment upon our habits hitherto and not without its injury to those who for the first time become aware of it, contains an element of encouragement in the bold and determined utterances that demand its suppression and its removal. The scattering of this evil by an aggressive warfare upon it by societies or the police under the spur of vigilant men and women, stirs the indignation of homes of purity against landlords and property owners and all who are in any wise involved in the wrong. There was an hour when conscience slept and the most importunate cries of this and other societies were considered but the hootings of night owls that ought to be suppressed.

(c) In the intelligent revolt from any system of State Regulation. Here and there one uninformed, now and then local bodies of people under some shrewd leadership are unwarily entrapped into endorsement of such a system. But a little information dispels the cloud. The mere reading of the text of any such proposed laws is sufficient to turn the stomach and rouse the ire of any right-minded person, and bring mind and heart into sympathy of opposition to it. And so there is wide spread resistance as soon as there is knowledge of the facts involved in this scheme and this is encouraging. Success when obtained is by secrecy and intrigue.

(d) In the uniform approval of this and similar organizations wherever they are known. The sphere of their operation is too limited and the circulation of THE PHILANTHROPIST and similar papers and leaflets is too small, but a constituency is created wherever the work is heralded. There never was an hour when so many people wanted purity everywhere as now, and the efforts organized and the noble names of workers that shine like a spiritual galaxy radiant with heaven's own light betokening the massing of an army for victory carry gladness to those who are praying for the dawn and the midday of social and individual purity in the earth. I find:

2d. An Aspect of Warning.

(a) Against all who love or profit by the corruptions of society. This evil is secretive and wary. It seeks to cover itself from sight and make the worse appear the better cause. It hides behind the permitted

33

customs of society which the good do not condemn and which the church tacitly permits. Vice can never be trusted. It always was and still is a LIAR. It breaks promises and deceives its closest friend. Those who publish books and make the way easy to sinful desires are roused by the growing opposition and are on the alert to evade the law and the detection of reputable vigilance. The disappearance here and there does not mean that the end has come but that there is a begining elsewhere. The sentence of the judge, the sermon of the preacher, the strong editorial, and the congress of workers will only make enemies more watchful and call for equal alertness of activity on the part of the friends of this cause in watching and combating the social bandits of the world.

b Against underrating the evil which we oppose. The fires have been burning in a debased humanity too long to be easily extinguished. The conflict is to be long and arduous but crowned with victory. Impurity is in league with all the diabolical forces of the universe. If the wicked spirits in high places aid anybody they bring their help to those who seek the corruption of youth for there they gain a masterly advantage. The hot blood that courses in the veins, the subtlety and fiendishness of spirits bent on the destruction of their fellow men, the greed of gain that counts nothing too good or holy to be bartered, the bulk of capital already invested in criminal pursuits, the STUFF that Mr. Comstock constantly finds and the persistency with which opposition to good is pursued utter a solemn warning against any under estimate of the present evil. The surrender of Satan is only at the end of absolute defeat.

(*c*) Against over-confidence in measures already adopted. For they are the objects of constant attack and this wary and alert enemy must be approached from ever new and unsuspected points. Not an advantage is gained in any community that is not instantly battled by all the combined forces of wickedness. The legislature is approached, the lobby is active with money and promises of political preferment, the physicians are importuned, the statistics are manipulated, the timid toilers are threatened with unpleasant notoriety, the high officials are urged to say that the common safety requires these vent holes for pent up bestiality.

That self complacency that counts victory already won receives earnest warning from the clear-eyed watcher on the heights of holiness. Hostility is organized, commands money for those who can be bought, reinforces itself steadily from the self indulgent classes of foreign nations coming to our shores, scoffs at "Puritanism," and allows no opportunity to pass to gain a point for its unhallowed ends.

Religion, the Christian Religion has unfailing relations to this whole effort in which we are engaged and its voice is without any nervous tremulousness when it speaks of impurity in life and thought and the proper attitude of the good towards it.

This Purity Movement represents and embodies the true aspects of religion towards all the corruption of the world. It assumes FOUR distinct attitudes.

I. IT IS MINATORY.

There is no latent sympathy between religion and corruption. The one will not grow into the other if let alone. The two will not flow together if undisturbed But there is everlasting repulsion between them. Th~ one has an eternal abhorrence of the other. They are mutually expulsive. Ferment instantly arises when they touch. Christ and Anti-Christ will clasp hands in peace when these two are found together.

Not only is there this natural antagonism but there is declared war. Religion calls for the extermination of the spirit of impurity and utters its solemn threats against it everywhere. No guilty head is spared. In the person of royalty it is as offensive as in the life of the obscure. In man it is as revolting as in woman. The threat covers the whole being. Religion threatens

35

the demolition of the sacred temple of the human body in which impurity riots. No cosmetics can hide, no medicine can cure, no physician can avert the spread of destructive forces in the body. Beauty vanishes, form and features change, the eye loses its lustre and the stamp of the beast appears. It takes the skill from the hand and the beautiful vision from the mind. It threatens the overthrow of the mental powers in the victim of this sin. The noblest endowments shall not be able to resist it nor the greatest genius escape its punishments. It threatens to fling the defiled from reputable society and reveal the hideous deformity of corrupting vices. Courteous manners, rare conversational gifts will only become the contortions of deformity in effort to hide what hastens to disclosure. It threatens the utter ruin of the spirit. Aspirations for lofty fellowship will give place to low and debasing companionship and the image of the divine will become the repulsive outline of the beast. Sweet affections will die and only cruel longings remain.

It threatens all alike. Man has often laughed at the fall of his weaker companion and bolstered himself up with the assurance that he could walk unharmed into the society of the good and pure while she was trodden under foot. Religion threatens a change when the impure man shall be as much an object of revulsion as the impure woman, when he shall be as publicly marked as she.

It threatens the rejection of the impure at the gates of the Heavenly City and bars out forever the corrupt from the fellowship of the good.

It threatens the overthrow of the nation where lust reigns unchecked and debauchery is tolerated and flashes "MENE—MENE—TEKEL—UPHARSIN" in fiery capitals before every eye.

II. It is MANDATORY.

It not simply advises, coaxes and pursuades. It not only invites with promise of blessing and assurance of abundant good. It not only threatens. But it is as stern as Sinai and speaks with unflinching command. It counts the corrupt person its subject and meets him with individual command. It thunders the law above his head and exacts the utmost penalty for disobedience. No one escapes. The law extends to words, thoughts, purposes and motives as well as to acts. It relates to the individual in private, in the home, in society, in contact with any and every living thing. It is as plain as when it speaks of idolatry or theft or murder. It allows no possibility of mistake or doubt. A "THUS SAITH THE LORD" attends each word as it comes like peal of thunder along the mountain crags. Law giver, prophet, psalmist, Redeemer, apostle speak by inspiration and every messenger of God through the ages has but repeated the sacred and unchanging counsels and commands for purity in body, soul and spirit and in every relation which each through the whole period of life sustains to all the world. It embeds its inflexible command in the decalogue and re-utters it in the Sermon on the Mount. It singles out the transgressor with a specific THOU ART THE MAN. The great Law Giver of the universe has not failed to make clear human duty in reference to purity of life and thought. Only the pure in heart shall see God. It is mandatory in respect to any plan of legal protection for sin and smites with withering blow all suggestions for a State Regulation of vice—When law becomes lawless, anarchy will follow

III. IT IS MERCIFUL.

It takes cognizance of the weakness of humanity, has tender words of forgiveness and provides a way of cleansing from defilement. The severity of the command is matched by the gentleness with which the penitent is received. But there is discrimination in the heavenly mercy. The lawless and hypocrites and incorrigible must meet their deserts. Mercy is not perpetual toleration. Religion is not softhearted, easily imposed upon, blind to faults but rather keen visioned, penetrating to the recesses of the life and quickly noting real sorrow for sin, and detecting the first pulse of real desire for purity. It extends the hand instantly to honest penitence and has no stone to throw at the humble supplicant for forgiving grace. It has clean water for the defiled and is ever ready to use it. The Master calls in loving tones and every true disciple longs for the recovery of all who have gone astray. The bitter denunciation, the fierce unwillingness to recognize the fallen sister, the heartless shrinking from any contact with the child of infirm purpose and feeble morality is all unlike Christ. The Purity Movement embodies the essence of Christianity in its mercy for the defiled that want to recover manhood and womanhood. It bleeds in its sympathy with those who are the unwilling slaves of masculine brutality and goes with hasty step into the abodes of crime and the low sections of cities and the far camps of the lumbermen and everywhere that the low cry of suffering and enslaved girlhood is heard with that tread of authority and that scourge of small cords that made the Master resistless in the temple court. It provides the home, the hospital, the farm, the retreat, the mother's arm, the father's embrace for the prodigal. It smites with withering blow the harshness that shuts the door against any child because fallen and seeks to restore to the beautiful paths of virtue those who have been torn and bruised in the highways of sin.

While we are unflinching in our attitude towards the enemies of virtue and have only blows of indignant wrath for all who seek to legislate into the nation's life cursed theories of protection to crime that decency and divinity alike condemn, and while we hate with increasing feeling the fashions of society that make cruel discriminations of sex, that flatter and fawn upon the impure man, while loathing the impure woman, and while we denounce the destruction of woman's imperial modesty in the adoption of any custom of dress or amusement that dethrones her from her regal place as head of the home and leader in the sweet civilities of life and companion in every noble relation, we still have compassion for all who will return and bathe in the fountain of innocence and abandon all wicked courses of conduct.

IV. THE PURITY MOVEMENT, LIKE RELIGION, IS MAGNANIMOUS.

It has not that austere, inflexible spirit of sinless, almost untempted, maidenhood in some parts of the country that has been enshrined in story and repeated again and again in actual life. For it recognizes the snares of wicked men, the terrible temptations of poverty, the horrible education of the crowded tenement house, the loose morality of many homes of luxury, the stimulus of wine and opium administered in hours of weakness by careless or lawless physicians, the fierce brutality of roused and ungratified lusts and with a divine pity for the erring, it like the Master has a place on its shoulder for the rescued. It will not only speak words of mercy, offer prayers for wanderers, build houses of refuge, secure farms in distant places, but it will restore to sweet and saving influences and build into the life again the regnant forces of righteousness and open the doors of christian homes with their re-fining atmosphere for the welcome entrance of purified spirits.

The Purity Movement is not iconoclastic alone, leveling to the dust all that it opposes; it is constructive. It gathers to itself the forces of the sunshine that fall-ing upon the heap of compost stirs it to loathsome putrefaction till it is removed, shining upon the ice cliffs melts them to rivers that fertilize adjacent fields, penetrating to rootlets awakens their latent life and brings them to flower and fruit, pouring its riches into the summer air and upon the still waters draws from muddy ooze the beautiful lily, causes it to lay its white petals on the silent surface and open its heart of gold to the sight of all.

So this great Movement makes impurity detestable, melts streams of thought and affection into human society, fertilizes the germs of justice in human legislation and brings to beauty the hidden possibilities of sunken and unfortunate humanity.

Minatory, mandatory, merciful and magnanimous, it cannot fail of the ceaseless blessing of the loving God of heaven till its sacred purpose is fully and triumphantly accomplished.

REV. W. T. SABINE, D. D.

SOCIAL VICE AND NATIONAL DECAY.

By William T. Sabine, D.D., New York City.

Social Vice and National Decay stand to each other as parent to child, cause to consequence, fountain to stream, the one begetting, the other begotten.

That Social Vice, by which we broadly mean fornication, prostitution, a defiance of the Divine law of continence, is the only or even the primary cause of National Decay would be too much to assume; but to affirm that the prevalence and increase of the Social Evil among a people is a sure sign and symptom of national degeneracy which it greatly promotes and accelerates, is only to utter an obvious and terrible truth; which history, reason, and experience alike set beyond dispute.

Vicious courses involve physical, moral, and mental degeneration for the individual transgressor.

Who—alas! can deny it, in view of the wreckage of humanity drifting by us and around us on the surface of life's sea?

Who so happy as not to have in sight among his acquaintance some terrible illustration of the truth that sensuality, to say nothing of the soul ; destroys the vigor of the body, clouds the intellect, and allowed to run its course, ends in the utter ruin of the man as a whole?

Any physician of experience and repute will admit that so far as he is cognizant of them a large part of the ills, imbecility and disabilities ; and among them the most obstinate and disgusting, with which he has to deal; originate here.

Here is the fruitful parent of epilepsies, tabes, syphilis; and as it is now asserted of leprosy itself.

Even persons comparatively ignorant of pathology do not need to be told of the dreadful ravages which those disgusting forms of disease; which are the product of incontinence and immorality: make upon the mental and physical powers.

A nation is an aggregate of individuals. An injury to the individual, is in its relation and degree an injury to the Nation of which he is a constituent part.

"If one member suffer all the members suffer with it;" is a law of life everywhere, from whose dominion there is no escape.

If the individual is anyhow incapacitated physically, morally, spiritually, to discharge his functions as a man and a citizen: the family and the State suffer in the degree in which his ability to render them has become impaired.

It follows, and there is no getting away from the conclusion, that where large sections of a population become physically and morally deteriorated through vicious and immoral practices, the strength and capacity of the State must be weakened in exact proportion.

If the evil, unarrested, continues to spread in ever-widening circles; with every passing decade involving hitherto untainted thousands in its curse; it is plain that the Nation itself must enter upon a period of decline, which allowed to proceed to its ultimate results can only issue in national ruin and extinction.

Such is the hypothesis to which a simple and direct line of reasoning infallibly conducts us.

It is the purpose of this paper to show that this conclusion is sound, as sound in history as it is in logic; that it is so proved by the facts, and that the experience of mankind in the past establishes it as a law of national life that *vicious and immoral practices in a people surely and proportionately engender national decay.*

The subject is one of the highest importance. It offers a fine field for the patriot, the philanthropist, and the Christian. We may be permitted to express surprise that it has been scarcely at all explored.

A great and authoritative treatise upon it is needed, which should be within reach of all legislators and students of political economy : a volume or volumes to the preparation of which one might worthily and usefully consecrate a lifetime.

I. In vindication of the statement that social vice involves National decay, our first appeal is to the *history of the past.*

This appeal will necessarily be largely a matter of quotation.

It is not too much to say that wide-spread social impurity hurried the great Empires of Antiquity into their graves.

Their decline and ruin is found to be coincident with their abandonment to vice.

Read the records of Babylon. The Greek historian Herodotus, in describing the social life of that great empire, details customs of such infamous bestiality, that for the credit of human nature we would gladly deny them.

Every woman in Babylon; we have the highest authorities for the statement; was compelled once in her life to prostitute herself and that at the choice of her seducer.

The annual festival at the temple of Bel terminated in the wildest orgies, and when the shades of evening fell upon the scene, the sanctions of religion were invoked for the indulgence of the basest sensual appetites.

This horrible national immorality was coincident with national decline. Too infamous to live, the Nation sank into extinction, leaving behind it a loathsome memory!

Under the caption "*Sodomite*"—speaking of those who practiced as a religious rite the abominable and unnatural vice, from which the inhabitants of Sodom and Gomorrah derived their lasting infamy as they derived their woeful doom, McClintoch and Strong's Cyclopedia says : "This dreadful consecration, or rather desecration, was spread in different forms over Phœnecia, Syria, Phrygia, Assyria, Babylonia: Ashtaroth, the Greek Astarte, being its chief object."

These nations are all dead; and it can hardly be disputed that these vices hurried on their doom.

Of Greece, which stood in the very forefront of the ancient civilizations, Dr. Tholuck writes: "We find no people on earth among whom immodest boldness was so united with mental refinement as the Greeks."

The great festivals, the Thesmaphoria, the Dionysia, the feasts of Cybele, were full of pollution.

The wealth of Corinth largely proceeded from the hire of vice.

Pythonice, who was notoriously an utterly abandoned woman, was a public character. At her death a great number of artists accompanied the bier to mournful music, while Harpalus, Alexander's lieutenant in Babylon, erected to her memory a princely Cenotaph on the way from Athens to Eleusis.

While the education of woman generally was entirely neglected among the Greeks, women of this class pursued every kind of science and art.

They were authoresses. They frequented the lecture rooms of the philosophers. They prepared books of laws for the conduct of their lovers.

They actually kept schools in which young girls were trained in the art of vice as systematically as the young men were trained in eloquence.

When these creatures died, such men as Aristophanes and Apollodorus made haste to write their histories.

A distinct connection is traceable between this state of public morals and the national decline.

These were coincident. Wide-spread immorality and public ruin went hand and hand down the decline.

Aristotle charges upon female licentiousness the disorders which issued in the destruction of the Spartan State; and when Thrasybulus delivered Athens from the Thirty Tyrants, her liberty came too late. The manners of her citizens were irretrievably corrupt, and honeycombed by avarice debauchery and licentiousness, that renowned city was diseased beyond recovery.

Thus Greece, for Art and Culture the most eminent nation of the ancient world; the manhood and womanhood of her people, sapped by immorality, sank into a ruin, from which she has never risen. Her history to this day offers awful warning of the perils of national vice.

We turn to a yet greater Empire.

Rome in her downfall repeats the same sad lesson. Mistress of the nations, without being mistress of herself, she conquered the world only to be conquered by her own licentiousness.

With advancing age and luxury the simple and austere morality of earlier times were discarded and even the death of Caesar could not restore that liberty of Rome, which had fled forever with her virtuous manners. "The last days of the Republic," says Ortolan, "were marked by an astonishing depravity of morals. The marriage of citizens had been abandoned or transformed into libertinism through annual divorces."

Sallust, who cannot be charged with any too prudish or nice regard for moral distinctions, writes of the last years of the Republic:—

" The lust of licentiousness, of low debauchery, of every sort of luxury did not less spread abroad; men offered themselves for the basest purposes, women publicly announced their virtue for sale."

46

Seneca, writing of the days of the Empire in its early decline, gives a terrific testimony:

"Women," he says, "reckoned the years by the number of their husbands," and asks: "Dost thou believe any age to have been more corrupt than that in which lust could not be restrained either by sacred things or by judicial procedures."

Juvenal speaks of those divorced before the nuptial garlands had faded, and whose chief distinction it was to have had eight husbands in five autumns, and again declares: "There will be nothing further which posterity may add to our evil manners; those coming after can only reproduce our desires and deeds. Every vice stands already on its topmost summit."

Speaking of the same age and its tendencies, Rev. Dr. R. S. Storrs, of Brooklyn, in a magnificent chapter on the Effect of Christianity on the Moral Life of Mankind, says of the same age: "Women of high rank even sought to be enrolled as common prostitutes that they might be unhindered in their lusts—the very temples became the resorts of lust. Buffoons and dancing girls attended on the feasts. They closed in the most licentious revelry, and whoever would have the image of one of them distinctly before him, may find it in that fearful picture of the Roman decadence, still, I think, in the gallery of the Luxembourg, and reproduced in occasional prints."

"Pantomines and buffoonery took the place of the delicate comedy or the serious tragedy of the earlier time. The scenes presented were full of adulteries and amorous intrigues. The pimp and the courtesan in Plantus plays had a popularity which Terence could not rival. The most frightful obscenities added relish to the performance, and the ballet-dancers danced nearly or wholly naked on the stage."

"The men of moral feeling, of intellectual desires, or of a generous public spirit, of whom there were still many in Rome, could only stand aside watching with

47

bitterness this infernal procession of all the lusts; always in peril of being caught in it or of being hurled by it into the unexplored abysm of death."

How completely these statements verify the representations of the Apostle, in the opening chapter of his Epistle to the Romans.

What wonder if as Matthew Arnold writes:

> "On that hard Pagan world disgust
> And secret loathing fell,
> Deep weariness and sated lust
> Made human life a hell!"

Dr. Storrs notes Mr. Lecky's significant affirmation that from this radical and permanent degradation of spirit the distinctive Roman people have never recovered.

The social vice of Rome; it cannot be successfully denied was very clearly responsible for her dreadful Fate.

"No nation," says Tytler with perfect correctness "has afforded a more striking example than the Romans have done of the necessity of good morals to the preservation of political liberty and the happiness of the people."

The list of witnesses is not exhausted. We might tell the story of Egypt, Assyria, Pompeii—the Canaanitish peoples, and every one of them will add force to this testimony of the Ancient world, that debauchery as certainly ruins a nation as its ruins a man.

But we hasten nearer home and to our own times, and

II. Our second appeal is taken to after-history and the experience of nations of later times: the immoral and enervated East; Turkey with its harems, France with its vast proportion of illegitimate births and its system of State regulated vice; read us the same sad lesson.

Time will not allow us to do other than suggest to those who have more time and opportunity the calling of these witnesses.

The examination of French, Turkish and Syrian history for the last three centuries, as indeed that of many other lands would afford undoubtedly most striking corroboration of the thesis we defend, but the limits of this paper forbid entrance upon this examination.

There is, however, one so preeminent and terrible illustration of the truth that social vice ensures national decay, now conspicuous in the eyes of the whole civilized world, that it cannot be passed over; on it so far as Modern History is concerned we may well rest the case.

We refer to the Hawaiian and neighboring Islands.

An article in the *Medical Record*, September 10th, 1892, on the *Etiology of Leprosy* by Geo. L. Fitch, M.D., of San Francisco, opens with the words, "What is leprosy, and what causes it? The answer I believe is; A fourth stage of syphilis."

This proposition Dr. Fitch undertakes to demonstrate from the etiology of the disease in the Sandwich Islands during the last hundred years.

The Islands were visited by Capts. Cook and Clarke in his Majesty's ships Resolution and Discovery in 1778.

Of the morality of the Islanders at this time Jarvis, in his History of the Islands says: "The ceremonies observed on the death of any prominent personage were extremely barbarous . . . Gambling, theft and murder were as open as the day; clothing was cast aside as a useless encumbrance; drunkenness and promiscuous prostitution prevailed throughout the land; no woman except the widow of the deceased being exempt from the grossest treatment.

There was no passion, however lewd, or desire, however wicked, but could be gratified with impunity . . . no other nation was ever witness to a custom which so entirely threw off all moral and legal restraints and incited the evil passions of men to unrestricted riot and debauchery.

"As a general thing there was no such sentiment as chastity;" indeed there is *no word meaning "chastity" in the language.*

Among a people thus given to utter sensuality, syphilis which existed on the British ships was introduced despite all the efforts of Captain Cook.

"Before the advent of the whites" says Dr. Fitch "in Hawaii Marriage as we understand the word, (one male and one female consecrating themselves to each other only) was practically unknown.

About the first lesson the Hawaiian mother taught her infant after it could walk was the *hula*, or national dance." This dance was grossly and beyond expression lascivious in its motions, and "the more lascivious the action, the more accomplished the performer."

Dr. Fitch further says, "Friends in visiting each other exchange wives over night, and strangers were accommodated with women as a matter of common courtesy.

Dr. Fitch on one occasion asked Queen Kapiolani what proportion of the native women had been true to their lawful husbands?

She replied—"Aole ukahi walhine likapu Ke la" (not one like that).

Here we have a population under absolute dominion of social vice. What is the result?

It is no doubt true that the introduction of syphilis among such a race must have intensified and accelerated its decay, but the introduction of syphilis only partially accounts for the ruin which followed.

The diary of Rev. Chas. Stewart, one of the early Missionaries to Hawaii, under date May 22d, 1832, says "Not to mention the frequent and hideous mark of a scourge which more clearly than any other proclaims the curse of the God of Purity and which while it annually consigns hundreds of the people to the tomb and converts thousands, while living, into walking sepulchres, the inhabitants generally are sub-ject to many disorders of the skin.

Still more impressive and significant in this con-nection are the following figures going back to 1823, when intercourse between Hawaii and the outside world received a great impetus.

The population mainly native was estimated in 1823 at 142,000. In 1832 it had fallen to 130,000. In 1836 to 108,000. 1853 it was 73,100. 1860—69,800. 1866—62,900. 1872—56,900. 1890—40,000.

If these figures do not lie how sadly and solemnly they seem to teach that social vice is a chief source of national decay.

A similar inference must be drawn from the statement of Rev. A. A. Sturgis, who found a few cases of syphilis in the Caroline Islands on his first visit there as a Missionary in 1851. Now all the islands are in-fected with it and about one in twenty of the natives are lepers.

Here we might rest the case. Could anything be clearer than this testimony of both Ancient History and Modern experience that it is as with a man so with a nation, the sin is sure to find the sinner out?

When a Nation sets at defiance the fundamental laws of morality ordained by God it invites decay, ruin and extinction.

III. But we are unwilling to leave a subject so im-portant without strengthening the truth by another and third appeal, to the longevity of peoples whose morality has been marked.

Going back to the early Mosaic legislation and the history of the Chosen People one is struck by the stringency of the Divine enactments with which the Decalogue opens and which so emphatically prohibit the least approaches to idolatrous worship.

Corresponding with the stringency of this require-ment was the attitude of God toward Israel in all her subsequent history.

No dereliction so quickly drew down upon her the Divine anger in its terribleness of chastisement and rebuke as the sin of idolatry. Again and again she suffered awfully on account of it.

It may be said that a due recognition of the Being, Unity and Dominion of God is basal in any correct system of law or morality.

This is true and will go far to account for the prominence given to this doctrine in the Divine legislation.

But another point must be considered. Wherein was Israel's temptation to idolatrous worship? Why did she so often prefer Clemosh Astoreth Baal to JEHOVAH, the gods of Amon and Moab to the one true and infinitely holy God? It would seem to have been an extraordinary, a diabolical fascination. We believe that the explanation is to be found in the *sensuality* of these wicked and false faiths.

They appealed to the lowest and basest instincts of the animal nature, and hence largely their enormous and seductive powers.

Lascivious dances constituted an important part of their ritual.

In the dusky shadows of their groves, the restraints of morality were cast to the winds, while within the precincts of the temples and around their very altars the practice of an utterly obscene and sensual worship proclaimed the gods they worshipped; gods of lust.

This certainly was characteristic of the worship of Moab as one must learn from her attempted seduction of Israel, (Num. 25).

The Septuagint renders the word "high-places" (Ezek. 16:39) by a term which in Greek signifies "a place of indecent resort."

It was not then merely, as concerned for the honor of His own great Name, and the preservation of the one true faith among men, but as well for the *physical and moral salvation* of the chosen people whose national life these excesses of an idolatrous worship would threaten with decay and extinction, that God made these enactments so strenuous and preeminent, and fenced them with penalties so prompt and terrible: and it is in good part to the operation of these laws directly against idolatry, incidently against sensuality, rigidly enforced by penalty, that we must in some degree attribute the remarkable preservation and longevity of the Hebrew race. A people scattered and peeled, wanderers without a home, yet a people refusing to die; while nations their superiors in wealth and numbers, honeycombed by vice and immorality, have descended to the grave of Empires and ceased to be.

In this same line of thought these words of Joseph Cook in one of the Boston Monday Lectures merit remembrance:

"There are many Saxon faces in this audience. The blue eyes, the white forehead, the blond cheek, the fair hair are signs of the Anglo-Saxon lineage. That Race rules the world to-day.

That Race has given to us Goethe, Milton and Shakespeare and Bacon and Kent and Hamilton and Edwards and Cromwell and Washington and Lincoln. It wrote Magna Charta, the Declaration of Independence, the Constitution of the United States.

It has bridged the Ocean with its commerce and traversed it with its electric wires. That Race in its German forests was noted for nothing so much as the spotlessness of its private morals.

While yet Barbarians our German fathers, as the Roman historians state, buried the adulterer alive in the mud. The adulteress they whipped through the streets.

"Non forma, non aetate, non opibus maritum invenerit." Neither beauty nor youth, nor wealth found her a husband. Out of this race sprung Chivalry. It is this race which has proved itself in the chivalric contests of a thousand years, both in peace and war

53

superior to all relaxed Italian and French tribes as the leader of all the world's civilization.

"The purity of the tribes in the German forests prophesied their future.

"The hiding of the power of the Anglo-Saxon race has been in the fact that it was at the first free from the sin of Sodom and Gomorrah.

"In the German wilds our fathers were, as the Romans found them, pure as the dews the forests shook upon their heads. The race has predominated in history because free "even when barbarian" from what elsewhere has been the commonest leprosy of barbarism.

"If the Anglo Saxon race has shown exceptional vigor the chief secret of its power is to be found in its reverence for a pure family life. It will continue to have that power and rule the world if it continues that pure life. Otherwise not."

In bringing this paper to a practical conclusion we must ask: Has History in all this no voice for our own land?

Is there any danger that Social Vice will work out, here and among our people, national decay?

There is such a danger. The study of statistics shows an alarming increase of vice in our communities.

The number of prostitutes has of late years in all our cities multiplied immensely; and the number of male prostitutes in a community is fairly reckoned at five times the number of female.

The Rev. Dr. B. F. De Costa has well said:

"The social evil is the greatest of all evils, because it is honeycombing society, undermining the foundation of the State, and destroying the public health. If one wants to know the number of impure men in a community, all that is necessary is to find the number of impure women and multiply it by five. * * * * Until the double standard of morality is destroyed, there is no hope for social purity."

But this is not the worst; forms of Vice, far more disgusting and pernicious, almost unnameable are known by the students of criminal life, to have existed among us for years, and as there is reason to fear are on the increase.

Montesquieu once affirmed that the principle of monarchy is *honor*, of despotism *fear*, of republicanism *virtue*, and General Washington, in his farewell address, reminded the nation he had done so much to found, that RELIGION and MORALITY are pillars of the State.

It is sad to think of our beloved Country; as we contemplate this loathsome and wide-spreading moral corruption, that, "gray hairs are here and there upon her, yet she knoweth not," as the Prophet Hosea said of his people.

Time was, not long ago, when we were wont to think that in the free and enlightened Institutions of our happy land the great problem of human Government had been finally solved, that a system so just, free, well-balanced and conservative of human rights had at length been secured, that its beneficent sway would last as long as men need government. Alas! if what we now hear is true this great nation may not live out half her days!

The same causes evermore produce the same effects. Our Country can hope for no exemption from the penalty which follows for the nation as well as the man the violation of Divine law.

Social vice unchecked worked ruin for Babylon; Greece; Rome; Hawaii. Despite their Puritan beginnings; despite a God-fearing and Bible-loving ancestry; despite the guardianship of just and righteous laws; despite a noble history; Social Vice, if it shall come to be regnant and unchecked will work the same ruin for the people of the United States; and afford the World and coming Ages one more melancholy illustration that as among the more degraded so too among the freest and most enlightened peoples; *Social Vice is the Parent*

of National Decay.   Years ago John Greenleaf Whittier
wrote, and his words are appropriate to us and here
to-day :

> "Our fathers to their graves have gone
> Their strife is past—their triumph won;
> But sterner trials wait the race
> Which rises in their honored place—
> A moral warfare with the crime
> And folly of an evil time.

> "So let it be.   In God's own might
> We gird us for the coming fight.
> And strong in Him whose cause is ours
> In conflict with unholy powers,
> We grasp the weapons He has given—
> The Light, and Truth, and Love of Heaven."

LAURA H. SATTERTHWAITE, M. D.

THE GREAT NEED OF THE MORAL CRUSADE.

By Laura H. Satterthwaite, M. D., Trenton, N. J.

One need only pause and listen to realize there is an urgent demand for a gathering of forces to march under the banner of purity. The work is too great for longer concealment. The ravages upon the human system from varying results of immorality are giving decided warnings of what the future may be if there is not an awakening. To the many desiring a betterment of the social status but standing aloof, believing discussion breeds an unhealthy condition in the minds of some who know nothing of this and need never know, permit me to suggest you are standing on a false hypothesis, as this incident illustrates. A lady guarding her children in every way to keep them ignorant of the great social evil though exerting herself to warn them of all others, was appalled to hear her thirteen year old boy tell her he had been repeatedly urged to enter a house of ill-fame and was aghast to find he knew what transpired within. As this woman's eyes were opened to the impossibility of keeping the knowledge from anyone entering the world, to do his or her part in life, or yours may be, and with a child lacking the naturally strong character of this one, too late. For what this boy learned on his short walk to school, others obtain there, from thoughtless servants and unprincipled caretakers. The only method to keep the information from them is to sweep the immoral blight from our land.

Probably there has not been a greater obstacle to a better moral standard and one claiming your attention early in the campaign, than the too generally endorsed idea that it is necessary to be lenient to one sex, according to the laws of health. Can we say there is a just God if we think a portion of humanity is condemned to save others, to suffer not as Jesus suffered, to have his reward, but in the belief of all adopting the teachings of the Bible, to everlasting damnation? For is this not the way of the lewd woman as Christanity views her? Charge your cannons with the truth and conquer this false reasoning. No individual has an excuse, except an uncontrolled passion for generations back.

A profound respect is held for the reverend gentlemen present and for every consistent Christian, and you working faithfully in the cause must not interpret censure, but as the whole field is surveyed there appears a pressing need for this crusade to moralize so called Christianity of to-day. You may answer how many church members we have, and how many standing before the Supreme Judge would have to answer in the negative, Hast thou obeyed the Seventh Commandment since connected with the church? Why are religious denominations so lax on this subject? We see persons holding high positions in their churches and meetings who could not stand the searchlight turned upon their morals one second. Yet there they are, equalling in authority their righteous brother and sister. Aye, often pointed to as worthy examples to innocent young minds, whose acute perception discovers their hypocrisy, and often is known their blackened character. No earthly power can convince me that the undefiled religion of Jesus can be embraced in anything but a morally clean body. Without this an otherwise clean soul must become infected and its professions of righteousness a superficial covering, which is far more harmful than open corruption. A religion not applicable to our every day acts and duties is a blackguard upon the name; and a church or meeting looking with placid countenance upon the two curses of this country—intemperance and immorality, so closely allied—do more to embarrass Christianity than the eloquent Ingersoll could ever do. There are some in all denominations who would keep an incessant commotion about obeying the doctrinal points of their body, dictated by man, but won't ripple the surface about the moral laws of God. Christians, to protect your religion as well as your people, you must bring the crusaders to the church doors and make an aggressive warfare until every church and meeting house is what it professes—a house of God.

This war is needed not for the erring only but the pure, if all knowledge was theirs, would cry aloud for quickened steps and powerful weapons. Most of you are familiar with that dreadful scourge of Biblical fame, leprosy, and would send into exile a case found among you. A disease which I can't conceive to be in some cases even second and certainly second only to leprosy in its obnoxiousness, is in your very midst. There are dying daily infants, children and all ages from its effects, caused by an inherited taint or an innocent acquirement possibly in their very household. Do you whisper, you never heard of such a thing? Quite likely. The physician's certificate seldom gives the first sown seeds of death or the unpleasant complications of an acute illness. Yes, a filthy disease is all around us and being rapidly spread by loose morals. We should be aroused to action, from the dire results falling not merely upon the guilty. Many authenticated cases show the wild oats of youth are reaped in after years; as that mother, marrying her healthy daughter, with every prospect of a brilliant social career, to the idolized son of another mother realized when she saw this innocent woman, after two years of suffering, succumb to the vile disorder contracted from her husband, who had lived but a few months of imprudence; and the mother of that husband then understood the unexplainable utterance of her son on his wedding day, that if he were not a coward he would shoot himself before he again met his bride. Can anyone not be personally interested in this agitation? If you have a son or brother do you not tremble at the possibilities in marriage? If you have a daughter or sister do you not

tremble at the greater possibilities in marriage? If you
have a babe seldom leaving your arms, in just one
unguarded moment a diseased germ may be implanted
upon an abraided surface of the child by a kiss. The
peril is so imminent the dealers themselves are becoming alarmed and ask for protection in seeking licensed
houses of prostitution, where rigid examination of the
female inmates shall be required. Such a partial and
unjust law should be overcome in its infancy.

Is it not time to cry halt in clarion tones when pure
men defend unvirtuous woman on the plea that men are
excused ? No greater discouragement was ever experienced by me than this defence for association with
an impure woman. It seemed an insult had been given
to the chaste sister, mother and wife as well as the one
addressed. If good men of standing were going to condone this offense because man's standard was low there
might be a surrender at once. The writer believes the
future of this question rests largely with man; woman
can do much but the virtuous man far more, in treating
the erring brother as the erring sister is treated. It has
been said " Virtue is the most precious jewel woman
possesses " and for the continuation of its value she
earnestly pleads and this crusade must fetter all such
declarations nourishing lewdness. The pedestal upon
which woman stands is not too high and she is not too
harsh upon this error of her sister. There is a tendency
to bring down one sex which as a body now stands superior and dim the splendor and glory of that masterpiece of
God, a true, noble, virtuous woman, by placing on the
same plane one of animal instincts. They cannot hold
that position, but pray you, men and women let not the
sacredness of motherhood be tarnished by their touch.
Fight as you never fought before to barricade unchaste
woman from securing a stand where she can flaunt to the
breeze the flag of defiance and our children taught to
look upon her with deference. For the sake of humanity in their social, business and political relations this

battle must be waged and the standard advanced all
along the line, because the force of Pope's lines,

> " Vice is a monster of so frightful mien
> As to be hated needs but to be seen;
> Yet seen too oft, familiar with her face,
> We first endure, then pity, then embrace,"

—'tis natural to predict has been appreciated by many
in observing men and women, apparently of good standing and sound thoughts, smother their conscience for a
few moments, to enjoy some they inwardly repelled, for
the sake of that studied flattery and nicety given them
for purposes, some baser than others. I know it is not
a popular thought, but many a woman is leading two
lives to-day as successfully as man. Ere long the time
for the hushing process increases and the minutes grow
into hours, and their minds become so poisoned against
their true friends, whose words as well as their being
become repulsive, and the successful tempters hold their
victims so strongly in their grasp and so dull their vision,
that they detect no difference, and we see them actually
scorn virtue and embrace vice. They know not why
their path in life has become so troubled, believing they
are the same individuals as of yore, until Satan sounds
the bugle for his agents, their followers and their friends.
Then the once upright man and woman look around.
An awful realization dawns upon them, and uttering
cries of remorse, believing their dual life will be overlooked as in the past, make a dash for their former
abodes in the midst of honor, only to find the doors to
respectable society have at last been closed and barred.
On them a bulletin announcing their lost reputation,
and that another must be made before the key will be
turned; and even then a back seat will ever be theirs.
This is a gloomy picture for anyone to contemplate, especially if beyond the prime of life, but unless something
is done to crush the growing power of these wily enticers
what family will feel secure from some of their number
being susceptible to their influence ? Their boldness in

defying public opinion is increasing, and if our good people sit with closed eyes and muffled ears and say we see and hear nothing, we are doomed. Does not this social serpent of vice call for solid ranks and telling ammunition? Cease not the care over the maiden but bestow more upon the youth traveling equally as dangerous a road, being ensnared by the superficial and insincere woman. The smoothed corrugator, and the delicate tinted powder, with other artificial appliances, make as many unhappy marriages as love for money, and such marriages being breeders of immorality the crusaders are called upon to slay their agents too.

If any think an unseeming harshness is shown toward my sex, I assure them the sin and not the sinner has been uppermost in the mind; and the minute the sinner casts aside the sin and proves a true repentance, by living a proper life, in the strongest terms would I say welcome them with open arms. But for the benefit of many withstanding with difficulty the outstretched hand of crime, the final reward of virtue must not be marred by having the once fallen placed above persons who have reached the goal without yielding. They who persist in living the life of degradation, help them as we can; but we shall be unable to enter into close association and keep clean ourselves. As a widow with a dependent family of children would be unwise and cruel to enter a house reeking with the germs of contagious disease, so would you be to the children of the world to enter into a friendship which would bring reproach upon you and destroy all future usefulness. Charity we must have, knowing many of us have our grievous faults; but intemperance and immorality, the lowest and most degrading of sins, handicap one from entering the race of life, and cause others to suffer more than the transgressor, impeding the progress of all humanity and presenting scars never to be erased from the life of the actor.

In closing may I repeat, the moral crusade is needed to kill erroneous ideas; to erect barriers for both man and woman against sullied associates; to fortify the pinnacle which the one sex now occupies, and to bring the other to her level; to clean churches and meeting-houses and eradicate that foe to *true* religion; to resist illegal bartering of young girls and children for unlawful purposes; to prevent our country from bringing another curse upon it by licensing houses of prostitution; to rid all from the dangers now threatening to weaken coming generations and destroy every vestige of honest and good government; to give us a clear, healthy, and moral atmosphere in which the babe from its day of birth will breathe an air which will not incite wrong-doing but stimulate the best in them.

No one can deny the necessity of this war when they witness the enemy; but some will say it is not necessary for them to enlist. The utmost strength of every individual is required to annihilate this many-clawed monster, and not the frailest frame can be spared from giving his or her mite, and not one of you rests upon a solid foundation, if you care for the welfare of your families or your friends; and as fellow-mortals you should be willing to raise your arm in defence of right, and give your voice in condemnation of the wrong.

Women, I beseech you, let there be no compromise. Stand firm and demand purity for purity, remembering Tennyson's lines:

> " The woman's cause is man's, they rise or sink
> Together, dwarfed or Godlike, bond or free."

JULIA WARD HOWE.

MORAL EQUALITY BETWEEN THE SEXES

By Mrs. Julia Ward Howe.

I shall begin my brief address by recalling to the minds of my hearers one or two of the trite sayings which remind us how near to each other are some things which we regard with very different feelings. "From the sublime to the ridiculous there is but one step." This proverb is very familiar to us, and no less is St. Paul's word that "in the midst of life we are in death." Even so, a simple step may lead from what is honorable in the sight of all men to the very depths of dishonor, and in the midst of our moral and social life lurk the seeds of our moral death. To speak without paraphrase, the relations of sex are either the crown of Society, or its ruin: they either build the State upon a sound and true foundation, or they set up fantastic structures upon quicksands which speedily become yawning chasms of loss and misery.

The rigid rule of our Puritan ancestors had, no doubt, some part in calling forth the reaction against ethical stringency which has been a feature in a part of our Nineteenth Century. The Puritans were, indeed, hard upon individual sinners, and much of their theology has passed even beyond controversy. But they did not exaggerate the danger which comes to the State with the admission of loose morals.

A false æsthetic has much to do with bad morals. We all live as much by the beautiful as by the useful, or more. The romancer of a period or of a special society may ingeniously divorce the beautiful from the good. In such a society the youth, whose ethical sense is as yet

immature, will run great risk of following the allurement of the false beauty.

For I need not say here that there is no real beauty
apart from what is good and estimable.

Young people in America read so much and so
miscellaneously that they will be apt to come often in
contact with the misleading sort of romance which I
have in mind. In American life, energy and the spirit
of adventure are largely developed, but home culture,
the most important of all, is abridged by the early age
at which young people leave the paternal roof to seek
fortune elsewhere. And this going forth to better one's
condition may often cultivate a barren egotistic spirit,
always alive to the chance of personal advancement, and
to little else.

We must cultivate in our young people a sense at
once of the strictness of moral obligation and of the
largeness of personal relation. We like to boast about
our country. It is easy to do that, but let us rather
remember what we owe to our country. "England
expects every man to do his duty," is a saying
which, no doubt, has had much to do with the
formation of character among the English people.
In the catechism of the Church of England duties
are set forth under two heads: Duty to God, and
to our neighbor—but we might add in the instruction of
the young, the question: What is my duty to my
country? I should answer, first, to learn to be a good
citizen, and secondly, to help, by influence and example,
to increase the number of good citizens.

Families are the wealth of states, and the ideal
family life is one which we Americans especially need
to cultivate. Let the romance of our youths look forward to married life on a plane of mutual dignity and
equality. In my view the sense of equality is a most
important condition in marriage, and the surest
guarantee of its sacredness. Do what you will, inferiority of ability will involve as its sequence inferiority

of moral responsibility. The interests committed to the keeping of women are too momentous to be entrusted by any man to his inferior. Such a feeling, latent in his mind, will always tend to lower the moral tone of the woman who looks to him for guidance and approval. We smile at the naïve device of the Vicar of Wakefield who, undertaking to place upon his wall a pen-portrait of his wife, adorned it with every high quality which he wished her to possess. I find a touch of deep wisdom in this. We all need to be reminded of the best that can be expected of us, and are hindered if not demoralized by the contrary course. There is surely in all this a logical sequence. The man, regarding the woman as his inferior, may consider it a light offence to work her dishonor. She, acquiescing in his view, will yield where she ought to resist. I am afraid that in such a case the woman will fall back upon Adam's excuse, and say: "The man tempted me." Out of such relations as these may be woven an intricate net work of vice and folly.

Let us bless our Christian religion for this above all else. It has explicitly stated and assumed the equality of the sexes. "In Christ Jesus there is neither male nor female," says the Apostle; and what said the Master: "He that looketh on a woman to lust after her, 'hath already committed' the sin," which in the woman we deem unpardonable.

All that to-day tends to the elevation of woman tends to dry up the sources of sexual immorality. But the Past has left us dread arrears with which the Present has still to settle. It has created for us numbers of degraded and unprincipled women who are content to take their tone from men, less outwardly degraded, perhaps, but even more unprincipled than themselves. Philosophy and Poetry in our day have sometimes appeared as the apologists of an evil which has come to us from the barbarous Past, but which has no apology in the civilized Present. I should say, pseudo-materialistic philosophy, unwholesome poetry, both of them unfit for a time of intellectual illumination like the Present.

For these evil views are a legacy from the old order of the domination of physical force. In this the power of offence was undoubtedly superior in the male sex, while power of endurance was greater in our own. This masculine ascendency has already in it one element of cruelty, that of sacrificing the weaker to the stronger, the ignorant to the designing.

I doubt whether the ferocity of the battlefield is as merciless as is the remorseless onslaught of unscrupulous passion. Oh, mothers, wherever you cultivate selfishness in your sons, and allow cruelty, you add something to the preponderance of evil in the world—you prepare unworthiness and unhappiness for them and for those with whom they will have to do.

I hold that equality of moral obligation is the one idea which lies at the foundation of any true democracy. This indeed is the only equality upon which we can insist. Intellectual and social inequalities cannot be done away with by any effort of human will. Every man cannot be a monarch, a genius, or a millionaire. Every woman cannot claim to shine by her wit, by her wealth, or in virtue of inherited position. To stand equal in justice before the civil law, equal in dignity before the moral law, this belongs to Christian democracy. And this positive idea will bloom into divinest beauty if we carry it, as our Master did, to its energetic issue—not only refraining from doing to others what we would not have them do to us, but going on to render to them the good offices which we should most value for ourselves, breaking from our personal limitations to embrace and serve the wholeness of our Humanity, which is present in the least of men as well as in the greatest.

The greatest poets have wrought in this spirit and to this end. Homer, Dante, and Shakespeare present to us no one sided view of humanity. And yet, some who have powerfully affected the imagination of the reading world have done otherwise. Even our Milton could say of our first parents:

" He for God only, she for God in him."

Thinking people have now passed beyond this limitation. Shall the woman see God in the man, and not in her own thought and conscience? Shall the human guide her in preference to the divine? Not so—let the sentence read: "Both for God only, in themselves—in each other."

The entertainment of the old unequal hypothesis has often seemed to me like the building of an arch in which one side should be reared in strength and strict measure, while the other should be built of unknown material, and with no perfect correspondence of direction. Society rests upon these arches. For one side you fit and smooth the stone carefully, for the other you take such material as comes to hand. How will such an arch stand? What pressure will it uphold? But if we bestow equal care upon the two sides of our arch then the keystone, Duty, will fit in, and our social fabric will stand so firmly that countless generations shall not cause it to move or fail.

MRS. REBECCA J. BROOMELL,

SECRETARY BALTIMORE BRANCH AMERICAN PURITY ALLIANCE,
BY WHOM MRS. HOWE'S PAPER WAS READ TO THE
CONGRESS.

THE RESPONSIBILITY OF WOMEN IN REGARD TO QUESTIONS CONCERNING PUBLIC MORALITY.

By EMILY BLACKWELL, M. D., NEW YORK.

The rapid development of Sanitary Science of late years, and the importance with which this progress has invested all questions of Public Hygiene, has created a growing interest in these subjects in the community, and especially among women.

The question of the best manner of dealing with Prostitution has long been recognized as one of the most difficult problems in municipal government in all the great cities of Europe, as it was in those of ancient times.

The growth of our cities during the past generation with the consequent increase of all the conditions upon which the evil depends, the extremes of wealth and poverty, the numbers of children growing up under unfavorable conditions, the difficulty of earning a living, are bringing this problem into similar prominence among us.

It is a question that has never been solved, but which will become ever more pressing until the principles upon which it is to be dealt with are finally settled.

Efforts have been made from the most ancient times to diminish this evil, to restrain its extent, and limit its injurious consequences, efforts which have become more systematic and more stringent as society has become more organized.

Every plan that is now suggested in the way of regulation and supervision has been tried in the most varied forms. No plan is now suggested that has not been put in operation somewhere and in some shape.

The one conspicuous result of these various efforts is their utter futility, their absolute failure. The fact stands prominently forth that the evil and its consequences are as great and as uncontrollable as ever.

This result would of itself be sufficient to prove that we have not yet reached the true principle on which to deal with the subject. Every mode of dealing with prostitution hitherto has treated it as a purely sanitary question, whereas the matter goes much deeper and involves the fundamental question of the relations of men and women. Right dealing with this subject means dealing founded on a true view of these relations.

The difficulty has been, and is, that every system of regulation is founded on the false principle of the inequality of men and women, in reference to moral obligations, to the almost universal belief that license is venial, even necessary to men, while Chastity is the one essential virtue of woman, the one quality in regard to which the least suspicion is fatal to her social respectability in any rank of life.

This view has come down to us as a relic of barbarism, from the old times when women were slaves, and their value and standing depended absolutely on their relations to men as decided by men. Slavery in every form yields slowly, and leaves an evil leaven behind which works mischief in society long after the apparent disappearance of its cause. This inequality of moral obligation in men and women is the last trace of the slavery of sex.

While this stage of the actual slavery of women has long been outgrown, we are still far from accepting and acting upon the idea that men and women are two equal and co-ordinate halves of the human race, with corresponding interests, rights and duties. We have not yet learned that there cannot be any real antagonism between the interests and requirements of men and women in any question that concerns both, that any apparent antagonism must necessarily arise from some false conception not yet outgrown.

One of the deepest and worst of these lingering falsehoods is this prevalent idea of the different attitudes which both moral and physical requirements are held to impose upon men and women in regard to moral obligations.

This popular view implies a logical impossibility.

The morality of women as a whole cannot exceed that of men as a whole; vice is only diffused in one sex and concentrated in the other. As a matter of fact purity is not regarded by society as an essential requisite of all womanhood, but only of a part of it. That wives and mothers should be pure, another class of women must have the whole balance of evil poured out upon them. The higher sense of mankind says that the family is the essential unit of the State. Our practice says the family plus prostitution is the essential unit.

Yet the moral sense of both men and women would revolt from the only logical conclusion of the present view, viz., that any people performing a necessary social function should not be degraded thereby, and that this most unfortunate class, instead of being made the scapegoat of society and driven into the desert with the sins of a nation on its head, should be regarded as an order vowed to sacrifice in obedience to a cruel social necessity; and their occupation should be regarded as legitimate and respectable, and should be surrounded by all the safeguards that may be required for its protection.

The only possible alternative to this view is to take our stand resolutely upon the ground of equal moral obligation, and accept no method of dealing with this evil that is based upon any other.

That men should not yet have risen to this point of view is not extraordinary when we regard the whole history of the growth of civilization. It seems at first sight more surprising that women should accept this double standard so widely and so zealously. This is, however, only another instance of what we find as the universal teaching of history, that any false social view wide spread and long continued, is gradually accepted by those whom it injures as well as by the dominant class. The Divine Right of Kings was a popular doctrine under arbitrary monarchs. Loyalty, the unreasoning self-sacrifice of the inferior to the superior, was one of the most popular virtues under the Feudal System, and so the subservience to a shortsighted view of men's requirements has come down ingrained in women from the times when their whole existence depended upon such subservience.

So women accept and act upon this popular fallacy without realizing the results of their action. Multitudes of good women would be startled by the assertion that purity is as possible and desirable for men as for women, and yet feel that loyalty to womanhood requires the utmost severity in the judgment of laxity of conduct among women. How many women are there in the country who really feel that vice is as derogatory to men as to women, who would turn the cold shoulder to a man on the same degree of suspicion as would lead them to drop his sister, who would be as distressed at immorality in their sons as in their daughters. Society does not allow such equal justice, the feelings of women do not impel them to it. They follow custom without reasoning upon it.

Women will not, however, much longer be able to ignore their responsibility in this question. Hitherto any false regulation on this subject has been the work of men alone. It is evident that this will not be the case in the future, and that in its final settlement women will inevitably have to share the responsibility. Two very marked tendencies have been developed among women in recent times that will play a constantly increasing part in social life.

The one is the tendency to combine and take united action in many directions. Women's clubs, societies and associations of all kinds have multiplied, and are multiplying endlessly; they are teaching women a much needed lesson, that union is strength, and that to gain it women must learn to act upon wider than personal grounds.

Again, the immense development of Sanitary Science, the management of Institutions and Charities, and our way of regarding and dealing with the great questions of Public Hygiene, is teaching them a second and equally needed lesson. This is that they cannot fulfil their duties even in the sphere universally conceded to them, in domestic, social, personal life, without following their interests outside the home, into the wider sphere of municipal and state action. The active interest manifested by many of our most conservative women in municipal reform, and municipal action in matters of public hygiene, shows that they are learning that they cannot satisfactorily work at home without following their interests out into the broader housekeeping of the city and the state, that they must become citizens as well as members of the family. It is very certain that these tendencies to wider action will increase and will bring women more fully into contact with this most painful of all social problems. It is of immense importance that women should assume the right attitude in this matter. We begin to see indications that this will not always be the case, and that there is danger that women, when first confronted with this question, may not always see beyond the false and shortsighted views which control our present customs.

The assertion that there can and must be only one law for men and women is usually met by men with a contemptous smile, as one of those quixotic conceptions of reformers which indicate their real ignorance of the world and human nature. Influenced by this deeply rooted feeling women often believe the assertions so constantly made that the only way is to palliate an inevitable evil.

Thus we find that in New Zealand, where women have recently obtained the suffrage, the "Woman's Liberal League" recently adopted and published a resolution endorsing the Contagious Diseases Act, and urging its adoption in New Zealand. A Woman's Rescue Society in Boston, last year, had introduced into the Massachusetts Legislature, and pressed, though happily unsuccessfully, the passage of a bill for the restricting of vice in Boston, and in Illinois we hear of a recommendation of the regulation of vice by a committee of women. In several other directions we find notices of action by women which show that they do not always at first sight appreciate the true bearings of such actions.

The first step toward diminishing a vice is to recognize it as such, and to stamp it with public reprobation. This is true notwithstanding the fact that we cannot hope to exterminate it by any mode of dealing with it. We have not succeeded in exterminating murder, theft, or any other crime by legislation. But the respect for life has greatly increased since public opinion has condemned dueling, and every other form of private killing. Drunkenness and Prostitution are the only crimes which we attempt to palliate by legalizing the conditions under which they may be committed.

It is often urged also that we take a sentimental view of this matter. That it is a question of individuals. That every woman knows the penalty of a lapse from virtue. That no woman need fall so low. That Prostitutes are a degraded and criminal body, whom their low moral sense, vanity, disinclination to work, impatience of poverty, etc., has led them voluntarily into their present condition. That they are hardened and shameless even beyond ordinary criminals, and that their unrestrained activity is a menace to society. Granting the truth of this judgment is it not inevitable that a class which is permitted to exist, but kept under the ban of society, must harden into defiant antagonism to social law ?

Women often fail to perceive what wide spread mischief this laxity of public opinion, in which they ignorantly share, works to them. To its influence is due in large measure every social and industrial disadvantage under which they labor. The isolation of women, their ignorance of the world, the necessity of surrounding girls with crippling limitations for their protection, the impossibility of allowing them freedom and independence, which prevents their acquiring self-reliance and power of dealing with the world if circumstances take them out of the protected circle of family life, these are only remnants of the old seclusion of women due to the danger of their free intercourse with men. The absolute relegation of women to the most narrowly limited private life, their general seclusion from all wider outside occupations and interests, which leaves the army of young women engaged in industry to the almost exclusive direction of and dependence upon men, comes from the same feeling that women cannot safely engage in anything outside of domestic life. The whole organization of society is built up upon the virtual separation of the sexes for the protection of the weaker. This makes the position of those women who must go out into the world the more difficult, because it separates them from older and better circumstanced women, deprives them of their natural leaders and counsellors. Moreover, upon this false view of necessity is founded the tacit permission to build up a trade in vice, to form a wide spread organization whose interest is to extend and supply it. Yet this vilest of all social classes is the very one which is made the accredited agent to superintend it in any system of legalization.

In whatever direction women are working to extend their openings for development, they are met by this permitted absence of moral obligation on the part of men as one of the great obstacles in their way, for it puts the relations of men and women and their whole way of dealing with each other upon a false footing, which works always to the disadvantage of women.

We want to bring all women to understand that the only true way to deal with prostitution is, first, to diminish the demand upon which it is based by stamping vice with public reprobation in men as well as in women. Secondly, to organize among women a broader and more effective form of rescue work. At present most of the effort in this direction is devoted to saving the fallen. Without in any way reflecting upon this benevolent work, it is yet evident that while the conditions which maintain vice exist undiminished, the place of every reclaimed woman is filled up by another pushed over the brink.

We want a still more active effort to save those "who are ready to perish." Girls' Clubs, Friendly Societies, Women's Protective Associations, Employment Societies, everything that brings to the poorest and most friendless the strength of combination and companionship, that brings the wealthier, more educated, better placed women into friendly social relations upon the ground of the equality of a common womanhood, are the most effective forms of rescue work, and every woman should feel bound to throw her help and influence into these efforts. Thirdly, every woman should resolutely oppose any form of municipal or state action that gives direct or indirect recognition or support to those who, as agents of vice, pursue the vile trade of encouraging it for gain. The fact that this is involved in every system of regulation should be enough to condemn the whole thing.

Women have had imposed upon them by society, and have accepted from their own moral sense the duty of embodying in their own lives the ideal of purity, and of standing for it in family and social life. They are pledged by every consideration of honor, of justice, of self-respect, to insist that what society demands as essential to every honorable woman should be made possible to all women. We need to make every woman feel that underlying and beyond her personal relation to the men of her family and circle, far deeper and more important than the personal interests or rivalries that may grow out of these, she has a vital interest in the question of the relation of women as a whole to men as a whole. If in every relation, in domestic life, as educators, as social leaders, women brought all their influence to bear to bring about a higher and juster moral attitude towards vice, their influence would be irresistible.

We want to make every woman feel that if through ignorance, thoughtlessness, or selfish indifference she accepts and acts upon the present false view of unequal moral obligations, she is tacitly instrumental in keeping up conditions which are forcing her weaker sister into the depths of degradation and crime. That she is not doing her duty to womanhood or to society.

Each sex owes it to the other to hold it to its own highest standard. It is no evidence of true regard for men to condone licentiousness in them, as it is no mark of respect of men for women to condone moral cowardice in them as an excusable feminine weakness.

It is to the interest of both men and women, that the highest standard of purity should be recognized as the one and only law for both sexes, and that no lower view should be tolerated in private life, or embodied in public statutes.

It is on this line, and on this line only, that the great battle against prostitution can be successfully fought, and to secure recognition of this fact is the one great end for which we must work.

J. W. WALTON.

YOUNG MEN AND MORALITY.

By J. W. WALTON, CLEVELAND, O.

The pure man is the ideal man. That impregnable fact is not in dispute. At the same time there lurks in our minds the feeling, unexpressed, undefined, that a Joseph is less to be admired than a Judah. We may not sneer, we may not go so far as to despise the man of virtuous self control, but deep in our hearts we are inclined to fasten upon him a certain effeminancy of character which is simply nauseating.

It is my purpose briefly to remind you that impurity of thought and life is utterly foolish and unmanly, and that no fellow who wants to make his mark in the twentieth century can afford to overlook this increasingly vital fact.

"To be carnally minded is death," alike to progress in this world and to hope for the world to come.

This truth, as old as the race, may well be repeated in the ears of each generation, for the reason that new facts, new discoveries, are constantly coming to light, which bear with great emphasis upon it. I am not one of those dark prophets who claim that the world is constantly growing worse. On the contrary there is strong reason to believe that the world is growing better.

Read ancient history, note how those old splendid civilizations rose and why they fell; then draw a parallax, if you will, upon our modern life. Note progress, even in the brief span of our own American history.

Can you for a moment imagine another Aaron Burr, brilliant statesman though he be, elevated to the second place in the gift of our nation?

Heaven defend us from the growth of a class at once rich and idle, the curse of any land, as both ancient and modern history demonstrate.

I have been all my life intimately associated with young men, and I know how to look at this subject through a young man's eyes. If you are bound to make shipwreck of life, I know of no swifter or surer way for you to do it than to give free rein to passion. If, on the other hand, you realize that we are to pass through this world but once and ought to make the best of it, then I have a word of friendly counsel for you.

The laws of nature are not playthings; they are stern, immutable realities. These statutes we may violate if we choose, but they carry their own retribution. Mercy may forgive the sin, but, so far as we can see, no tears, no length of time, no, not even Omnipotence itself, can avert the awful penalty.

You may break the costly mirror, you may rub the down from the ripened peach, or brush the dewdrops from the rosebud, but can you replace all these? No more can lost purity be restored by force of will. Thoughts of evil will come back to you, like foul birds, in your holiest moments, and no skill of necromancy, no supreme effort will put them down.

There is an instinctive sense of chivalry due from every man toward every woman, as such, a lofty ideal, a sanctity, a feeling of responsibility for defense and protection, of loyal devotion to the sex.

The voluptuary has killed all these finer feelings. The romance, the charm of the world is gone. He has committed moral suicide.

Whether known only to yourself and your Maker, or whether your guilty knowledge is shared with another, " Be *sure* your sin will find you out." It *is* found out when you know it yourself. You cannot thereafter look at yourself in the glass without the reflection, " I am a degraded man ! "

Perhaps you are saying that your wrong doing has proceeded no further than your thought, that it has not wrought itself out in any deed of evil. Nevertheless the root of the whole matter is there. It is just as true to-day of the American young man as of his forerunner in the days of Solomon. "As he thinketh in his heart, so is he." You look for malaria in the vicinity of swamps, and find it. Loose thinking is invariably followed by loose living. It is only a question of time.

Did you ever reflect upon the power of a man's imagination in headlong flight without a guiding rein? Its break-neck pace increases with every bound. No amount of sensual gratification can check its wild career. On, on it rushes, goaded by its own insatiable passion, toward the awful precipice in its path, over which it must surely plunge—and then! Ah! what then?

Do the laws of the universe change when we shed these tissues which we term the body? Is there any reason to think that the fact of death causes a revolution in your undying character? I shall not attempt to dwell upon the consequences of secret vice. Physicians will tell of impaired vision, of tottering steps, of incapacity for connected thought, followed in time by mental collapse. Nature, kinder to the offender than he has been to himself, decrees of him that development shall cease and that the candle of his race shall be extinguished.

Or it may be that your violation of the law of purity is shared by another.

Shall this be an innocent victim thrown from the high pedestal of pure womanhood into the fathomless mire of an evil life?

> "Let fair humanity abhor the deed
> That spots and stains love's modest snow-white weed!"

More commonly young men transgress in company with those who make a business of sin. The consequences are not long delayed. Self-respect, once lost, can never be fully regained. Each surrender to passion weakens your power of self-control. The appetite grows by what it feeds on, but satisfaction lies not that way.

It is only a question of time when the young man who surrenders to passion will have to reckon with disease, in spite of precaution, and in spite—I had almost said because—of so called health certificates based upon medical examinations, worthless except as false lighthouses to lure men on to the rocks.

That shameful maladies are abroad in the land, shameless advertisements of quack nostrums only too broadly demonstrate. These harpies grow rich, and their fortunes are in the main drawn from young men.

A wide-spread disorder, more dreadful than cholera or yellow fever, is prevalent, confirming the truth of inspiration, "Her house is the way to hell going down to the chambers of death." Any large hospital furnishes an object lesson on the text, "The way of transgressors is hard." We have seen young men setting out with splendid prospects, who became prematurely old and shriveled and helpless, loathed by themselves and by those who through duty or affection became their care-takers, sinking hopelessly into dishonored graves when they should have been at their best in life, dragging wife and children with them. Can you imagine a stronger foretaste of hell than to look into the face of a helpless child—your child—whom in a moment of wild passion you have sentenced to a life-long struggle with suffering and disease, perhaps with deformity or idiocy? Your thought was that your sin was covered, but it has come out before all the world in the next generation, which with weakened will-power will probably still further go down until the stock itself runs out. Said a late distinguished alienist to me on this subject : "Think you that a disease which eats through skin and muscle and bone and marrow will spare that most delicate of all organs, the brain ? Be sure it will not. Mental disorders most commonly follow. Tell the young men that this matter of lewdness is a marked sin." Every candid medical man will reinforce all that I have said, and more.

Would to God I could pass over this most unsavory subject more lightly, but the truth has only been approached, not laid bare. A word to the wise is sufficient ; fools will go on sinning and suffering until they die, and their memory shall rot.

There is another disease which commonly follows in the train of social sin, a disease which I need not name, but which is often the subject of light jest on the part of young men. "As easily cured," they say, "as a cold in the head." Is it ?

Science with its microscope and its patient investigation has been making some important discoveries just here, especially during the past few months. Ask your physician, and if he is at all abreast of the times he will tell you that in the remorseless march of evolution Nature has decreed of those who contract this so called lighter malady, "Write these men and women childless." Hopeless sterility for yourself and for the wife of your bosom is not the invariable but probable result.

Thus are the iniquities of the fathers visited upon the children unto the third and fourth generation, or else the generations themselves blasted, their places are taken by the sons of those who by their own election are found worthy to perpetuate the race.

Let us turn, now, to the brighter side, the reasons for a virtuous, sensible life.

I like that word "virtue." It comes from the old Latin root, "vir,"—a man. There is much in language to denote the common thought of mankind. Our very words speak the high regard in which we hold the man of self-control. First of all, his conscience is at rest. Madame Guyon, though a prisoner in the Bastile, could say, "I care not what my outward circumstances may be, so long as the little bird is singing sweetly in my bosom." Nature itself, to say nothing of revelation, is in harmony with your better self.

Virtue prolongs as well as ennobles life. Without virtue, on the testimony of thousands, life is not worth living.

> " Virtue, the strength and beauty of the soul
> Is the best gift of heaven; a happiness
> That e'en above the smiles and frowns of fate
> Exalts great Nature's favorites; a wealth
> That ne'er encumbers, nor can be transferred."

It is only fair to her whom you choose for your life companion. Is there any valid reason why you should refuse to bring to her the unsullied mind and life which you demand from her ? Marriage is, in its very nature, a mutual thing.

He who guards the purity of his young manhood is delivered from the fear of much that must haunt the *roué* or the unhappy victim of secret sin. He can look his pure bride in the face with calm assurance. He has earned the respect of the world at large. " Virtue is bold, and goodness never fearful."

" He is most powerful who has himself in his power."

In the language of holy writ: " He that ruleth his spirit is better than he that taketh a city."

His children and his children's children shall rise up and call him blessed.

I am convinced that these reflections furnish a powerful motive of restraint to young men. I beg you will grasp and hold them.

Then, again, the virtuous man, and he alone, is worthy of the friendship of pure and virtuous women. Young man, the older you grow the more potent will this fact become. Friendship is a master passion in life. Whom do you choose to be the friends, the companions of your declining years? Fit yourself for the higher companionship of the purest and best, of whom the world is not worthy.

The elect of God and man shall walk in white, their countenances reflecting the pure light that shines from above.

The noble of the earth will recognize in you a kindred spirit, and you will be welcomed to their fellowship. We may strive to deceive ourselves and others, but we succeed only in deceiving ourselves.

Our place in the esteem of those we value most is fixed, not by circumstances, but by ourselves.

An ancient Latin author has said:

"His own character shapes the fortunes of every man."

Again, the practice of virtue is a triumph of the higher over the lower nature. By it, and this alone, the soul becomes worthy of its origin and destiny. These thoughts, repeated a thousand times, are not mere platitudes. They are profound truths that take hold upon our lives. They involve the very aim of our existence. "The pure in heart, and only they, shall see God." None others can. Impurity, like a hot iron, destroys the very eyes of the soul. I leave it to the theologians to explain all the depths of this profound revelation. I am convinced that He who spoke the sermon on the mount was most kind in his warning.

> "What then?   What rests?
> Try what repentance can.   What can it not?
> Yet what can it, when one cannot repent?
> O wretched state!   O bosom black as death!
> O liméd soul! that struggling to be free,
> Art more engaged."

Suppose we were to wake up in the great hereafter and hear the mighty voice of the great Captain ring out the command: "As you were!" That is the substance of the Revelation:

"He which is filthy, let him be filthy still, and he that is righteous, let him be righteous still."

They who have overcome temptation here, shall go onward and upward, evermore growing into the likeness of the Model Man, purity personified. Then shall we be satisfied.

I should be untrue to Him were I not to recommend Him as a helper to reach this ideal. Mere struggle against vice will not prevail. You need to replace vice with positive virtue. Throttle temptation at the start, but do more than this. Be beforehand with ennobling thoughts and useful occupations. Exercise body and mind. I welcome the modern Young Men's Christian Association, which does not coddle young men but gives them what they need, exercise of every power of body, mind and soul, to drive out all sorts of morbid imaginations.

Young man, brother man, learn to "overcome evil with good."

"Be in the end, what you wish to be to-day."
—*Dean Stanley.*

THE SOCIAL PURITY ALLIANCE OF GREAT BRITAIN.

By Miss C. M. Whitehead, London.

" The experience of the past is the best hope for the future," and truly we find that it is so when we turn the pages of history, and mark for our consolation and encouragement the course and development of great moral movements.

The "Ascent of Man" is not true scientifically only but also spiritually. Step by step the race mounts onward and upward ; and we trace with gratitude, which ought to make us calmly expect victory in the future, that catastrophies and shocks in the moral world have contributed to that higher progress.

Each revelation of wickedness has roused man to take a higher step in demanding a remedy, to insist that it shall be found.

In pessimistic, faithless moments perhaps a dim idea flits across the mind of man that former days were better than these; but the searchlight of a truer knowledge turned upon the pages of the past reveals a condition of shameless immorality patiently accepted, and dispels that dim idea.

At least that one point has been achieved.

The conscience of mankind has been so awakened that abuses are revealed only to be repudiated, contested, and sooner or later removed. Men and women, their moral consciousness kindled to a burning glow of enthusiasm for purity and holiness, have not been wanting to vow themselves to the cause of rightousness if need be to the death.

They did not deem it sufficient themselves to wear and cherish "the white flower of a blameless life," but

MISS C. M. WHITEHEAD.

with the cry of the old crusades upon their lips, "It is the will of God," have flung themselves into a new crusade against iniquitous laws which were founded on the principle that vice was a necessity for man. It is not too much to say that the fight against those laws, commonly known as the Contagious Diseases Acts, has brought the nation to a much higher point of purity than was ever known before, shown in an increasing demand for an equal moral standard for man as well as for woman.

Many have been directly and indirectly the departures into new channels of energy which have dated from that great struggle for the recognition of an equal standard involved in that contest, and the Social Purity Alliance came into existence when the fight was at its height, in 1874, and its objects are well set forth in words quoted from the retrospect of its early history, taken on its attaining its majority this year, 1895: "It was soon felt it would not be enough to repeal these degrading Acts; they were themselves the outcome of a degraded standard of social purity. It was commonly held that immorality which was shameful in a woman was in man very pardonable if not necessary. This was the root of the evil. The new Society firmly took its stand upon the principle that the law of purity was as strongly binding on every man as upon every woman." *More*, it felt the spirit of a *crusade* was needed, and therefore the Alliance was formed "for the recognition of the duty of a combined social protest, the duty of an active instead of a merely passive opposition to the inroads of vice."

These twenty-one years have seen, as was natural, many vicissitudes. Other Societies have arisen which have perhaps diverted public attention from the steady work which has gone quietly on in success and failure, mainly educational, seeking in the warning and instruction of young men to lay a deep and solid basis of sound national purity.

It has held firmly to its original charter, and therefore it was fitting that the groundwork of that charter should have been reiterated of late, making a total and declared repudiation on the part of its Committee of any lurking sympathy with the principles of the system known as the State Regulation of Vice a necessary condition of holding office.

The Society in its constitution has held firmly to its declared principles, for, contrary to the rule of so many old foundations, it has from the first associated men and women together, and found in their joint work and consultation a source of mutual strength and encouragement.

There have not been wanting those who have said that the need of the Society was over, that other associations were doing its work, but to those who see more deeply its need was never greater that at the present moment. Because this is the hour of all hours when the principle of mutual union of men and women in the cause of purity needs to be insisted on.

Again and again in England we have the curious anomaly of men, in societies for the rescue of women, legislating, acting on committees, giving women no voice in what surely is beyond all doubt their natural sphere, the helping and succoring their sisters who have been beaten down into shame and despair by men. It is time that an efficient protest was raised against such one-sided and mistaken action, and in the existence of a Society where men and women have from the first been banded together in a righteous cause on equal terms is found the best antidote to the spirit which would have excluded women from touching this matter, or at least from sharing the councils of men even where their own sex is mostly concerned. On three principles preeminently the Social Purity Alliance bases its operations, and can be confidently recommended to the cordial support of those who value those principles as the groundwork of all right action Social Purity is not a solitary fragment of life divided off into the strict keeping of the Seventh Commandment, but it is a web of many strands, chief amongst which predominate those eternal principles of justice, truth and courage.

Was it not because those principles were allowed to slip in the past that the Alliance was needed to proclaim *one* moral standard for men as well as for women instead of the unequal judgment which then prevailed?

To unequal judgment even now the failure of much rescue work may be attributed. How can it be otherwise? How can you go forth to raise and rescue the woman if you believe in your secret soul that vice is a necessity for the man, and that the purity you recommend to her is impossible to him? Your hand outstreched to help your sister to rise falls paralyzed at your side if you believe for one moment that her ruin and that of hundreds more is a necessary if sorrowful condition in the scheme of human economy.

And yet we find that subtle falsehood poisoning the minds of many to-day!

How does it work? We see many who would shudder at the bare idea of taking a fallen woman into their homes (repentant though she might be) for fear of the contagion of her presence, have no dread of the malarial poison distilled by the low standard of morality held by many men who unblushingly avow one law for themselves and another for the women they degrade.

It is apparent, when men speak at meetings in the face of physical facts as if women were the sole offenders, as if *they* could and did sin alone. It tells again in the excuses offered for a man's nature, as if a woman's brought no fierce temptations to be fought down in hours of weak health, weary duties and dull monotony.

It only needs to point to our law courts to emphasize this habitual view, and in more ways than we enumerated social purity demands justice.

Naturally that principle leads to another, for to judge justly truth must be made clear—truth which is knowledge which must *know*, and will not decide blindly in the dark.

Judgment grows wider, more discriminating, more tender as it sees further.

How hard, for instance, is the judgment of a woman who lives at ease, knowing nothing by experience or imagination of the awful temptations of the work girl who starves on three shillings or half a crown a week.

Knowledge then is needed to get at truth on this pressing problem, till we learn that somehow, somewhere, consciously or unconsciously, we all touch the fringe of this evil,

> " That even the loneliest one must stand
> Dependent on his brother's hand,"

—and that our economic policy is at the root of the whole matter, and the comfortable woman who buys carelessly and underpays her dependents, has to answer for her share of the social evil just as much as the sweater.

Also a foolish idea has prevailed that ignorance is innocence, and boys and girls have gone forth in absolute blindness as to the great facts of life which it most behooved their salvation to know.

This point may well be stressed in speaking of our Alliance, for it has made the education of the young —boys going forth to the dangers of school life, work girls to the perils of a great city—its special work, striving to give the needful information just when and where it was wanted, simply, frankly and purely. Some of its best publications have been written for parents and guardians of the young, showing them how best to safeguard the young heart against the perils of our day and generation.

Not less is the work done in warning young men in meetings held specially for them by the secretaries of the Alliance, work carried out with singular tact and enthusiasm, which has been instrumental in bringing fresh adherents from all parts of England.

With the knowledge of danger comes also the sense of sympathy, of comradeship, and the realization it is not a lonely struggle against overwhelming odds. In keeping silence as the good have done far too long they seem to have forgotten that evil is not dumb, that the boy in his school, or the young man in his bank, is assailed by plausible and specious arguments in favor of self-indulgence to which a traitor within the citadel— his own surging nature—bids him yield, against which he has not been fortified. How powerful good *can* be against evil has again and again been proved, in cases known where one word of warning given almost by chance has been a very panoply of protection against the fiercest assaults of evil. The Alliance seeks to give that word of warning which shall prove a support in the hour of need, and nerve the heart with courage—our third great principle—to stand firm in the moment of attack.

The Alliance calls on its members to nave the courage of their convictions, courage to break through the "conspiracy of silence" by which the good and pure have too often played into the hands of those who wish for evil and try to spread it.

It bids those who are sorely pressed in the fight take heart since they are not fighting alone, but are comrades in a great company, bent not only on saving their own souls, and keeping their garments white, but in "aiding those who fall, and strengthening those who do stand."

So in the threefold strength imparted by unfaltering allegiance to these three great principles—justice, truth, and courage—the Alliance has concluded the twenty-first year of its existence and looks out hopefully into the future, recognizing that its work of education was never more needed than now, when these principles ought to be taught through the length and breadth of our land.

A subtle danger lies in victory, it is *capua* which enervates, and many, in the face of the great moral triumphs gained in the Repeal of State Regulation of Vice, and in the passing of the Criminal Law Amendment Act, are tempted to forget the lessons of the past, and do not remember that if we are to keep what we have gained, the rising generation must be educated up to a true, moral standard.

In literature, in drama, we see that the sex question is stirring society at large. All Europe, as Professor Forsyth truly says, is moving on to a settlement of it, and justice demands, therefore, that the woman, who has such a vital interest in the matter, as she bears her own penalty for any false step, and frequently the man's share as well, should be free to put forward her own claims for consideration and her demand for equal justice.

The rising generation needs to be taught that her demand is a *just* one; that knowledge can be fearless where ignorance would cower in terror, for truth is the foundation of true courage.

Faith in the justice of the cause of purity, as the "Will of God" for man as for woman, desire to make that truth widely known, courage to act on that faith, *these* principles inspired by God Himself from a three-fold cord which will not be quickly broken, but bind our Alliance to fresh efforts and fresh victories.

HELEN H. GARDENER.

THIRD SESSION.

HEREDITY AND ETHICS

By Helen H. Gardener, Boston

I shall ask this Congress to look at the question with which I shall deal, upon strictly natural and scientific grounds. To eliminate all religious bias and to think of the entire subject in its relation between man and man and not at all as a question between man and a God. When we discuss heredity in any form we rob our work of all scientific value if we proceed upon the basis of thought which assumes that some outside "higher power" regulates or changes or interferes with the fixed order of nature. It is true that we do not know, absolutely, what some of the laws of heredity are; that we do not know exactly *how* to modify or change a strain which we discover. But there are facts and laws which we do know and if we will but exclude all emotionalism and vagary there is much more that we can learn. That physical characteristics and tendencies are transmitted no careful student or observer can doubt. No biologist of standing questions the fact. No stockman doubts it. Every finely bred horse or hunting dog proves it, and, strange as it may seem, we can learn more facts of value in the consideration of these questions as related to the human race, from horse, and dog and cattle raisers than from any other source. Why? Simply because they have tested and studied the topic without a veil of mystery, mysticism and prudery before their eyes. They know that the colts of a "vicious" or tricky animal

99

are likely to have the same mental or moral traits. Perhaps you are surprised to hear me use the word moral
when speaking of a brute animal. But if you will but
stop to think you will know that animals below man
vary as surely in their mental and moral life as does man
himself. They have a sense of responsibility or a lack
of it ; they have loyalty, faithfulness, affection, honesty,
or they lack these qualities. Now in their application
to a wider range and scope are not these qualities or
their absence what we mean by morals or ethics in man?
There has been a habit of mind and speech which has
led people to assume that what is "instinct" in animals
below man is "reason" or "intellect" in the human
animal. With this view I think no competent scientific
observer can agree. In degree we differ from them but
we partake in kind of their physical and their mental
characteristics and possessions. Everyone knows, then,
that physical characteristics are transmittable and transmitted. How often do we hear, "Oh, yes, I should have
known he belonged to that family, the likeness is so
marked," or some such similar proof that we all recognize, the transmission of physical qualities. Now we
have but to reflect a bit more deeply to be able to assume,
at least, that since our mental (and therefore our moral or
ethical) life is but the result of the expression of *one side*
of our physical quality, we have a good working theory.
It is beginning to be well understood that degeneracy,
whether of mind or body, is upon a physical basis.

It is not a healthy, normal, pathologically whole
brain-mass in the skull of either an idiot or a criminal.
Idiocy is a *physical* disorder. So is insanity. So is
criminality. Famous criminologists are beginning to
give us the "ear marks," so to speak, which they have
learned to expect upon certain kinds of offenders against
the canons of morality—that is to say, against the
natural basis of ethics, which all peoples and all re-
ligions recognize and which therefore form a natural
basis of morals—the basis which applies between man

and man, strictly. All peoples hold that murder, theft, arson, etc., are wrong. That is because all people object to being murdered, stolen from or burned out. As we develop in brain capacity these few primary qualities are added to and elaborated until we have a vast code which it is deemed "right" or "wrong" to follow or to avoid. Often one race develops these in one direction; another in another line; but ever and always it is the more or less wise effort of those who are struggling toward what they *believe* will secure the highest social harmony. That is to say the most wholesome and endurable relationship between man and man. Of course many blunders are made and have to be unmade, and hence the moral or ethical code is never stationary and is ever shifting, ever reaching out toward what we believe will better the condition of man. This very struggle leaves its physical marks. Witness the facial grimness of the "Pilgrim Fathers"—still visible, but modified—in New England. Witness the debonair countenance of the Cavaliers and their descendents of the South.

It is very generally recognised in these days that crime and criminals are not accidents. They are naturally produced and may be naturally prevented. Reformatories and prisons are mere palliatives. The protection of the nation against an increasing penal population lies in another direction. But first we must grasp fully the causes and sources of crime. That we have failed to do this accounts in large measure for the fact that we have found no cure. Just so long as we permit ourselves to drift vaguely in the matter of cause and effect just so long will cure be impossible and palliatives be necessary evils. We pride ourselves as a nation upon the fact that our prisons, insane institutions and hospitals are many and large and finely equipped ; that our blind and deaf and imbecile asylums grow in numbers and efficiency, and so long as we have a large population of unfortunates it is, of course, our imperative duty to see that every possible relief be given them; but more imperative still and back of this duty to ourselves and to the nation is the duty to know *why* we need all of these institutions and consider if it may not be possible to lock the barn door before the horse is stolen. To give health and sanity and a useful life to these cripples of society, to make them self reliant, self supporting and socially and economically useful factors instead of burdens to themselves and on the State, is far more important than is the most perfect hospital and prison system possible to devise. This needs but to be stated. No one will question its truth but strange to say there are few who have appeared to recognize the fact that it is possible to prevent, in large part, rather than care for or cure such human wreckage. There are two lines of action open to us; the improvement of, first, the heredity and then the environment of the submerged classes. But can we improve the heredity *until* the environment is made better? Can the birthright of a child be secured if the parents are ill nourished, surrounded by filth, crime and disease? Is it possible for children to be mentally and physically whole and morally and ethically sane, who are born into unwholesome surroundings and from parents either or both of whom may be tainted in body or diseased in mind? We inherit our ethical as well as our physical caliber and quality. There are many persons who are intellectually bright who are born morally insane—what is called "moral idiots." This lack of ethical or moral grasp varies from absolute idiocy, as in the case of the Hathaway woman now in prison in New York for wholesale murder, on and up through the grades of moral tone or the lack of it, which would compare with the infinite grades of intellectual grasp or the lack of it, from the type of an absolute imbecile to the ablest minds of the ages. The grocer who sands his sugar, the farmer who sells light weight, the milkman who waters his milk, the banker who "borrows" trust funds, the R. R. president who works his men to the limit of endurance on starvation wages, the politician who trades on his position, one and all are in varying degrees morally obtuse, ethically near-sighted or blind. Let me illustrate: In a school or college there are all grades of *mental* stupidity or alertness. One boy is so dull he is dubbed a dunce; another is a bit brighter, but still he is far below the mental average; another is just an average boy whose mind labors slowly and more or less accurately over not particularly difficult problems or questions; a higher mental type grasps quickly and fully his lesson, while still a higher comprehends not only the lesson as it is, but in its relations to all else that he has learned. The grades and types of moral quality vary quite as widely *and are as innate*—as much a matter of birth—as is the unequal mentality, yet we rarely take this fact into account. One man is morally, utterly obtuse, idiotic. He may at the same time be mentally unusually bright. Just as the very dull boy mentally may be and often is the soul of honor and honesty. That is, he is morally sound but mentally slow or dumb. Conversely, he may be and not infrequently is, intellectually above the average or even brilliant and at the same time stone blind in his moral nature—or in parts of it. It is time that we recognize this fact and, at the same time, that we search for its cause and aim at its cure.

The foundation of all that is diseased in body and mind is laid in the wrongly adjusted family relations. These defects may be, and of course often are, developed afterward by outside means, but the seed is sown and the plant sprouted in the home, and before the child is brought into contact with the outside social environment which develops the final blossom. It is held to be an awful crime to take human life. May it not, under many conditions, be a far greater crime to *give* human life? Is that not worth thinking of? Is it less than a capital crime to thrust unasked upon a human being a diseased, a polluted or a crime soaked nature? To push out into the world a helpless atom whose future is mortgaged to idiocy, insanity or vice? Do you not know that the living lies men are, in their relations with their wives, helps to account for that tendency in children? Do you not know that the pretended subserviency but resentful acquiesence of wives helps to account for the mendacity of their offspring? Perhaps it is all this and more that you have in mind to deal with, and if so it will be useless to simply try to rescue those who have already thoroughly developed their inherited trend toward social immorality. It is important first of all to teach men and women that inside the marriage bond, even more than outside, is crime and disease bred. The majority of morally and mentally diseased children are born of those who are married. There is a cause for this which social purity workers cannot afford to ignore if their work is to be more than the merest surface plaster. An "owned" maternity at the mercy of a licensed paternity is a menace to mankind. The command to "increase and multiply" has been read always as a command to bear many children, whether physically, mentally, or morally fit for such a task or not; but suppose even religionists should pause to see if it might not have meant to "increase, multiply and *replenish* the earth "—that is, to till, fertilize and make fruitful the earth? Why not? *If* it were the word of a God (assuming that a God is wise and merciful), he surely could not have meant to have the brutal, insane, dull, diseased and criminal fathers and mothers (whether married or not) curse the helpless unborn by thrusting life upon them. The belief of woman in the necessity to obey that command has filled the world with idiots, criminals, insane and vicious human pawns to whom life is a cruel mockery and because of whom this organization exists in large part. Consider that. And consider what is back of it and how it can be met.

REV. MARY T. WHITNEY.

THE LAWS OF PARENTAGE AND HEREDITY.

By Rev. Mary T. Whitney.

This is a world of cause and effect.

We come into the world knowing nothing. We either blunder into facts, or are taught them. People have walked the earth for ages, but have only lately learned to travel by electricity. No new forces have come into existence; it is only that we have newly found them out. We are increasing our knowledge and making valuable discoveries in every other direction, but here is a whole realm about which we know nothing. We study gravitation and other natural laws, but not the laws that govern this vital matter.

In teaching our children, we leave a blank just here. We teach them arithmetic, all there is of it; we do not go as far as proportion and then stop. But in physiology, we teach them thoroughly up to a certain point, and then there is a blank. In Sunday School and elsewhere, we teach our children honesty, we teach them all the virtues but one, thoroughly, and then we stop. We teach them any kind of business thoroughly; but in regard to the greatest business of all, marriage and parentage, they have no teaching.

Then consider life-culture. How carefully floriculture is studied, and with what wonderful results! The florist or gardener can make you almost any kind of rose or apple you want. It is the same with stock-raising. The stock-breeder can make you almost any kind of a horse to order, the heavy draught horse or the swift race horse, because he has studied the subject and works according to the law of life. But when we come to the culture of human life, we find a blank.

There is no place where wisdom is so much needed or
ignorance so disastrous as just here; yet we do not
even think of studying it; the whole subject is left in
midnight darkness.

I respect legislative and rescue work; and I have
been thinking how brave Mr. and Mrs. Powell were to
begin this work years ago when people did not dare to
speak of these things. But the first thing needful now
is the careful, thorough, scientific study of this matter.
A prominent minister said to me once, "All the
knowledge we have about this subject we have blundered
into;" and we have not blundered into much. We have
got to study the law of the sexes thoroughly and scientifically, as we do electricity.

We shall never get rid of prostitution outside
marriage till we have got rid of it inside marriage. We
must begin with the inside, not the outside. We shall
never get rid of prostitution while the fathers of our
children support disreputable houses. The keeper of
one of these houses was asked: "Who supports these
establishments? Is it the young unmarried men?"
"Oh, no," was the answer. "They are supported
mainly by well-to-do married men, whose wives move
in the best society." What does this mean? It means
that the children of these men will inherit the same
tendencies and weaknesses. We have yet to learn in
any broad, general sense, that in heredity, the father is
as important a factor as the mother. We shall never
have a pure and chaste generation till we have pure and
chaste men as the fathers of our children.

It was inevitable that the Social Purity Movement
should begin with rescue work, and I honor the brave
men and women who have fought this hardest of all
battles; but we must now change the direction of our
thought a little. We must now take this subject from
the gutter up to the highest place. The law of sex is
not just like the law of gravitation or that of chemical
affinity; it is above them: it is the law by which God

107

creates all life. You in this audience are all workers; none of you have come here out of curiosity. I urge you to study the laws of parentage and heredity, and then to go out and teach; for people are eager to learn. I do not doubt that before many years this subject will be intelligently taught to all young people, and that they will grow up with serious views of marriage, and will enter into it seriously and intelligently, instead of blundering into it.

SAMUEL C. BLACKWELL.

THE MUNICIPALITY IN ITS RELATION
TO VICE.

By Samuel C. Blackwell.

Among the apt and noble words which we inherit from our forefathers is this great word, the "Commonwealth." It expresses the object of free government, the government of the people, by the people, for the people. This is the pole star of the American citizen, never to be lost sight of amid all paltry politics, falsely so called, meaning the strife of parties for the salary and perquisites of office. The American who loves his country will never forget that office, rightly understood, means service, the loyal discharge of a trust whose one great end is the public good, and its substantial and enduring reward the gratitude and honor of his fellow citizens.

The municipality, that is, the local self government of the American citizen, is especially charged with the promotion of the welfare of its own constituency, by the maintainance intact of those institutions upon which the good of every individual citizen depends, in the suppression, by its collective power, of those overhanging or undermining evils which attack the welfare, the freedom and the happiness of every citizen, evils with which the citizen, alone and unaided, cannot cope.

For the discharge of this duty the municipality is equipped, by its local statutory board of aldermen or commissioners, its executive, mayor or chairman, its judiciary of local judges or justices of the peace, and its local constabulary or police.

No one of us dare overlook his own responsibility, for nothing good will come out of our civil and town governments that we do not first put into them. The tide will not rise higher than it is lifted by the ocean.

We laugh at the vanity of the French king who exclaimed, "L'Etat, C'est moi"!—the State, I am the State! There is no occasion for laughter but there is immense significance in the fact that the American citizen may say, must say, my local government is what you, I and our fellow townsmen make it.

What now is the relation of the municipality to great public evils?

First of all, the municipality owes it to its constituents to take and to hold the attitude of defence of all that works for the public good, and of resistance, constant and consistent, towards all that work against it.

We know the worth of a high example. How a great school of young men and women are guided and strengthened by the character, kind and firm, of a teacher who commands their respect and trust. How mere public whim, expressed in fashion, can change the very cut of the garments of a whole community with the passing season.

Much more the public sentiment expressed in common usage shapes the conduct of high and low. Still more potent is this object lesson, seen by all, the attitude of the local government. If it be indifferent to public virtue its constituents tend to indifference. If the local home government is vascillating, weak and compromising in its policy, demoralized by bidding for base votes, as a means to clutch party spoils, this cannot fail to quicken all the seeds of vice.

But if its policy reflect the uprightness of its manliest citizens, the better sentiment of the community will respond like vegetation to the sunbeam. The vigilance of the municipality will command the hearty co-operation of all men and women of good will, in its thought and action for the common weal.

So much for the normal attitude of the municipality towards every prevalent vice, but, considering its duty and its opportunity in dealing with the terrible evil which confronts us on this occasion, every suggestion applies with added force.

For this is a vice that not merely tends to evil, but consummates it. It differs from intoxication, which tends to evil; it is in itself a suicide, both physical and moral; it differs from anger, which impels to violence; it is in itself murder, both of the outward and of the inward life of man and woman. It is vice that has become crime.

It is a vice that tends to undermine marriage, the basis of enduring nationality and the guaranty of progressive civilization, as well as the central ethic of Christianity. Marriage is the one relation that may identify the affection, the interests and the hopes of man and woman for life. It is fitted to survive the parting of all other ties and to endure when youth itself has fled.

This vice delays or utterly defeats the normal tendency of youth to marriage. It unmans the boy and cheats him of his Creator's kindest gift, the identification of two unsullied lives, and this unspeakable impoverishment, for a wretched counterfeit, which surrenders his human birthright to his lowest animal instinct, a mere instinct that requires no soul.

Upon marriage depends the Family, that brotherhood derived from a common parentage beginning in infancy, strengthening throughout youth, maturing in manhood, and normally lasting to the end of life. From such brotherhoods associated have grown the Clan, the Town, the State, the Nation, and, in such associated brotherhoods, following our Creator's method of develment, lies the promise of international fraternity, the brotherhood of mankind.

Has not the municipal government a duty, to arrest the growth of a vice which tends to subvert Marriage and the Family, those foundations of the welfare of its people? The slaves of this vice know not what they do.

Its indulgence is suicide for the perpetrator and murder for the victim.

This is no phantom. We are not beating the air. This vice has indeed become crime. The Honorable Elbridge T. Gerry and Police Superintendent Burns, in 1893, estimated that there were then, in New York alone, not less than 40,000 abandoned women. We speak of these crushed and trampled beings as a class; but think of them rather as 40,000 women, once possible wives, who might have represented 40,000 homes, now rendered impossible forever. This in one city. Every other city contains a similar pitiable class, in proportion to its population. Ruined and helpless prisoners, confined by despair and alcohol within a deadline patrolled by famine.

There are those who say, "These women are already lost, these at least are fair prey." Where is our manhood gone? Is this the type of real manhood, the manhood that will not break the bruised reed?

But this large class of women, themselves made hopeless outcasts, deprived of self respect and sympathy, and of all opportunity for honest self support, driven by destitution, once tempted by men have now become in turn the tempters of men.

And now, reflect that a much larger class of men, averaging four or five times the number of their victims, are lured to degraded lives of secret sensuality by the practice of this vice. More than 160,000 men in one single large city, drawn aside from upright private life to a private life of deceit and untruthfulness. Instead of being helpful to others, become dangerous destroyers of the helpless.

Can this sad fact exist and continue without the most disastrous effect upon the welfare of the community? Does not it challenge the most serious thought and efficient action of the municipality?

I do not for a moment think or say that we must rely chiefly upon law and police for the cure of this evil. Municipal responsibility cannot lessen individual and professional duty. Parents must sedulously elevate the moral character and strengthen the self control of their children; and; beyond all other ennobling influences, they should make their own lives attractive object lessons of domestic joy.

Every minister must think on the temptations which surround the unwary, and must protect them by uplifting the human standard of ennobling domestic life in order to shame and silence the demon whisper of mere animal instinct.

Every physician must remember that his patient has a mind as well as a body, a mind fitted to guide the body, and that normal human nature must crown the mind as king, or body and mind both will fail of their real welfare.

Every man of good will, young or old, must treat all women with respect: not with mere lift the hat display, but with sincere, considerate courtesy, for the sake of their womanhood. By such an example each man can best teach every other man this first characteristic of true manhood.

Every woman must estimate character above fortune in her choice of friends. And the basis of character is truthfulness.

And all men and all women who forgive and honor the returning prodigal son, should do no less by the returning prodigal daughter.

So much for individual effort, which must continue while the world lasts, and so long as successive generations come upon the stage, all inexperienced, with the angel and the demon on each hand.

In dealing with an evil, prevention is better than cure, and in prevention lies the special power of the municipality.

What can the municipality do?

I would urge, first and foremost, one leading fact which must be always borne in mind in the application of preventive methods. This enormous evil originates in an enormous wrong. As a rule, each one of these 40,000 outcasts was misled before she fell; cunning, flattery, money, deceit, falsehood, possibly force, led her to a fate which she did not choose.

This is a vice in which two participate, and the originator and maintainer of its fearful work is the man rather than the woman.

It seems to me that the inefficiency of every municipal effort to district, or to regulate in any way this vice and crime, has lain in the fact that it has contemplated only one-half the evil and ignored the other. Can the farmer succeed in protecting his sheep by merely fencing them in? Is it not still more necessary that he *chain the dog?*

The duty of the municipality is not amelioration but repression. This vice will grow rather than starve, by efforts of amelioration. We cannot ameliorate theft or murder, we must repress it.

Every effort to confine this evil, by districting it, has failed by ignoring the iniquity of the vice. The municipality has permitted and condoned in one street what it pretended to condemn and punish in another. It has lent its sanction to the originating wrong, and this has tended rather to encourage than to repress it, and consequently to increase the resulting evil. Every effort to ameliorate this evil by attempting to regulate it, has rather stimulated the vice instead of repressing it, because it has permitted it, and has held out an illusory idea of greater safety in its practice.

The effort of the Catholic Church to district the vice in Rome was tried, and abandoned as impracticable. The "Contagious Diseases Acts" of Parliament, proposing to regulate this evil in England, after sixteen years of vain experiment, were repealed by Parliament in 1886. The statute to regulate the evil in Missouri, passed by the Legislature of 1870, was repealed by the Legislature of 1873.

The preventive power of the municipality may be secured through its several departments by suitable selection of its common council and judges, its mayor and its chief of police and by careful instruction of the rank and file of the police as to their faithful performance of duty, to be rewarded by promotion and their inefficiency to be followed by dismissal.

A primary duty of the municipality is to extinguish the *trade* which this vice engenders, for avarice seeks money profit in furnishing facilities for its practice. All schemes for pecuniary profit to be derived from pandering to its demands and all efforts to obtain fresh victims from the innocent of either sex, should be punished as among the gravest of crimes. Neither tenant nor landlord should be spared in the impartial vigilance of the police, and all condonement or blackmail should lead to immediate dismissal.

Public *solicitation* to vice should subject the offender of either sex, alike, to arrest and to equal punishment; and punishment, as a rule, should be by imprisonment rather than by fine.

The sanitary duty of the municipality demands the utmost vigilance. The approach of cholera or smallpox, from abroad, is recognized and averted with the utmost care, but cholera and smallpox desolate for a time and pass by. Malarial and typhoid fevers, originating in our midst, require and receive constant sanitary examination for their extermination. No less must the utmost sanitary vigilance and the most decisive sanitary measures be employed in this case, to stamp out by repression the hideous plague, loathsome as the leprosy, by which the human constitution protests against promiscuous sensuality. For this becomes hereditary, and among the 160,000 fallen men of New York, how many, faithless to their marriage vows, may transmit the dread contagion to innocent wives and to the helpless children of another generation.

Medical examination and sequestration for hospital cure, when found necessary to prevent the spread of disease, should be applied equally to both sexes with strict impartiality. Sufferers among the poor should be subjected to compulsory hospital treatment and private practitioners should perhaps be required to report all cases under their charge until cured, as they do cholera and smallpox, in order that they may meanwhile be subjects of surveillance by the sanitary authorities.

The *charge of women*, arrested for whatever cause, should be entrusted to suitable matrons and to physicians of their own sex, whether in police stations, prison or hospital. The municipality, in all its departments, should seek to preserve and to promote the decent self-respect of all women under their cootrol.

Buildings and flats should be periodically examined and when manifestly unfit for lodgement with decent privacy and cleanliness they should be vacated and condemned.

The *distribution of books* and advertisements and the display of placards plainly designed to make money by demoralization should be recognized as a crime, and should be checked by a prompt notice for their suppression or punished by severe penalties.

Of course this line of municipal policy must be pursued with good sense, so as to deserve and command public approval, yet it must be constantly, consistently and impartially maintained, if we would have the municipality exert its power to lead public sentiment and to fulfill the object of the American Commonwealth.

Nelson at Trafalgar signalled his fleet, "England expects that every man this day will do his duty." Peace also hath her victories and her preceding conflicts. Standing on a wider battle field, confronted by a more insidious foe, America expects of her municipalities, her home guards, that each one will do its duty.

ORGANIZED PROSTITUTION—HOW TO DEAL WITH IT.

By Mrs. Dora Webb.

The immensity of this subject cannot be conjectured, even by those who have had experience in dealing with it.

The length, breadth, height and depth of this iniquitous business has never been uncovered by any individual in the work. I doubt if hell itself measures more that is devilish than do houses of ill fame.

Every house of ill fame is organized prostitution. Bad men and bad women combine to run them for money. They systematically plan for the ruin of young girls, that they may get coutrol over them and make merchandise of them.

Their methods to obtain victims are as varied as they are devilish.

They especially take note of unprotected working girls and set traps for their unwary feet. One of their successful methods is to send out circular letters to working girls, offering large wages for light work. Thousands leave honest work to accept this offer and find themselves in the hands of villains.

These places combine with assignation houses, where only rooms are let for base purposes. These assignation houses, many of them, are luxurious in their belongings. Music and gaiety which is bewildering to the tempted girl, who is ignorant of the character of the place to which she has been invited, together with the serving of the finest confectionary and SOFT DRINKS, soon cause her to yield to the seductive influences and thus, step by step, the way is paved for her to become an inmate of the brothel.

MRS. DORA WEBB.

These places combine together for the purpose of protecting and extending their business. The mayor of one city said he always had to plan to raid a number of houses at the same time or he would fail to succeed with more than one, as warning would quickly reach the others.

They form syndicates for the purpose of supplying fresh victims. A few years ago it was stated to the House Committee, which was investigating the immigrant question in New York, by the President of the Woman's National Industrial League, that "syndicates exist in New York and Boston for the purpose of supplying fresh young girls from immigrants arriving in this country, for houses of ill fame; agents of the syndicate go abroad and assist in this nefarious business. Immigrants arriving in New York City furnish 20,000 victims annually."

I am informed by good authority that within a few years there existed in Chicago a syndicate which confederated with a fortune teller in Montreal, Canada, to furnish girls for the business.

These places are a community by themselves, and when a girl once gets into their toils it is almost impossible for her to extricate herself or for her friends to find her. Indeed, she is about as lost to the world as if the earth had opened up and swallowed her. There is a constant exchange of girls carried on by these places in order that the basest desires of their patrons may be gratified. In one of our cities, at a broker's office, there came a message for a supply of tickets. Said the broker: "That means that a fresh lot of girls are being sent to the houses of ill fame."

Young girls are kidnapped, entrapped by deceptions; young girls are bought and sold, for cash, like slaves for this "market of lust." *Is it any wonder there are so many fallen women?*

These places plan to ruin our boys. Not satisfied with the open door and the regulation—for every one of these places carries out a system of inspection which says to the young man you may sin with impunity. They send out agents whose sole business is to solicit patronage. Our boys are solicited at every turn to enter these doors of hell; even our college boys are not exempt. At one of our colleges in Ohio, an agent from one of these houses in a neighboring city came to young boys under eighteen with offers and promises that would make their fathers and mothers tremble with indignation and fear did they know of it. Messenger boys, errand boys, boys who deliver dry goods and groceries, all must come in contact with these places.

One young man who was serving as collector for a large business firm, resigned his position rather than suffer the insults which were unavoidable by reason of his being obliged to collect from these dens of vice.

Last year, in the city of Cleveland, it was found that some boys were frequently absenting themselves from school. Upon investigation it was learned that they were carrying flowers to houses of ill fame, to sell to visitors. AND OUR BOYS ARE FALLING BY THE THOUSANDS.

An eminent lawyer said to me, " It is my deliberate conviction, based upon facts coming to my knowledge in the course of twenty years' practice, that more boys are converted to drinking habits in houses of ill fame than in the saloons."

Hundreds of these leprous places are allowed to exist and ply their business in every city. And just so long as these places are tolerated, just so long will there be an effort to license and regulate them.

How SHALL WE DEAL WITH THEM ?

As they now stand, the laws on our statute books recognize the running of a house of ill fame, or the renting of property to be used as such, as only misdemeanors and placed alongside of minor offenses to be tried in the police courts and, with but few exceptions, the police courts draw the line against diseased women only. As a rule, city and police officials prefer the existence of houses of ill fame for the revenue and political influence they may gain therefrom. I believe I am telling the truth when I say our greatest hindrances to the enforcement of law against these places are the officials themselves.

We need to get laws on our statute books that will make the running of a house of ill fame and assignation houses a *felony*, to be punished by imprisonment in the penitentiary. Why not?

The individual who runs a house of ill fame is an abettor to every crime known in the "Catalogue of Sin." Murder, drunkard making, lying, stealing, gambling, buying and selling human beings, obtaining property under false pretenses, adultery, rape, and crimes against the body too shameful to mention, are included in the business. I could give facts to substantiate every charge had I the time. The proprietor of a house of ill fame is a criminal in its largest sense and should be punished by imprisonment in the penitentiary, and the mayor or official who regulates this unholy business is accessory, and we should have a law by which they could be punished by imprisonment also.

I don't believe this to be impracticable. Give women the right of suffrage and we would help very soon to solve this vexed problem of "municipal misrule."

In every city and town there should be an auxiliary to the American Purity Alliance, whose business it is to bring about agitation, education and legislation against the existence of houses of ill fame. Literature should be freely circulated. Public meetings and mass meetings should be held where information upon this subject can be given.

People are so ignorant concerning these and indifferent because ignorant.

Inform the people of the traffic in girls caused by these places. Inform them of the traps set for the feet of their own loved ones.

Agitate, agitate; educate, educate; then we can legislate and enforce legislation.

Society is saturated and honeycombed with the idea that nothing can be done to eradicate this evil.

If Christian people would but awake, and put on the "Whole Armor," given in 6th chapter Ephesians, they would go forth to conquer this enemy.

This octopus, whose lecherous grip has well nigh strangled justice, which has bought and sold virtue, which has robbed manhood and womanhood of all that is sacred in life, which has ruined more homes than has the liquor traffic lo these many years, can be wiped out of existence.

Will we do it?

If God be for us who can be against us.

ADDRESS BY FRANCES E. WILLARD.

FRANCES E. WILLARD, President of the World's and National Woman's Christian Temperance Union, who had recently arrived from England, visited the Congress, was warmly welcomed, and, in an impromptu address, spoke substantially as follows:

"These are good days. I am surprised to see that you could muster such a Congress to talk upon such a theme. It shows a bright outlook for humanity. There is nothing new in the topic. Ten years ago we dared not talk about it nor even tell each other what we thought. Our great hope is that we shall dare in the future to tell each other that we do think about the sacred problem of the relations of the sexes. We shall have then a basis of principles and argument, of science and common sense that will build up a stalwart cause for purity, for the equal chastity of man and woman, for the protection of home and for the training of the little child that toddles at our feet.

"Ten years ago, I say, we women did not dare speak of social purity. We hinted at it mildly and gently between the lines. And it was one man's splendid chivalry that unloosed our tongues and gave us courage to speak out the thoughts of our hearts.

"Whatever blame may be laid at the door of William T. Stead for his methods, he certainly did a great work for purity when he published his exposures of London immorality. It was that cyclone of moral power started by him which, crossing the seas, gave courage to us white-ribboned women so that when in session at Philadelphia, we organized our purity department.

"The bill for the protection of women was becalmed in the British Parliament but Mr. Stead's work caused the passage of this bill and made every little girl in Great Britain more safe from brutal men.

FRANCES E. WILLARD.

"In this country we have carried on a similar fight. This is the age of petitions, rather than votes, for women, and we spent several years in getting up petitions to the various legislative bodies in which we asked for adequate protection to women and children from the assaults and designs of wicked men. The National Congress, at our instance, placed a law upon the statute books making the age of consent sixteen years, and many other states have raised the figures as you know.

"Thus the movement has gone forward in its multiform powers and rising strength. We are only in its dawn, and there may be some of us who will live to see the glorious daylight. We want the wider companionship of men and women; we want the world to enjoy the "meeting of two in a thought," as Emerson says. And the prospects are bright for this. In 471 colleges in this country there are but 41 now which exclude women from their classes. And in the schools for women there are 30,000 girls who are becoming the intellectual equals of the best educated men.

"This is all a much brighter state of affairs than in the Old World, where men still go to school by themselves. In the famous public schools of England, where young men are isolated, I have been told that the tragedies of vice are too terrible to be even named. Look at Germany, with its sabre-cut, beer-drinking students. Has America anything like that? And yet even Germany, with all its opposition to woman's advancement, is coming slowly to its sober senses. Last week at its socialistic congress a woman was one of the chief speakers and on educational and progressional lines some progress can be seen.

"In joint athletic sports I am sorry to say that England is ahead of us. In almost every game, sport and play, youths and maidens are side by side in healthful out-door enjoyment in that country.

"The girls are growing taller as a result of it. They are on an average three inches taller than the generation which preceded my own. And the boys, I am sorry to say, are stunting their growth by the use of tobacco. The best medical testimony says that. It is a cause of grave alarm among the the military people because they will not have such well-formed soldiers.

"The bicycle—well, I think that is one of the greatest allies of purity and temperance the world has ever seen! In England this summer I often saw the sign, 'Milk for Bicyclers,' and when you can get men to drink milk it means well for temperance, for the home, for purity. In Chicago, the city from which I come, and a city of which I am very proud, my friends write to me that people who keep saloons, tobacco stores or Sunday theatres, are loud in bewailing the losses which the bicycle has brought upon them. I would not ride my own wheel on Sunday in any public place, but I am glad to see a man do so if it will keep him away from the theatre or the saloon."

LETTER FROM MRS. JOSEPHINE E. BUTLER.

MRS. ANNA RICE POWELL, Corresponding Secretary, read to the Congress the following letter from Mrs. Butler:

1 KING STREET, WESTMINSTER,
LONDON, Oct. 3, 1895.

MY DEAR MRS. POWELL:

I fear my letter will be too late for you to bring a message from us to your Congress. I was much fatigued for some days after the Colmar Conference and was some days later recalled to England by the news of the death of a dear sister, which event has engrossed and distressed me much.

We had a most useful and successful Conference. I personally felt the absence of Mr. Powell as a great loss. America was represented, however, by your brave and able compatriots, Dr. Kate Bushnell, and Mrs. Andrew, whose addresses made a deep impression.

We had had some fears of disunion, owing to the facts of this being our first International Conference held in Germany, and that German opinion in general is more in favor of severely repressive measures than we think to be right or safe, measures which have the inevitable tendency to be carried out against women alone, without regard to their male companions in wrong doing.

We were, however, rejoiced to find how much less these opinions prevailed (at least in Alsatia) than we had expected. There was just sufficient divergence of view on the subject of proposed future legislation to give a vivid interest to the discussions, while perfect harmony and brotherhood prevailed, and the standard of principle of the Federation was held up firmly and clearly and was heartily accepted by all. You will receive full reports shortly of most of the addresses, and later I hope to send you in pamphlet form the most able and interesting discourses of M. Felix Bovet and Professor Louis Bridel, jurists. These defined the limits of state action in dealing with sexual vice and marked sternly and clearly the lines beyond which the State and the Law *cannot* usefully go. When the law in this matter ceases to be useful, it tends to become positively mischievous. Other forces must be brought into operation, notably the force of a changed and purified public opinion, which can accomplish what no laws or police measures can ever accomplish.

From the Colmar Conference our sympathies went forth to you, our fellow workers in the States, and to our fellow workers in all lands. Personally, I can only once more beseech our friends who have accepted the principles of the Federation to be firm, very firm, against every form of compromise. Many of the offered compromises are fair and harmless in appearence; but if carefully studied they reveal the subtle intention and the half concealed machinery to carry out the intention of bringing certain women under the control of men for the most selfish and degrading ends.

Believe me ever most warmly yours in this noly cause,

JOSEPHINE E. BUTLER.

THE AMERICAN PURITY ALLIANCE AND ITS WORK.

By Mrs. Anna Rice Powell, *Corresponding Secretary.*

The nucleus of the American Purity Alliance was formed in the summer of 1876 and was then called the New York Committee for the Prevention of State Regulation of Vice. The revered Abby Hopper Gibbons, a daughter of Isaac T. Hopper, was its president. It was organized in response to an appeal that came to us from the International Federation for the Abolition of State Regulation of Vice, of which a venerable and influential English physician, Dr. J. Birkbeck Nevins, of Liverpool, is President, Professor James Stuart, M. P., of London, is Honorary Secretary, and the honored and beloved Josephine E. Butler of England was and is the inspired and inspiring leader. The delegates sent over by the Federation were the Rev. J. P. Gledstone, of London, and Henry J. Wilson, M. P., of Sheffield. The winter previous to their arrival, some of us in New York had been active in protesting against an attempt, in our Legislature, to introduce the immoral system of legalized vice. We were therefore better prepared to welcome the message of warning which they brought, and which it was their great concern to have widely extended in our country. They had good evidence that it was the purpose of the Regulationists abroad to extend the system internationally, and the issues involved were then little understood here in America.

They left some of their literature for us to circulate, which we did to the best of our ability. But we

MRS. ANNA RICE POWELL.

soon found that we needed to publish for ourselves what was specially suitable for local needs, as it required constant watchfulness to thwart the schemes of those who were persistently plotting to obtain the obnoxious legislation.

We gave no strength to organization; we simply worked on from year to year, doing what we could, not anticipating so long a service. But the work grew and enlarged upon our hands. Through our publications, our constituency, not large in numbers, but choice in moral quality, extended in most of the States of the Union. Still we were not in a concentrated form to gain the strength we needed from them, and a year ago we broadened our basis and took the name of The American Purity Alliance, hoping thereby to do more and better work, and to come in closer touch with our allies and supporters.

While our first active efforts were directed against the attempted legalization of vice, it soon became apparent that this was but a symptom of a deep seated disease in the body politic, which could not be cured without constitutional treatment; and that the people must be made to understand the need of it.

We have had our rescue homes, and alas! there are never enough of them, but there has been too little rescue work done for fallen men. We must plead for justice as well as mercy, and bear a united protest against the double standard of morality—one for women, quite another for men.

Let us, by all means, multiply our rescue homes, opening doors of hope for the sinning woman bearing for her the message :

> " O, wronged and scarred and stained with ill,
> Behold thou art a woman still ! "

But let us not forget that the appeal we make to her womanhood needs also to be made to the fallen man, in pity as well as condemnation, for the honor of his manhood.

HENRY J. WILSON, M. P.

It is the purpose of the American Purity Alliance to impress the thought upon society that it is a grave injustice to boys to allow them to be weighted with the belief, in their struggles with temptation, that they cannot live as pure a life as their sisters. When they are taught to resent such a view as an insult to true manhood, temptations to impurity will lose much of their power. We live according to our ideals and wrong thinking results in wrong action.

Many a man mourns in secret to-day over blemishes of impurity left on his soul in boyhood, because he was not helped to believe in his higher and nobler self. The best atonement for such regrets may be found in service to save others from like transgressions.

While, therefore, it is the mission of the American Purity Alliance to help to redeem fallen womanhood, it has a special concern, as the best safeguard for girlhood, to save boyhood and manhood from the false and Godless doctrines which tempt to the sacrifice of purity and make a victim class of women enslaved to vice, possible.

We charge upon this dual standard of morals the need we see for legislative reform, especially for the protection of the young of both sexes. Only a few, comparatively, realize the nature of the "age of consent " laws, so called in legal phrase, by which the plea of the consent of a mere child of ten years to her own ruin, may shield her betrayer from punishment. Much ready sympathy is expressed by those who can be reached when this is explained, but it does not prove an easy task to move legislative bodies to change the legal code ; or to secure convictions when it is changed. It will take time and persistent effort ; and it needs the concentrated power of organization.

Many are the individual expressions of interest that come to us from all parts of the country when the injustice of the double standard of morality is proclaimed, showing how hearts are burdened and

REV. J. P. GLEDSTONE.

oppressed by it and how much the promulgation of a better gospel is desired. Individual testimony is valuable, but a united protest will reach farther, and the propagandists of evil will feel in it a power that can resist their stratagems, and hear in it a voice that speaks for the voiceless, and for those who are made an easy prey because of their dependence.

Any person who approves these principles may become a member of the Alliance by the payment of $1.00 a year; be entitled to vote at its meetings, and to receive its annual report. We invite memberships from all parts of the country of those interested in the promotion of its work.

We have relied largely on the types for the dissemination of our principles. The Alliance publishes THE PHILANTHROPIST, a monthly periodical devoted to the promotion of purity, the better protection of the young, the repression of vice and the prevention of its regulation by the state. Its price is $1.00 per year. Our leaflet literature covers the various phases of this painful social problem. It is designed to reach and elevate public sentiment ; to gain a regeneration of thought on these matters, and to inspire an affirmative faith in the possibilities of chastity as a basis for the reform needed in all ranks of life.

While the police and citizens alike choose to assume ignorance of the existence of the up-town house of sin and its patronage from fashionable circles, little can be gained, in the advancement of good morals, by raiding the low dens of debauchery in the slums. Therefore, while we aim to do all we can to secure repressive measures, we realize that our movement must be educational and preventive in a specific, radical sense to be permanently effective.

We need jurors who have been trained in White Cross Societies, and we expect, in time, to have them. Our faith is primarily in the higher law engraven on the hearts of men and women alike.

This may seem to some Eutopian, but looking back only a few years, we see marked evidences of progress, and great cause for encouragement to hold up these principles.

No thoughtful student of this movement can fail to see how it is forcing itself upon the consideration of those who have heretofore ignored it altogether. The silence of centuries is being broken. Women with men are watching legislation to secure moral safeguards never understood in times past. All this represents that agitation of thought which must precede any great reformation.

We can each bear some part in the important work to be done.

THE DESERTED CITY—LEGALIZED VICE.

By Rev. Joseph F. Flint.

Our age excels all that have preceded it in heeding the first commandment ever given to man: "Be fruitful and multiply, and replenish the earth and subdue it; and have dominion over every living thing that moveth upon the earth." An army of trained scientists is questioning, and exploring and prying into the vast domain of nature, and with the aid of microscope, retort and scalpel, are wresting one secret after another from her reluctant grasp. Every nook and corner of the earth is being explored, surveyed and ransacked with the avowed purpose of augmenting the richness and fullness of human life.

Another army of men are equally intent upon discovering the best methods of distribution, insisting that the good things of life are not for the privileged few but for the needy many. Men are searching for general principles, for universal truths, and seek to strengthen the bonds of a common brotherhood. The eighteenth century was individualistic, the nineteenth century is organic. Then the soldier was first, now it is the citizen. Then the classes held sway, now the masses are valued. Exclusiveness, egotism and superstition are being superceded by inclusiveness, altruism and universal enlightenment. We hear the sweet, the far-off song, that hails a new creation. Cain has had his day, now the Good Samaritan steps forward, and acknowledges himself his brother's keeper. We are entering upon the cosmopolitan era when international law, exact science and spiritual truths are awaiting the coming of time's grandest product—the world citizen.

REV. JOSEPH F. FLINT.

In view of these things, ladies and gentlemen, what shall we say of the daring attempt made to turn the dial of time backward and fasten upon American cities one of the worst evils of the old world, namely legalized vice? In this age of light and water and soap, to countenance so vile and dark a nuisance! In this age when the submerged tenth of England, the sweat-shops of New York and even the children of the Gretto receive a sympathetic hearing, to give legal standing to what is wrecking manhood and destroying homes! Can anything exceed such folly? Looked at from all sides, legalized vice is the quintessence of all the deviltry and meanness the world has ever known—the greed of the auction block, the cruelty of the inquisition, the secrecy of the robber's den, the confinement of the Bastile, and the horror of the Tower of Silence—and all to gratify the abnormal passions of bad men at the expense of the week and erring. If there is any good in legalized prostitution, it must stand the test as a general principle—by their fruits ye shall know them. It was my fortune to visit a community founded by Communists —what was the outcome of the experiment? Squandered fortunes and a demoralized populace. I recall a western village from which churches were carefully excluded—what kind of a place was it? It was unsafe for a man, much less a woman, to be on the streets at night.

I wish to show that legalized vice, when left to work itself out to its logical conclusion, speedily proves self-destructive, and it has occurred to me that perhaps it would prove a welcome change to the audience if I gave what I have to say, in the form of a brief sketch entitled the Deserted City:

The city of Vanity Fair was intensely American in antecedents and traditions. Full well had the pioneers laid its foundations in thrift, industry and righteousness, and now after a century of existence, their descendants were reaping the rich fruits of the early bountiful sowing. Wealth flowed in on the people in golden streams, and in the wake of wealth came luxury, display and selfish ease. It was the ambition of the citizens to begin where their fathers left off, not foreseeing that they might end where their fathers began. At first the dwellers of Vanity Fair were greatly intoxicated with the wealth of good things flowing in upon them, then a little later luxury came to be taken as a matter of course, making it entirely reasonable to interpret life in terms of pleasure and not of duty. The next step in their history was quietly to discard orthodoxy and adopt "naturalism" as their religion with the one article of creed, "Let us eat and drink and enjoy ourselves, for that is the chief end of man." Certain old fogies that still persisted in preaching Christian stoicism were laughed out of court, or rather out of church, while speakers that prophesied smooth things, were voted capital good fellows. The most popular resort at this time was a dancing academy; none of your ordinary affairs, observe, but a select French establishment, presided over by a hooknosed Parisian of charming manners and faultless attire. Not to be up to all the doings at the academy was to be hopelessly belated and dull. And as for art, it was suddenly discovered what a divine thing is woman's form, some of the ladies evidently not agreeing with Theano, a Roman matron, who, as she was putting on her shawl, displayed her arm, and somebody observing, "What a handsome arm," replied, "But not common!"

One day there came to our city a real live count, fresh from Europe. The *fin de siecle* ladies pronounced him perfectly lovely, and the local dudes went into ecstacies over the delicate tint of his necktie. And then he had such a knowing, worldly-wise air that quite captivated the natives. They gathered about him in groups, drinking in his double-edged stories and cabalistic lore with gratified approval. The moment being favorable, this unclean bird of passage assumed a knowing look and expressed his amazement that so progressive a city should yet lack one thing.

"And what is that?" came from all directions.

"Why you blockheads," he replied, "can't you guess? Unless my eyes deceive me, you are without that crowning convenience of a modern city—a temple of Venus. In Paris we do these things better." Then he went on to picture in glowing terms what would have brought the blush of shame to the cheeks of a purer generation, who would have kicked the scoundrel into the street.

My first point is, that should any American city ever give legal standing to prostitution, it will prove a traitor to its own past history. For not only was this nation founded by righteous men who lived the life of the spirit, but so also were our cities. The pioneers were true men, who took life seriously and set a noble example to their children. But the citizens of Vanity Fair were emancipated, you see; they looked upon the body not as the instrument of a conquering will, to be subdued and toughened to hard work, but as the proper source of pleasure. Hence they saw nothing objectionable in the plan unfolded by the stranger, especially as he convinced them of its perfect safety as well as of its desirability.

Now it happened that while the leading men were contemplating the new move of enthroning Venus, one of the local papers reported an instance where a prominent young man had been accosted by an impudent and noisy siren of the streets, who robbed him of his hat and then tried to decoy him. The editor called attention to the frequency of these disgraceful scenes, and asked if nothing could be done to clear the streets?

Now we know what a former generation would have done; they would have dealt severely with the individual offenders and then called for a general revival of righteousness. My second point is, that as long as the heart of a community remains sound, as long as the Parkhursts and Roosevelts hold sway, there is no danger that legalized vice will ever root itself among us. The issue lies not with the rabble but with the respectable citizens.

But as already said, Vanity Fair was progressive; they believed in the higher Pantheism, that finds all alike good, including the pandered human body, and being the disciples of Comte, the philosopher, they concluded to set up the worship of humanity, more particularly woman, and what woman was so worthy as she who made of herself a martyr to shield her sisters? Did not the French revolutionists enthrone a harlot as the Goddess of Reason? And what would clear the streets so quickly as gathering these girls into one place? Happy thought. The people were bound to worship something, and as the men declared that the worship of God was too high and exacting, why not substitute naturalism in its most pleasing form, the form of woman? The rude and lawless rabble had long clammored for greater license; here was just the thing to satisfy everybody—raise the fleshly Venus into a religious cult, make a State religion of it, with laws and regulations.

Yes, a temple must be built with a statue of Venus before the altar and with such historic worthies as Cleopatra and Henry VIII. and Napoleon the Great as titular saints. No sooner said than done. A stately dame was soon found, vulgarly known as the queen of the demi-monde, whose graceful poise and lofty air and exquisite taste in dress fitted her to be the high priestess. She was not long in gathering about her a choice bevy of assistants, vised and approved by the authorities. To be sure the girls did not understand the meaning and outcome of it all, but they were pleased with the costly robes and bright ribbons, and were they not free from drudgery and anxiety for daily bread? What gay, hilarious times they had, these second cousins of the old Roman Vestal Virgins. They were so knowing and clever. They claimed to be perfectly " straight " and insisted that they were respectable, and were envied by every happy wife and mother for their knowledge of the world. The world they saw was of course the only true world. They know the names and price of every drink, they could spot a tenderfoot afar off, and held in reserve a wicked little laugh for any young fellow that was too reserved and puritanic to worship at their shrine, sanctioned by the State, as it was. Why, if these goddesses were so worldly-wise, they had to be treated like the inmates of a kindergarten, and even held as tearful prisoners, was never explained.

Meanwhile the authorities were immensely pleased with their manifest success. The treasury was full, lavish prodigality prevailed, and multitudes of worshippers thronged the shrine of the new State institution. No need of church bells to call them together; all were singularly enthusiastic from the first, and were sure to come again. What strapping high-pressure fellows they were, these worldly devotees. They gave nature credit for making them what they were, they could not help being otherwise, though to be sure that good creature, whisky, and high feeding helped the matter on not a little. Their watchward, "Back to nature," was something the fanatics could not understand, who insisted rather in going forward in the spirit. Many of the old-fashioned citizens moved out of town, taking their families with them. Sadly they shook their heads and exclaimed, "Ephraim is joined to his idols, let him alone." Fire and brimstone did not rain down upon this modern Sodom: it was simply left to its fate in the relentless grasp of natural law! And here it is well to note the fact that no amount of bravado, or sophistry, or the clamor of mere numbers can ever take the place of scientific facts and the results of experience. If ever vice is legalized in our cities, it will be because the rabble have overborne the voice of reason and truth.

Having once committed themselves to the new cult, the authorities were very willing to be left severely alone, for was not everything going as merry as a marriage bell? Speaking of marriages, it was admitted that the old-fashioned weddings were falling off to an alarming extent, and many a sweet maiden was left to pine away, because her true love never came, but over at the Temple they were having great times. As the love for quiet home life decreased, the liking for the more exciting life at the State institution increased. The populace was so well gratified that they gave a banquet to the illustrious foreigner already mentioned, the latter taking occasion in an eloquent address to laud Vanity Fair to the skies, comparing it to Berlin, Vienna, and even to Paris the only! What an immense advance over the Simple-Simon ways of the past when people were afraid to eat of every tree in the garden!

But the brilliancy of the occasion was somewhat marred when the very next day it was vaguely whispered about that all was not well over at the Temple of Venus. More than one of the goddesses has suddenly died amid unutterable agony, and others were heartily sick of their position; instead of being elevated and ennobled thereby they were robbed of the last vestige of modesty and happiness. The matter was kept as quiet as possible, and the high priestess rolled her eyes to heaven and murmured something about the victims having received a martyr's crown, to which the officials nodded a pious assent. Upon investigation, it appeared that a sort of unquenchable fire had broken out upon the altar of Venus, which outsiders called by the vulgar name of venereal disease. Nothing of the kind had ever been known in well regulated homes, and this strange fire could only be compared to the fires of Moloch that devoured the sons and daughters of King Ahaz, and the eternal fires that burned before the shrine of slaughter in the ancient temple of Montezumah, and whereas in the abomination of the Amorites the youth were first slain and then offered up to Moloch, the ceremony was here reversed, it being the duty of the Temple assistants to continue in service as long as possible, without actually perishing. Some pitiful sights were witnessed, as the vestals, unlike their Roman cousins, endeavored to escape the ravishes of the fire while unwittingly keeping it burning.

Everything under Heaven was done to check the devouring and painful flames, specialists were employed, who repeatedly claimed to have found the proper extinguisher, but again and again the smouldering coals burst out beneath the ashes, as virulent as ever. Becoming thoroughly alarmed, the authorities quietly sent a committee of investigation over to Europe, only to be told that the Venus worshippers over there found the same appalling fire devouring its thousands every year: but it was added, with a knowing wink and a wicked smile, that "as Europe swarmed with poor girls, easily allured and trapped into their temples, the supply always equalled the ceaseless demand." This only added to the perplexity of the commissioners, who were aware that Vanity Fair had long ago been quarantined from the rest of the world, for the purpose of fully testing the outcome of the new cult.

However, arriving home they put on a bold front, crammed out the fine phrases and new arguments learned abroad, hung up the seductive works of art imported for the Temple, and thus for a time renewed the waning enthusiasm. But balms and lotions and logic all failed to stay the ravages of death. When it was finally hinted that the men should supply half the victims, the idea was indignantly spurned. What, the lords of creation, for whose special benefit the state institution had been established, shall they make sacrifices? Never! Why were the girls fed and housed and officially enrolled if not to be offered up for their betters? This splendid logic, of course, settled the matter; a girl more or less was no serious loss. It never occurs to the friends of license that their premises are wrong, hence the conclusions they draw therefrom must be also false. Beginning with the brutal assumption that the body is supreme, no place is left for the spirit: no wonder, therefore, that every rational principle of ordered human society is outraged, including the right of woman to her best life.

Gladly would our friends have foraged upon outsiders had not their former neighbors withdrawn their families. As it was, the Temple police were ordered to compel the faithful themselves to furnish the maiden tribute. The agents found no little difficulty in the way. A physician who was one of the first to advocate the new cult, indignantly refused to fill his own prescription, as it were, by giving up his daughters; and so with a preacher, who had said, "It is better that one girl die than that the whole city be tainted," not foreseeing that the death of one would finally involve the death of all, even the fairest of the flock.

To make a long story short, the emancipated city of Vanity Fair, too proud to acknowledge its mistake, with an energy born of despair and a devotion worthy of a better cause continued the slaughter of the innocents, playing the role of Jephthah and his daughter on a large scale. Of course these drastic measures could not last forever, but as long as the grist held out it must be poured into the hopper to satisfy the hungry mob that remained blinded and stubborn to the last. No tongue can describe the horror and desolation of the scene. The very sunlight seemed to shun the doomed city: the perfume of flowers, the song of birds and the gay prattle of children were memories of a happier past. Broken hearted mothers followed their stricken daughters, to fill with them unmarked graves, struck down by the same awful scourge.

As for the men, they doggedly insisted that they were sound in limb and consistent in conduct, while all the while the secret fires of their own kindling were gnawing at their vitals. A leprosy worse than that of Naaman the Syrian had fastened its fangs upon them.

One morning when the sweet springtime came up from the south and the king of day spread his golden light over the earth, a scene met his gaze out of saddest harmony with the fresh awakening life of the world. Vanity Fair was a deserted city, a charnel house. Nature, which the votaries had professed to adore, had taken terrible vengeance on her outraged majesty. Before the shrine of the fleshly Venus lay the prostrate form of the high priestess, a look of utter despair upon her distorted features, now pale in death. With imprecations upon their lips the once proud and confident advocates of legalized vice breathed their last. As the last deluded mortal expired, the fire that had so long haunted the weird temple flickered and went out. As the final whiff of blue smoke curled its way through the silent chamber, it traced these words on the blackened walls:

" There is a way that seemeth right unto a man, but the end therecf are the ways of death."

MRS. CHARLTON EDHOLM.

THE TRAFFIC IN GIRLS AND FLORENCE CRITTENTON MISSIONS.

By Mrs. Charlton Edholm, Chicago, Ill.

Mrs. Edholm began her speech by asking all to bow their heads in silent prayer that Christ would put upon her lips just the words He would have her say, and that the Holy Spirit would so descend on every heart that we should hear His divine call, "Go ye out quickly into the streets and the lanes of the city and bring in hither the poor and the maimed and the halt and the blind." Rising from her knees she said: I shall always thank God that through Evangelist Charles N. Crittenton, that magnificent "brother of girls"—the name given him by our peerless Woman's Christian Temperance Union leader, Frances E. Willard—I was brought into the rescue work. Once when he was holding evangelistic meetings in Oakland, California, which I, as a newspaper woman, was reporting, he said: "Sister, I believe God wants you for the rescue work." I said, "Oh, Mr. Crittenton, I can't do that. I love these girls at arm's length, and as a newspaper woman have written many articles pleading for the same standard of purity for men as for women, which is, after all, the solution of this whole problem; for when every man has the chivalry of the Lord Jesus Christ in his heart there cannot be in all the world such a thing as an outcast girl, and I have written many articles pleading that the rescue homes might be supported, so that girls should have a chance for a better life. But, Mr. Crittenton, for *me* to go down into a haunt of shame and put my arms about one of those girls and point her to Jesus, oh, I couldn't do that. Don't you know they might say something about *me*, and I'm willing to give God everything in the world I have but my reputation, but I can't give Him that." I shall never forget the kindly look in his eyes as he said, so gently, "Sister, don't you remember it is written of Jesus, "He made Himself of no reputation? Now can't you do as He did? Can't you follow where He leads? And let me tell you something: you give your reputation to God and He will take care of it. You try to keep it yourself and you will be sure to lose it." But still I did not want to come, and so I made another excuse. I said, "Mr. Crittenton, you know I am a working woman and must support myself and my boy by my newspaper work, and I can't go into this work in the slums where there is no money." And again he said, so gently, "Well, sister, God never yet called anyone into His work to starve them, and I know if you go out, throwing yourself in faith upon Him and the generosity of His people, I know you and your boy will be taken care of."

Then, beloved, as Mr. Crittenton described the awful horrors of the lives of those girls—my little sisters and your little sisters—it seemed to me as though I could see them, kicked and beaten, 230,000 of them, and they outstretched their arms to me and cried out, "come over and help us," and I threw myself upon my knees and my own eyes were full of tears, and I said, "Oh, dear Saviour, if you can use me for this work among the girls, here I am. I consecrate myself to it from this time forward." And, beloved, I am so glad He took me, for I've never had such joy as when I have taken some poor little sister in my arms and led her from a life of sin in a brothel to the Lord Jesus and a home in the Florence Crittenton Mission.

And how true Mr. Crittenton's words proved. I did give my reputation to God and He has taken care of it. And although I have been in the haunts of sin of most of the large cities and spoken before conventions and conferences of ministers, God has made the hearts of the people so kind that I have not had a word of criticism.

Then God takes care of finances, and while I go out simply for free will offerings, not only does God put into my hands enough to take care of myself and my orphan boy, but He has put into these hands hundreds of dollars that have gone right back to the Florence Crittenton Mission work. Why do I speak of these personal experiences? Because God is calling some man or woman here to the rescue work, and I beg of you, beloved, don't make excuses, as I did, but come into this work and find the greatest joy of your life in saving souls.

About six months after this talk with Mr. Crittenton I went to the New York Florence Mission, for I wanted to get the data for our book, "The Traffic in Girls and Florence Crittenton Missions," and night after night found us in the slums, and oh! the horror of those nights!

One evening we visited quite an aristocratic house of shame, and as I stood in the doorway of that parlor such a sight met my gaze as froze my heart with horror. There sat eight or ten of the most beautiful little girls I ever saw, and not one of them was over sixteen years of age. There they sat, dressed in their little short dresses, just as mother dressed them, with their hair braided down their back, just as mother braided it to send them to school. And as I looked at them I could think of nothing but a lot of little lambs waiting for the slaughterer's knife. And, beloved, if some man had taken a knife and drawn it across the throat of every one and left her weltering in her blood on that splendid carpet it would not have been one ten-thousandth so bad as what she was waiting for. As I looked into the eyes of these beautiful girls I thought of a little girl I have up in heaven waiting for me, and I pressed my hands across my throbbing heart and said, "Oh, God! what if it were my little girl." Then, beloved, my heart broke for the mothers of those girls. It seemed to me I could see them in their desolate homes, mourning for their children and, like Rachel, "they would not be comforted because they are not."

Then I put my arm about one of these girls and said to her, "Child, does your mother know you're here?" And oh! that cry of pain!—sometimes I hear it in my sleep, and I wake up and don't sleep any more that night—as she said, "Oh, mother's heart would break if she knew I were here." Then I said, "Well, won't you tell me how you happened to come, dear?" "Well, we lived on a farm up in the northern part of the State, and there were a good many of us and father had a pretty hard time to get along, and I thought if I could get a good position in housework in New York I could send most all my wages to papa. So I watched the New York papers and I saw an advertisement where they wanted girls for housework, and I wrote to the man and told him I wanted a good place so I could help papa." And he wrote back and said he had a good place for me, and if I would come on a certain train he would meet me and take me right to the place where I was to work." And she said, "I did come and he did meet me and he brought me here and I've been here ever since." And, beloved, I stand here in the presence of God to say that of the 230,000 erring girls in this land three-fourths of them have been snared and trapped and bought and sold as that little girl was. For when that man placed that child in that haunt of shame and the key was safely turned on her and she was a prisoner and a slave, he received his price for her, and how much do you think he received? What do you think little American girls are worth in the shambles of shame? Only $25 to $50. Why you would pay more than that for a Poland-china pig. I said to her, "Dear, I don't believe you want to stay here." "Oh! no," she said; "this life is hell upon earth." Then I said, "Come with us, dear, to Florence Mission. Hundreds of girls have been saved there and gotten back to mother's arms and mother's Jesus." Willingly she came to the Florence Crittenton Mission, was lovingly welcomed by our dear "Mother" Prindle, who loves these girls as her own daughters, and through the blood of the Lord Jesus she was saved.

When Mr. Crittenton found there was an organized traffic in girls and that through false employment advertisements, mock marriages, the cursed wine rooms, drugs, dancing, and starvation wages, thousands of girls are annually trapped in those dens of infamy, he said, "For God's sake let us get this information in shape so the fathers and mothers and ministers and teachers may warn the girls so they may be saved from falling into these awful snares." This has been done, and in our book, "The Traffic in Girls and Florence Crittenton Missions," is detailed those traps that are laid for the girls of our land. I wish every father and mother would read it, for I know many precious girls would be saved. I know your blood will tingle with horror as you read, that you may not be able to sleep for a week. I wasn't when I found out these things, but surely it is better to lose your sleep for a week and save your darling than not ever again to have a good night's rest because she is lost.

Then as you read the beautiful story of the founding of the Florence Crittenton Missions, your tears of indignation will turn to tears of joy. Mr. Crittenton, a wealthy merchant of New York city, was summoned by telegraph to the bedside of his baby girl Florence. When he stood inside the doorway of his child's bedroom and saw the flush of scarlet fever upon his darling's face, he knew he would not have her long. They put the little girl in his arms, and, as though she knew her death was to be his conversion, she said, "Papa, please—sing —the—sweet—By-and-by." With choking voice he sang the beautiful words, which seemed more like a funeral dirge than a pæan of joy. As the beautiful eyes closed on earth to open in heaven, his great heart broke. For six long months he struggled with his grief, and at last he threw himself down beside his bed and said,

"O, dear Christ, I can't stand this another minute; I must know that I will spend an eternity with my little girl, and I won't leave this room till I leave it a Christian man." After a little prayer the wonderful peace came in his heart, and as he went down stairs this verse rang in his ears: " Go ye out quickly into the streets and lanes of the city and bring in hither the poor and the maimed and the halt and the blind." So down into the slums of New York he went; and one night he was pleading with a poor erring girl to come to Jesus, repeating His words, "Neither do I condemn thee. Go and sin no more." She sobbed out, "But *where* can I go?" That question went through his heart like a knife thrust. In that big Christian city of New York, with its thousands of Christian homes and hundreds of Christian churches, there was scarce a door, save the door of sin, open for her. He made up his mind there that there should be such a home, and in the memory of his little Florence he founded the New York Mission, where for thirteen years those precious girls have been pouring in and being saved. Hundreds have been returned to the arms of their loved ones, hundreds are married and in happy homes, and many are earning an honest livelihood, and scores have swept into the arms of a pitying Saviour and are waiting for Mr. Crittenton to come. Then Mr. Crittenton's heart went out to the girls everywhere, and he has now founded twenty-one of these Florence Crittenton Missions in as many cities of the United States, and at the earnest solicitation of Lady Henry Somerset one will be founded in London.

The work has now grown to such large proportions that it is now organized into the National Florence Crittenton Missions. Florence Crittenton Rescue Circles will be organized in bands of ten, on the plan of the King's Daughters Circles. It is Mr. Crittenton's hope that at least one such Circle shall be organized in every church in America, and the rescue work thus accomplished may be reported in church annals as a regular part of church work. Many of these Circles will be composed of holy women and men who feel that God has called them to the special work of seeking and saving these poor lost girls by weekly visits to the houses where they live, talking and praying with each girl, and always leaving a touching little leaflet that shall have the address of the nearest Florence Crittenton Mission upon it. In this way every girl in a house of shame can have the message of the loving Saviour carried to her once in two weeks, and thus hundreds of these precious girls would be saved; for God's word is true: " My word *shall not* return unto me void, but shall accomplish that which I please." These Circles of young ladies could gather weekly and make garments for our girls and the tiny little ones in our homes. Surely in the construction of those dainty baby wardrobes, with here and there a bit of embroidery or lace, will give scope for artistic taste and be the Master's "fancy work," for it will clothe His little ones and bring to the maker such a blessing as He has promised to those who minister to the least of His children. Then another ten could be the peace makers, and find the young man who has betrayed the girl, and by kindly persuasion show him the awful wrong he has done and get him to repair that wrong to mother and child by marriage. Many such marriages have taken place in our homes and are most happy. Sometimes, too, a glimpse of Penitentiary bars has a very persuasive influence on such a young man. Then another Circle can hold Evangelistic meetings two or three times a week in our homes. Another Circle can make the solicitation of funds and supplies for the Florence Crittenton Home their special work. Circles of young men can push the White Cross work and raise the standard of manly purity to that of the Lord Jesus. Some Circles can be legislative, working for better laws for purity, and especially in raising the age of consent or the age of protection. Every Legislature in our land ought to be besieged by good women and men till a girl's virtue is protected at least as long as her property. Membership are, annual, $1; Sustaining, $5 annually; Life, $25. Half of this goes to the support of the State Florence Crittenton Home and half to the general work of keeping Evangelists in the field and founding new Missions. For all information address Mr. Charles N. Crittenton, 21 Bleecker Street, New York City. It is earnestly hoped many of Christ's followers will join us in this grand work.

With such organizing methods many new Missions will every year be founded, and ere long every large city in America will have one of these Homes where the tempted girl may find food and shelter and clothing and human love that shall lead her to the dear Saviour and a consecrated life for Him.

But, dear friends, the best way to help the rescue work is to prohibit the saloon. As long as we have the traffic in drink we will have the traffic in girls. Surely American mothers, when they realize that they must give not only 100,000 boys but 46,000 girls every year to die drunkards' deaths, will join the Woman's Christian Temperance Union and help to save *their own children*. Surely, sometime, fathers will quit authorizing saloon keepers to make their boys into drunkards and their girls into that pitied thing whose name our shuddering lips refuse to mention. If I voted for the saloon to make somebody's boy into a drunkard, I'd *expect* to have my boy made into a drunkard. If I voted for the saloon to send some mother's beautiful girl to the streets, I'd expect to find mine there. God help the 4,000,000 Christian voters to vote as they pray, and prohibit the liquor traffic, when the traffic in girls will cease and Florence Crittenton Missions not be needed.

LETTER FROM HON. THEODORE ROOSE-VELT.

The following letter from President Theodore Roosevelt, of the New York Board of Police Commissioners, who was to address a Good Government meeting in Baltimore, and who was invited also to address the National Purity Congress, was read by the President, and warmly applauded;

POLICE DEPARTMENT,
NEW YORK, Oct. 14th, 1895.

AARON M. POWELL, Esq.

Dear Sir:—I am sorry to say that I shall only get on to Baltimore a few minutes before the meeting, and will leave immediately afterwards, so I could not possibly speak elsewhere.

You are entirely at liberty to quote that I re-affirm in the most hearty manner what I said before. I will not have one law for men and one for women ; they shall be treated exactly alike, so far as I am concerned.

Very truly yours,

THEODORE ROOSEVELT.

O. EDWARD JANNEY.

THE MEDICAL PROFESSION AND MORALS.

By O. Edward Janney, M. D., of Baltimore.

The physician holds an influential position in society. In the capacity of medical attendant of parents and children, he becomes to both, and especially the latter, a loved and trusted friend, to whom, as they grow into manhood and womanhood, they appeal in matters medical and non-medical requiring the exercise of trained judgment. The medical profession, moreover, is composed of well-educated and thinking men, students of the questions of the day, on which they bring to bear their trained mental powers.

For these reasons physicians stand high in all communities. Their opinions and example have great weight with others, and their decision in medical and sanitary matters is final.

Such being the case, it is of the utmost importance that physicians carefully study moral and social questions as they arise, in order that the views they come to hold in regard to the proper solution of these problems may be righteous, for, should their opinions be incorrect, many will be led astray.

This is especially the case with those social problems which are semi-medical in their nature; those which have to do with health, or whose study requires a knowledge possessed only by the physiologist, and particularly with those problems, most perplexing in their nature, which deal with the relation of the sexes.

Perplexing as they are, these problems press upon the conscience of the observant and the thoughtful and demand the right solution. The time for decision and action has arrived. These evils which have thrust their hideous presence upon us from time immemorial must be banished from the earth. No longer are men and women willing to call them necessary evils. No longer can we hear unmoved the cry of anguished and helpless girlhood, and our heart-strings are torn with the oft-repeated story of their wrongs. An aroused conscience demands that a righteous attitude toward moral degradation be maintained and looks to the medical profession for enlightened co-operation.

Such co-operation will be afforded, doubtless, by the majority of the profession, and yet there does exist within its ranks a certain element from which no assistance in this moral crusade need be expected. It is the element which upholds the idea that chastity is incompatible with perfect health and teaches men so.

When physicians assume this position, they do so either from ignorance, which is inexcusable in a learned profession; from policy, because they know that such advice will prove acceptable to many young men, or else from an intrinsic wickedness which thinks evil of all men and allows them to take no interest in efforts for the elevation of the race.

Upon this class of men arguments and illustrations have little weight ; but an enlightened public opinion will reach them at length, and therefore an effective means of correcting this evil is to help to form such a public sentiment and trust to its general expression to effect the desired reform.

To argue that a continent life is not a healthful one is to stand in opposition to the known laws of nature. One has but to recall many familiar instances among animals to perceive its fallacy. Everyone is acquainted with men and women whose nature is fully developed physically, mentally and morally, and yet have lived single lives. Examples illustrating this point could be mentioned in great number, but only one need be given, the great Example, whose name is mentioned with reverence—Jesus of Nazareth.

This fact is now understood and accepted by the better part of the profession: Witness the following declaration, indorsed by a large number of the best known and most eminent physicians of both schools: "In view of the wide-spread suffering, deplorable hereditary results and moral deterioration inseparable from unchaste living, the undersigned, members of the medical profession, unite in declaring it as our opinion that chastity—a pure, continent life for both sexes—is consonant with the best conditions of physical, mental and moral health."

It may be wise at this point to consider some of the results of giving improper advice to young men in regard to the matter under discussion, whether such advice comes from physicians or others.

Scarcely a day passes that an account of the suicide of some young man does not appear in the public press. Many of these result from following such advice. Prompted by such counsel, he enters into evil company and evil places and before long, finding his moral tone lowered, his self-respect lost, his body diseased, his hope of a life of usefulness darkened, his conscience a coal of fire, he seeks relief from his sufferings in death. Oblivion, he thinks, is preferable to such a life. But is oblivion obtained? Only God knows.

But, perhaps, in his desire to carry out the advice given, instead of seeking evil company, he cultivates the acquaintance of some innocent young girl. In such an instance there is a possibility, too often realized, that there will be added to the load of iniquity he is to carry, the ruin of another life, and the despairing cry of a lost soul drives him to destruction.

Not always, however, is the nature of man so sensitive, and he with ruder instincts may choose to live, and live to be a curse to womankind.

But suppose a man has "sown his wild oats" and has not experienced all the evils that follow, what can be said of him? In the first place it may be said that such associations as he has had have blunted his moral sensibilities. It is true that "the punishment fits the crime," and such a man is not and never can be the man he might have been had he led a pure life. His wings are scorched and will not lift him into the purer upper realms.

Follow his further experience in life. He would marry, and here it is to be observed that he does not seek a companion fallen like himself, but one whom the faintest breath of suspicion has never touched. This man, with his unsavory past and with the seeds of disease in his system, does not hesitate to unite, in the holy bonds of wedlock, with one who is pure and innocent. Has the medical profession no protest to utter in these cases?

The following instances from actual practice may serve to illustrate what often follows such marriages:

W. B., aged twenty-four, a healthy young woman, married a young man whose life had not been pure. Within two years she began to suffer with a local diseased condition, which after causing great distress, finally demanded a surgical operation and this resulted fatally.

F. A. was a lovely young woman with fair complexion, bright color, excellent health, happy disposition, and with every prospect of a long and useful life, when she married. He who promised to cherish her was one who had followed the evil suggestions so often given to young men, and brought to the altar a wrecked constitution, under a fair outward semblance. As months passed the friends of the bride noticed that her cheeks were losing their bright color, that listlessness had succeeded animation, and they feared that all was not well. A year passed and one night there came into the world a little, wasted, immature child, with life poisoned before it was born. This same poison, which had been working in the mother's system for a year, now swept her with a force no remedy could stay, and the mother and her child were laid in one grave.

And the cause of this lay with him who had promised at the altar to *love, honor* and *protect* the innocent and confiding being who there committed herself to his keeping.

Suppose that child had lived, what then ? One evening a young man called to be treated for a peculiar form of skin affection. His sister was affected in a somewhat similar way. Almost as plainly as if it had been on a printed page, could be read a history which told that a parent or grand-parent of these young people had followed the bad advice against continence and had brought upon these innocent young people a curse that is beyond power of removal and which they, in turn, may transmit to their offspring.

No wonder when such cases as these appear in the daily practice of physicians, they are impressed with the necessity of taking a stand in this matter and show a willingness to co-operate with those who aim at reform.

The physician has a certain duty to perform toward the public. It is his high privilege not only to cure the sick but to prevent sickness. Now it is well-proved that when a man has once suffered from any of the diseases of impurity he never fully recovers, but carries through life the power to transmit disease. It is claimed with reason that this is the cause of a large proportion of the diseases of women which produce serious local disorder and often require dangerous operative procedures.

In view, therefore, of the physical and mental suffering often amounting to torture, to wives and sometimes to children, that follows, physicians should assume and firmly maintain a position of opposition to the marriage of a man who has ever suffered from a disease of impurity, even the mildest.

Should this attitude be understood and supported by the public, it would almost solve the Purity problem.

In the advocacy of purity reform the chief error that medical men are likely to fall into is the adoption of some improper, half-way measure, such as the State regulation of vice, a system which vainly aims to protect bad men, while holding in hopeless slavery all suspected women; and preventing the saving of those who have been unknowingly entrapped by the designing, or the reformation of the penitent. Let no physician advocate any such iniquitous scheme, but with high moral courage demand the abolition of the whole evil system of social wrong !

May the members of the medical profession, "with firmness in the right as God gives us to see the right," stand in opposition to all such vice and advice, and so wield their mighty influence as to further the cause of virtue, and, like knights of old, so place their shields as to protect the weak and the innocent.

TEMPERANCE AND PURITY.

———

By Mary Clement Leavitt.

It sometimes happens that a reformer is so thoroughly engrossed in his own cause that he loses sight of the importance of other reforms, and even of the help that others might be to his. In a few sad instances he has been known, figuratively speaking, to throw stones at others who are really helping him.

Among all the reforms that engage our attention at the present time, none are more closely allied than purity and temperance, no vices more closely related than impurity and intemperance. No reformers can or ought to be more mutually helpful than those engaged along these two lines.

In this country I believe all who are engaged in either are friendly to both, but in England there are persons doing earnest work for purity, who are unwilling to investigate even the effects of alcoholic drinks upon chastity, while on the Continent of Europe some of the purity workers are utterly opposed to total abstinence, as are the masses of religious people and nearly all the clergy, Protestant and Romish.

In the course of the long journey I made all over the world, which lasted from July 13, 1883, to June 18, 1891, although I started for the sole purpose of organizing W. C. T. U.'s, I soon found that I must help in the Purity Reform or fail to do my duty. In this way much additional light was thrown upon the close connection between the two evils.

I have indeed come to believe that in Christian countries, where alone religion holds up the correct standard of purity, the two vices are intertwined at the

MARY CLEMENT LEAVITT.

warp and woof in the web. Where the religion of the country presents no barrier to sins of impurity, if drink adds its incitements, the results are fearful beyond description

The desire to lead a pure life must arise from instinct inherited from a pure ancestry, from a knowledge of God's plan, the only high, holy, joyous plan, for the conduct of sexual life, the fear of evil results from a wrong course, or the union of these motives. In the latter case we have a young person well fitted to go through life with a face open as the light, a life as pure as the stars.

Comparatively few such young people would go astray if their powers were not thrown out of the normal balance.

Alcohol (opium and tobacco as well) is capable of doing this, and then saddest results follow.

"I never should have yielded to him but for the wine he persuaded me to take," is the wail of thousands of young girls who had no wish to go astray.

"I could not support the horrors of this life (in a brothel), without the spirits I drink. It deadens my feelings and then I don't care," is constantly said to workers by these poor fallen sisters.

"I never wished to sin with women till after I took to drink," is the frequent confession of men who have turned back from a sinful life.

"One thing I know, you cannot carry the purity reform till we fellows leave off drink," said a "society" man to the White Cross advocate who was laboring with him.

These are not isolated sayings, but repeated so often that they may be taken as *formulæ* for great classes. All through Maine, Massachusetts, Vermont, New Hampshire, no sooner had prohibition been put into operation than inmates of houses of ill fame began to steal away, and soon the houses themselves to be closed, and it is a constant sequence of prohibition.

Naturally the question will be asked, "How does alcohol bring these things to pass?

For a clear understanding of the case it is necessary to state what alcohol is. I use the words of the late William B. Carpenter, of England, who to the day of his recent death was the first toxicologist of the world. He said, in an important and well considered lecture, given in a scientific course before the Lowell Institute in Boston, and afterwards printed: "Alcohol is a deadly, irritant poison, not a true stimulant. Through this narcotic power it first attacks, then weakens. and, if the alchoholic habit continues, destroys the will power."

Next, it constantly confuses reason and judgment.

Thirdly, it produces, especially if taken in the form of malted liquors, an abnormal excitation of the sexual desires.

If the last named result only took place, the higher powers of reason and judgment might still point out the only right and safe line of conduct, and that rudder of the human being, will power, keep him walking in it. But, alas, while evil clamors for indulgence, all these higher powers are drowsy, and the fall comes.

When in conversation with a well known English lady residing in Naples, she spoke of the very common infidelity in marriage by wives of all classes, as well as husbands, declaring that more than one-third of the marriage vows taken were broken by husband or wife, or both. I remarked that the universal habit of wine drinking probably had some influence in bringing about that state of affairs.

"Oh, no! It is the forced, loveless marriages," said the lady. To that I replied, " Suppose a young wife has no love for her husband; suppose she falls in love with another man who has conceived a passion for her. If neither drank they would yield to reason, decide to see each other no more, and will power would hold them to that course." When I had finished the explanation as given above, the lady said, " I believe you may be right.

I have not understood before how alcohol acts on the different powers of the mind."

John Ellis, M. D., author of "Avoidable Causes of Disease," "Deterioration of the Puritan Stock," etc., says upon this subject: "I am satisfied that the chief causes of the social evil . . . are the use of intoxicating drinks and narcotics . . . and the fashionable modes of dress among women."

A lady in one of our large cities whose husband is a quiet but indefatigable worker among wicked fashionable young men, told me that again and again men said to her husband, "If I am to live right I must give up balls, society, everything. The wine, the undress of the ladies, are too much for me every time. We rush from the ball to the brothel. Every great ball prepares a harvest for that sort of place."

An American gentleman who has recently spent much time in France, observed very carefully the effect of wine upon young, even little, children. As all children drink at *table d'hote*, he had plenty of opportunities to observe. He saw so frequently a plainly marked excitement in this direction that he became convinced that wine is an important factor in bringing about the early and common impurity in the country. In view of these facts I appeal to the supporters of this Congress who are not yet identified with the temperance movement, to give us your voice and vote to remove this potent stimulant to sexual vice, not only in our country but all over the world.

Most of us must give ourselves mainly to one reform only, but occasions frequently arise when one Society can give countenance and help to another, and we can always help each other at the polls. The W. C. T. U. in all State and National legislation the Purity Association may undertake, will help you to the limit of our power and influence, while every step we gain is breaking down the obstacles to your ultimate triumph.

And now, as I have not, in reading my paper, consumed all the time I may fairly claim, I wish to bring forward three points vital to the success of the Purity Reform.

First: Woman was not created to be an adjunct of man, but co-ordinate with him; responsible to God only just as man is, in doing God's work of peopling the earth, subduing it, and carrying on the world. As long as the opposite idea prevails, as soon as a man listens to the seductions of sin he will feel at liberty to thrust this being, created solely for his use, into whatever condition pleases him best. Hence polygamy, concubinage, divorce at the will of the husband alone, as in Japan, Egypt and other countries, and hence harlotry. The co-ordination of men and women must be taught to the young, especially to boys, everywhere and always.

Second: All boys must be taught that personal purity of thought, word and act, all through life, is as glorious and indispensable in man as woman, and as obligatory upon him; that he commits an irreparable wrong not only against himself, body, intellect and soul, but against his future wife and his descendants, down to the third and fourth generation, if he transgresses the law of purity. We must teach that it is as necessary for a boy or young man to keep the marriage vow as well before as after marriage. Girls must be taught the frightful consequences to themselves and their children if they marry impure men.

And thirdly: We must change laws and constitutions, if need be, in order to punish adequately women and men who make a trade of betraying innocent girls into the clutches of vile men, veritable Minotaurs, fattening upon the bodies and souls of virgin girls.

Let us remember that the constitutions, whether National or State, as well as the laws, were made by men, have been amended and can be whenever advance in thought, in knowledge, in justice or humanity demands it. The needed change is to forbid these persons to be released on bail, between arrest and trial; if convicted, not to sentence them to pay a fine, but to prison for a term of years for the first offence, and for life on the second conviction.

As it is now, the rich customers go bail, the rich customers pay the fines, and the wretched panderer to vice gets off with a few hours in the station house, a few hours more in the court room, and with no pecuniary loss. Should not this trade in virgin innocence be put on a par with treason and murder, the two unbailable offences? When you return to your homes to night, which would be the more terrible news to you: that a beloved daughter lay murdered in her saintly purity, or had been stolen, sold to a villain; you could not find her; your eyes would never see her more, but she would soon be sold again into a brothel, there to lead a life of the most revolting slavery this earth has ever known? If your daughter is safe because of your standing in society, will not you make the daughters of the poor man in the back street, or of the poor widow who once lived next door to you, or the poor girl who stands alone in the world, with no man or woman to protect her, as safe as your own?

MARTHA SCHOFIELD.

SLAVERY'S LEGACY OF IMPURITY.

By Martha Schofield Aiken, S. C.

This subject is so full of disagreeable, heart-sickening facts, that the truth should only be spoken to awaken a desire to help the *many* who do not yet realize there is in them a spirit "made in the image of God."

We who were called to labor in our country, darkened by the blight of slavery, find the roots of *impurity* so deeply imbedded in the animal nature that a generation has made little progress in weeding them out. Thirty years of missionary work in the South forces the conviction that the *blackest* shadow lies on the *white* race.

Impurity robbed the slave of the sacredness of parentage; it destroyed the holiness of motherhood; it separated those whom God had joined together and put their children, created in the love of the Lord, on the auction block for gold. It tore asunder the *home;* it rent in twain the families that God had set together; it robbed men of their divine right of fatherhood; it gave children to women whose fathers they would not have chosen.

It whitened African blood without law or gospel. Impurity was permitted and often encouraged between sexes and colors in little children, and thus at an early age they began to increase the slave market; many a young man's "first-born" was sold to the highest bidder.

The mother of six children when asked why *her* mother had not taught her how to cut out a baby's dress, or iron the clothes after washing them, replied: "*My* mother could teach us nothing; she was too good a field hand and too good a *breeder;* she brought nineteen children to her master;" then added in a most pathetic tone, "she was only allowed nine days when we was born, then sent back to the field. An old woman took care of us, sending the baby to the field to be nursed. They made *me* marry at fourteen years of age, told me nothing, and when my baby was born I wanted to kill it; I wouldn't look at it for two days. I hated it, cause of my pains."

The market value of every coming child was calculated as a dairyman does his Jerseys.

This terrible *excrescence of animalism* can only be overcome by an education that teaches there is *no sex* in *sin*, it is neither male or female, and that the Lord holds a man responsible for his children whether he feels accountable or not.

A sad part is that a profession of Christianity puts little restraint on what too many ministers, especially of the colored race, call "*nature.*" This is the excuse in the minds of wrong doers who have been well educated in theological schools by money donated to "educate ministers." The ministry used as a stepping stone to an education and with no struggle of mind or manual labor to meet expenses, loose rein was given to inherited tendencies. While studying for the ministry honest labor and manual training would have curbed the surplus of animal passion. Oh, that those good people who gave of their substance had been *wiser* and required those being educated for the ministry to labor with hands as well as brains. On *this* rock many smart men out of slavery have wrecked their own moral character and been followed by church members. Purity of life was not a requisite to become a member of any denomination in either race. When a young man was reproved (he was the son of a minister) for wasting his money on women and asked if he was not a church member he replied, "Yes, I grew up in Sunday School and have studied my Bible well, but never found where

Adam and Eve were *married*, yet they had children."
He was asked if he knew what Jesus said. "Yes, that
was adultery with another man's wife, but these women
ain't married—got no husbands." This, with many
worse facts, proved to us that the Bible is often used to
cover and lessen the responsibility of sinning. It is a
two edged sword in the hands of babes, and it takes
courage to warn regarding the possible wrong of giving
it to children or to men with minds not developed and
trained to rule the animal nature. The rebound of
slavery left two races to guide themselves by *feelings*
instead of principles.

There are no young lives in America that have as
much to contend with as the young *colored women*, often
pretty and attractive and more solicited when they can
read and write notes for appointments, or tales of "undying affection," and have been under refining influences.

We stood by the coffin of a beautiful girl of twenty
years, whose rich English father had died suddenly and
the property he left her colored mother, since dead,
lessened in the lawyers' hands. Her boarding school
knowledge and inherited refinement (father and grandfather white) added to her attractiveness. We looked
on the still face and felt she had been called with her
babe to "go and sin no more." Then arose within us
a strong pity and compassion, with yearning to help the
young white men who were sharers in her shame,
whose arms had caressed her and whose money had
decked her body and paid for the costly coffin.

In an interview with the white clergyman where
they attended church, and offering to help save them,
sons of respectable parents, he said, "nothing we could
tell would equal what he *knew*."

The communion bread and wine had been offered
in white churches by men who led colored school girls
from the path of virtue, and most of the men in the
congregation knew it.

What minister dare touch the sin of slavery and remain in the South during its existence! *Free speech* of the *truth* of impurity is still barred and bolted by custom and inheritance, while the messages of the Lord wait for utterance.

Did these things end with slavery? No! no! *no!* The trail of the serpent is everywhere. A Northern teacher had to write to a public official, saying a certain young woman was a teacher in her school because, he had made a vile proposition when she went to the court house on business about the land she had earned. That official moved in the best society. One cannot conceive the feelings of modest, retiring, educated and refined colored women who know they are never safe from the insults of white men, or the temptation to a life of ease, luxury and a comfortable home, often with an affection that lasts for years, for the fathers frequently support and educate their children.

The pitiful part is that the best families are not yet awakened to the shame of such wrongs. First-class lawyers have been known to go to a colored man in a campaign and say, "I know you are my half brother now I want you to vote for Mr. ——."

There is a *darker side* yet, fulfilling the truth of the words that the sins of the fathers shall be visited on their *children*. It does not say on *sons* only, and daughters inherit from fathers and have become mothers of babes whose fathers were mulatoes. These girls were often in the care of men house servants or coachmen, and after the birth of the child it was given to a slave woman and both put in the market. It is unnecessary to multiply cases or give more startling facts; the social evil is written everywhere in the *color* of the children born since the war. The city schools are bleached and most of the boarding schools whitened with it.

The stain of this Legacy of Impurity will outlast the bondage of body and stripes to the flesh.

Rays of light are coming in by the active work of the women in that clarifying organization, the Woman's Christian Temperance Union. In their broader intelligence and aroused abilities they are sharing a weariness of so much talk and preaching about keeping *race* purity. They know what enemy is in the household and through them it must be cast out. Their work combined with the educational efforts to lift *colored* women to a higher wifehood and holier motherhood is *one* of the means. The still greater need and only safe building for the future is to teach *boys*—yes, *boys*—the danger and the wrong, and lift men to the responsibility and nobleness of fatherhood and to respect *all* women.

The men are slow to recognize that as church members and professing Christians, their own lives must be pure, and on combined effort depends the blotting out of the darkest legacy ever left by one generation to another.

REV. A. H. LEWIS.

THE SACREDNESS OF FATHERHOOD.

By Rev. A. H. Lewis, D. D.

God has absolute power to give life. All creating centers in Him. He has conferred infinite honor and infinite responsibility on man, by giving him power to re-create and perpetuate his kind.

Fatherhood is a most sacred function. In this life alone its exercise is fraught with measureless results for good or evil; considered in view of the endless life on which all men have entered, the possibilities and results are beyond conception or computation. The ignorance and indifference which abound among men—otherwise well informed—concerning fatherhood and its obligations are startling and criminal; while the wickedness which degrades this function to the low level of animalism is a shameful badge of degradation.

It is a sad commentary on this ignorance and indifference that men lead in social impurity, regardless of their higher duties and holy responsibilities. They furnish the money which creates the commercial power of this evil. Enough will be offered upon the altar of lust in this city to-night to build many churches and relieve thousands who are in distress. The fires of animalism turn the forces which belong to pure fatherhood to bitterness and ashes. The history of social vice is the history of depraved manhood. Under the false and cruel "double standard" of morality which has shielded men and trampled on women, men have been the greatest sufferers as well as the greatest sinners against themselves, their sisters and the God of purity. There are now at least three fallen men to every fallen woman. In the sight of God these men are "lost ones," quite as much as the women are.

Prostituted manhood and outraged fatherhood are among the darkest stains in the history of the "social evil." To call it the "degradation of manhood" would be more appropriate. To claim that it is a necessity for the protection of virtuous womanhood against the animalism of men is an insult to all manhood and to fatherhood.

Science has fully demonstrated the value of fatherhood in fields lower than those which men occupy. The world accepts these conclusions of science, and places high commercial value on fatherhood in horses, cows, chickens, and poodle dogs for foolish women to fondle. Race horses and fox hounds must be "well born;" how much more *immortal men!* If earth-born fatherhood is thus valuable, how more than priceless is that by which men project themselves through time and the eternities for good or ill? Oh! the everlastingness of results.

In the largest sense, fatherhood includes motherhood. Parenthood is co-re-creation. Much is said of the sacredness of motherhood, and men demand purity in wives and mothers as a first and never-to-be fogotten factor. It is only just and logical that as much be demanded of men. This we do demand, and on this demand we base all pleading for the faithful recognition of "The Sacredness of Fatherhood."

DEFINITION.

Under God, fathers are subordinate creators of immortal life and eternal destiny. God instituted marriage, monandrous and monagamous, when time was young and Eden was sinless, that human life might be kept strong and pure in continuous perpetuation. Through this divine endowment man's creatorship involves body and soul, all being and all destiny. Through it all generations link and mingle in enduring unity. The heart throbs of other centuries are still felt in our own, and ours will mingle with those of generations yet unborn. Character and destiny are ever attendant on fatherhood. Thus is that law true — so glorious in obedience, so terrible in disobedience—which the Finger of Fire wrote on Sinai, "Visiting the iniquities of the fathers upon the children to the third and fourth generation of them that hate me; and showing mercy unto thousands of them that love me and keep my commandments." In the presence of such truth we can better understand the deeper meaning of the words, "No man liveth unto himself."

PREPARATION FOR FATHERHOOD.

Ideal fatherhood, such as the dawn of the twentieth century ought to see, begins with perfected physical life. To be valuable for fatherhood a horse must be a "magnificent animal." So must a man. This is especially true as to everything which touches that form of life we call "nervous force." Whatever impairs this unfits for fatherhood. Hence the shame and sin of bestial lust. Hence the crime of men against themselves and their children in the use of alcohol, tobacco and all like poisons; the wickedness of placing the pleasures of an animal indulgence over against the demands of fatherhood. The question is not whether men intend to wrong themselves or their children. It is not a matter of purpose, much less of option. The law of cause and effect works ceaselessly, whether we will or not. If it were not imperious the best results could not come. Because it is imperious evil results will follow from evil causes. "Whatsoever a man soweth" both he and his children must reap. Men must give to the future what they possess. They must transmit what they are. A man never escapes from himself. The ideal father is the ideal upward looking and upright walking animal, the true *Anthropos*, and not the lustful beast. The earthly dwelling place of the immortal one, which has so much to do with character and soul development, should be well born. Narcotized nerves and lust-poisoned bodies cannot furnish fit fatherhood for that which is highest and best in each succeeding generation.

Why is it that whiskey and tobacco must resort to lust-provoking pictures to quicken trade? Why must these put a premium on vileness in order to succeed, more than bake shops and meat markets do? The pictures which accompany the cigarettes that are tainting the fountain of fatherhood in the boys of to-day are fit counterpart to the nameless symbols which defiled the streets of Pompeii, when the pagan vileness of decaying Rome was at its worst. This terrible harvest is enough to appall the friends of purity, without considering the awfulness of those diseases which lust entails and perpetuates.

PURE SOUND MENTALITY.

The ideal father is not until the " magnificent animal " becomes the thinking and reasoning man. The quality of intellect goes with fatherhood as surely as physical characteristics do. Fatherhood gives trend to thought, as it gives contour to features and color to eyes. Hence no man is at liberty to be content with low intellectual powers or attainments. He is bound to make the most of himself and for himself for sake of those who may be born to him through fatherhood. He should seek that which is highest in thought, richest in intellect and noblest in conception touching all things, all questions, all duties. To be indolent and non-thoughtful is to fall below all real manhood. To be content with mediocrity is to be worthy of condemnation. To labor continually that he may attain higher heights of knowledge and of intellectual culture is the least a man can do, if he would be true to his possible mission as a father.

THE WORSHIPING IMMORTAL.

Body and physical life, mentality and intellectual life are only the foothills which lead toward the mountain

top of ideal fatherhood. This mountain top is reached
when a God fearing, truth seeking and humanity loving
spirit posesses and sways the whole man. Whatever is
noblest in purpose, richest in purity and holiest in endeavor belongs to fatherhood, and is demanded by it.
This demand is above "creed" and party. It is above
computation in value and beyond question in its im-
perativeness. If a man could forget himself and be
indifferent to his own destiny, he must not forget his
children and his children's children. If he could be
careless of body he must be mindful of the eternities
which await him and his. Strong and clean physically,
rich in culture and nobility intellectually, reverent and
Christ-loving spiritually, the ideal father stands nearer
to God in fatherhood than in any other relation.

THE SPHERE OF FATHERHOOD.

When the morning stars sang the first wedding
march in the sinless Eden, God set the bounds of fatherhood and motherhood within the sacred temple of
monandrous and monagamous wedlock. To seek fatherhood otherwise contravenes the highest laws of human
life and relationship. To incur the unfitness and degradation which come through promiscuous lustful indulgence is a crime from which every noble man will
shrink.

Judged by the highest law, the lust-indulging man
ought not to become a father. He has no right to put
weights on body and soul which his innocent child must
carry through weary eternities.

We talk of the glory of motherhood. Art puts the
aureole upon the head of the Madonna; this is well.
But fatherhood has equal glory. When a pure husband
knows that another heart is beating beneath the heart of
his wife, that another life belonging equally to both is
preparing to step into full birth, that he has thus begun
to project himself into the history of all life and all time,
then as never before he begins to put on the crown

of manhood, and to take part with God the Everlasting in the work of creation; then the angel who writes the "vital statistics" of the universe places his name among those who have entered the sacred temple of *Fatherhood.*

Men, you who are already fathers of sons, bow your heads while God grants you new annointing, that you may fulfill your mission thus well begun by teaching your sons their high and holy place in the universe and among men. Let no false delicacy keep you from revealing to them, as the years demand, the sacredness of those wondrous powers which are to fit them for co-creatorship with the Universal Father in heaven.

Young men, you to whom fatherhood is yet to come, begin anew from this hour that preparation which will enable you to look upon your first born with thanksgiving rather than regret. Prepare yourselves for the divine mission, the matchless honor and the endless destiny which lie enshrined within the portals of your waiting fatherhood—high, holy, sacred fatherhood!

ADDRESS TO THE NATIONAL PURITY CONGRESS.

FROM THE "COMMITTEE ON THE PURIFICATION OF THE PRESS," OF THE BALTIMORE YEARLY MEETING OF FRIENDS, PARK AVENUE.

BY PAULINE W. HOLME.

In presenting this report of our Committee in the midst of as important and interesting papers as are claiming the attention of this Congress to-night, a sense of the value of every moment of time compels brevity.

In 1889, during our Baltimore Yearly Meeting of Friends, a very general concern was felt in the Women's Meeting that the greatest care might be taken to guard the young against improper reading. In this connection the influence of the daily press, which is felt in every home and is so important a factor in moulding the character of our boys and girls, was considered, and as was recognized its power to elevate our people in virtue and morality, by ever preserving a high, pure tone in its delineation of facts, or to degrade and debase, by pandering to the demands of the lower elements of society, it was deemed advisable to appoint a committee to co-operate with the noble minded among our editors and journalists in the endeavor everywhere to obtain a purer public press. That committee was appointed and for six years has continued its labors with unabated zeal.

During the first year, an appeal pleading for the omission of details of vice and crime and other objec-

PAULINE W. HOLME.

tionable items from our daily papers, was sent by them to 79 editorial organizations of the United States and Canada, from whom so numerous and hearty responses were received that the committee were encouraged to pursue their work. Having been reappointed the following year, they presented the needs for this work to more than 400 editors and publishing associations. Each year a printed report of the work has been circulated. These reports, with various appeals, have been sent to about 4,000 editorial offices. The personal replies received and the various editorials promulgating these pure principles, give evidence that the simple efforts of this small committee are already bearing fruit.

The committee elicited the co operation of some of our most prominent educators and other influential citizens by obtaining the signatures of more than 100 well known college professors and teachers, doctors, ministers, lawyers and leading business men to an appeal for the exclusion of detailed and sensational reports of the evil doings of the day, and all immoral or questionable advertisements from our newspapers. A copy of this appeal and the signatures was sent to every newspaper office in our State.

We also sent a copy to leading reformers in other States, desiring them to do for their own locality a similar work to that begun in Maryland. We have also presented our plans of work to other Yearly Meetings of Friends, to the annual conference of the Methodist and the Unitarian clergy and to many ministers of the various denominations in Baltimore. They have at once recognized the importance of these endeavors and have heartily endorsed them.

We have also communicated our efforts to the National Woman's Christian Temperance Union, and to National and International Leagues and Press Clubs; and through their resolutions endorsing the action of this committee our work has been reported not only to the journalists of America, but it has been brought to the notice of the European press.

Our experience with editors, from whom we have invariably received the most courteous consideration and such endorsements as encourage us to continue our endeavors, leads us to this conclusion:

If those who deplore the standard of the public press would raise their voice against the clamor for excitement and sensationalism, and uphold the hands of those worthy journalists who are endeavoring to raise the standard of public opinion, they would help make way for a better day in journalism. There is a work for all. The demand for sensation is imperative, and the first seeds of morbid desire and impure sentiment are often sown in the mind of the innocent and ignorant by the details of the evil doings of the world, so vividly portrayed in the newspapers that daily enter the home. Let parents and all educators note this danger and unite with other good people in an earnest effort to maintain a pure press.

Each subscriber has the right to call the attention of the editor to what he deems objectionable in his paper, and this privilege, wisely exercised, would doubtless be very effective in raising the standard of the daily press. Too often the perusal of the vivid descriptions of sinful conduct has enkindled in the young of weak character latent evil propensities; or an improper advertisement has opened the door to a corrupt life. Then what more worthy undertaking for purity workers!

It is with this feeling that our cause is one that we have ventured in this brief manner to present our work to-night to the National Congress of the American Purity Alliance. We realize that this cause of purity, in the interests of which we are assembled, can be furthered in no way more rapidly than by the efficacy of a pure public press; while an impure press can blight the noblest efforts of our best workers. Therefore we appeal to this powerful organization, whose influence is so potent and extended, to include among its many laudable endeavors the promotion of this worthy cause by helping to banish those sensational sheets which tend to sow broadcast seeds of impurity and immorality, and by sustaining and aiding those who are endeavoring to make the press an educator and source of pure entertainment.

DR. ELIZABETH BLACKWELL.

FIFTH SESSION.

ENGLISH EXPERIENCE AND PURITY WORK.

By Dr. Elizabeth Blackwell.

My Friends:

I would gladly be with you on this important occasion, viz., the first meeting of the National Purity Congress of the United States. But as this is impossible, I hope you will allow me to offer you some of the experience gained in England, which may be of service to the Purity movement now growing up in the great New World.

I have spent the last twenty-six years in England, taking an active part in the important moral movement which has grown up there, and have seen some of the causes which have brought it about. At the same time I have watched the growth of what is called free love and free divorce in the United States. I have thus learned to recognize the important effect exercised by law, *i. e.*, by human laws, upon the relations of men and women; and I increasingly realize both the difficulty of the problems before us and their fundamental character.

I see how necessary it is that thoughtful men and women of the same race but of varied experience, on the two sides of the ocean, should unite in seeking a wise solution of this vital problem of our sexual relations. I trust that out of this important Congress active, permanent committees may be formed, including both men and women, who will seriously study the various branches of this great question of Purity. These include the sexual education of the young, the questions of fornication and promiscuous intercourse, of marriage and divorce, of police regulation and State legislation. By the formation and union of such active committees a great social force would be formed to develop and enforce the application of the principle of equal justice.

Among the potent causes of moral deterioration in England is the English law of divorce. It is as long ago as 1858 that the present unequal law was established by Parliament as the law of the land.

This new law practically denied the unity of the moral law by its unequal condemnation and treatment of men and women, for it made adultery a criminal offence in women but not necessarily an offence in men. It was a direct attack upon the sanctity of the family relation.

The injustice thus taught to the rising generation during thirty-eight years by human law bore its inevitable fruits in a deterioration of social morality. This was shown in 1865 to 1868, when the iniquitous "Contagious Diseases Acts," dealing with female fornicators, were passed by Parliament.

Gradually, however, the sense of justice, which seems to be inherent in our slow Anglo Saxon race, was aroused by the gross injustice of these acts and the scandals that arose in their application, and twenty-six years ago an arduous struggle began, which ended in the abolition of these last bad laws in 1886.

During this long and intense struggle for the repeal of the "Contagious Diseases Acts," the relations of men and women were subjected to a popular criticism, such as has never occurred before in the history of mankind, for they were brought before the judgment of the two halves of the human race—women as well as men.

It was then perceived that the "Contagious Diseases Acts" were a symptom and a result of a false and dangerous error that permeated society. This error was the belief that it is possible to maintain a double standard of sexual morality in any country that claims to be a Christian country. It was clearly seen that the false doctrine of one law for women and another law for men must be exposed and swept away, and the truth established that men and women of the same race must be guided by identical moral principles, if the progress of advancing civilization in that race is to be maintained.

ORIGIN OF THE SOCIAL PURITY MOVEMENT.

On the realization of this fundamental truth, viz., the unity of the moral law, began that active effort in its defence which is now known as the Social Purity Movement.

The first Society, under the title of the "Social Purity Alliance," was formed in 1875 by the banding together in a public organization of some of the most active men and women opponents of the "Contagious Diseases Acts."

From this apparently insignificant beginning this fight for justice has gradually extended into every civilized country, until to-day we are able to rejoice in this noble Congress, the latest and most hopeful development of that great transforming truth—the unity of the moral law.

STEPS OF PROGRESS.

In the past "Contagious Diseases Acts" contest, it was especially necessary to protect women from the short-sightedness of one sided legislation, and maintain the sacredness of potential motherhood.

Now, however, in the new crusade of purity we are in addition called on to defend the honor of men and maintain the sacredness of fatherhood. It has become urgently necessary to expose the gross materialism which can believe in no spiritual power higher than the physical instincts—a materialism which would resort to cannibalism were there no other way of satisfying the imperative instinct of hunger. But we, recognizing the equal nobility of the masculine and feminine natures, are called on to defend men from the aspersions cast upon them by their own sex.

Young men are now taught the false physiological doctrine that the biological difference in the structure of the sexes is so great and so unequal that the male cannot be guided by the same high law of self control as the female.

This false and dangerous error is now accepted and promulgated by "men of the world," by many physicians, legislators, professors of moral science, and even by clergymen and women tutored by them. We, as purity workers, deny this atheistic doctrine. On the contrary, profoundly respecting the noble work which men are called on to perform in the world, we reject the assertion of the fatal subjection of men to such false and unworthy theories. We believe that men equally with women possess strong souls as well as bodies. We declare that will and conscience are not chimeras, but are intended to direct the growth of the human organization, physical as well as mental. We state that it is a physiological falsehood that chastity must be injurious to health; and we maintain that it is an insult to the human male, as well as a blasphemy against our common nature, to assert that men are dependent upon the selfish use of women for the maintenance of their individual physical health.

SOUND PHYSIOLOGY.

Physiology, which includes biology, when intelligently studied with unprejudiced consideration of *all* the factors involved in the problem, proves conclusively the following important truths:

1st. The parallel physical and functional structure in the two halves of the human race.

2d. The equally powerful moral force of sexual attraction in those two halves of the race.

3d. The indispensable influence of the parental relation in the gradual elevation of the race.

Through these truths of physiology we learn the important practical lesson that in neither half of the race is the exercise of the creative faculty indispensable to the maintenance of individual physical health, whilst at the same time its exercise is essential to the continuance of the race. We learn, also, from physiological and social observation, that the rational exercise of the parental function is a precious means of human development in both men and women.

These three great biological truths, viz., individual independence, race necessity, and social development through parentage are essential Christian truths. They form the strong foundation of our purity work.

It will be observed that they centre around the great fact of parentage as their determining principle. They demonstrate to our intelligence that the exercise of our creative powers must be guided by their relation to the responsibility of parentage. We must grow into the perception that it is the abuse of a great trust to subordinate the higher to the lower use of this trust.

In all our efforts as purity workers we must seek to harmonize these three biological facts by their rational, *i. e.*, their religious adaptation to the divine order of growth.

In seeking enlightenment respecting education, marriage, divorce, legislation, these vital subjects must all be brought in their practical applications to the tribunal of these essential facts.

THE CAUSE OF SEXUAL EVIL.

The disorder at present existing in the special relations of men and women is owing to our failure to subject the most powerful attraction of sex to the enlightenment derived from the higher law of parentage. For the preservation and advancement of our race it is absolutely necessary that the narrow impulse of individual selfish indulgence should be enlarged and exalted by thought for others and by enthusiasm for the advancement of humanity.

We learn from the records of past history, as well as from the direful evils of the present day, that sexual evil lies at the root of all national decay.

It is in the spirit of reverence for the race that the first necessary instruction to the young should be given at the important epoch of puberty.

THE LAW OF PROGRESS.

As all permanent national progress centres around the family group, which is the *social* element, the Divine Law of progress requires that each factor in that group shall receive the consideration which is needed for its healthy development. This power of healthy development constitutes the necessity, or fundamental "rights," of each individual. Only when these necessities are recognized and provided for will a noble and progressive parentage of the race be possible.

Now the sacredness of motherhood has always been recognized to a certain extent and in a more or less confused way, in civilized societies. The responsibilities and rights of motherhood are being gradually established; and women themselves are beginning, in Christian countries, to realize their responsibility as creatures in *direct* relationship to the Divine Creator.

So also the sacredness of childhood and the protection due to its freshness, helplessness and unfolded possibilities, are gradually taking possession of the adult mind.

The weighty importance, however, of fatherhood, that first essential factor in the social element, is not studied in our day with that profound consideration that advancing science requires. The continued power of fatherhood, in its mental as well as physical potency; its effect on gestation; the mighty magnetic and moral influence of the father in the wonderful work of promoting the advent of a human being; the indispensable influence of the father as well as the mother, in infancy, childhood and adolescence,—all these facts involved in the sacredness of fatherhood have not yet received that reverential and careful consideration that God, speaking through nature, demands for it.

Our children now come, too often, half orphaned into this world, and fatherhood too generally is regarded as a temporary and comparatively irresponsible or insignificant act.

This slower consideration of the full meaning of fatherhood seems to be inevitable. In the gradual emergence of the human race from the rough and hard conditions of savagery, the male has necessarily been the strong and brave physical pioneer of progress, protecting and dominating the female, on whom the wonderful but hidden burden of creation seemed especially to rest. It was inevitable that in this division of the world's work a certain amount of arrogance on the part of the protectors to the protected should grow up, before the higher realities of the spiritual life were unfolded. We see this quite unconscious arrogance transmitted through the ages. It appears in every department of life. It is observed even in our religious teachers, from Moses to Compte. It makes the one divine life and *direct* teaching of our Lord Jesus Christ stand out in striking contrast, as a prophecy of the future, presenting the ideal towards which we must reach forward.

It is the brightest feature of the present age that this narrow selfhood is giving way to the large and joyful hope of free co-operation, as we see here to-day, when men and women become true fellow-workers for the manifestation and advancement of divine order.

SYMPATHETIC JUSTICE.

The ideal of Christian justice is sympathetic justice. This is the latest and divinest development of the human mind. It requires that the individual (or the community) that seeks to be just should enter into the life of his neighbor, as if it were his own experience. He must realize the limitations, the temptations, the special conditions of environment of his neighbor, as well as the higher object of life and its ideal, before a just practical judgment can be reached. Just judgment between men and women cannot be made until a sympathetic appreciation of each half of the race by the other half is gradually attained.

The law of Christian or sympathetic justice must be applied to each factor in the social element (man, woman and child) if the family group is to grow up into the strong creator of a healthy race.

The needs of the man, the woman and the child must be sympathetically studied. The man must learn to realize the mighty force of love which, germinating in the womanly nature, may grow into wisdom under natural laws of development. The woman must learn to respect the strong, active force of men, which will grow into wisdom when permeated by the unselfish power of love

THE ROOT OF PURITY.

I have spoken of the unjust divorce law of England. It is a subject on which English public sentiment is gradually maturing. It is a subject on which we shall gladly learn from wise American thought. But we cannot abolish one injustice by inflicting another; and this would be done by introducing the laxity of divorce existing at present in the United States—a laxity which dangerously imperils the sacredness of the family relation.

My own strong belief at present is that no true solution to the various problems which now surround the sexual question can be found until we learn to realize that virginity on entering upon the marriage relation is as obligatory on young men as on young women.

In both it is virginity of soul, as well as body, that is required. We must realize this need in education; and education begins before birth.

It is for this reason that I have ventured to call attention to that all-important aspect of this subject, which seems to me involved in that great force—the Sacredness of Fatherhood.

Virginity is essential to true marriage. It is a realm of infinite possibilities. It includes reverence, self-dominion, unselfish thought for others and recognition of the sacredness of parentage.

It is only when the boundless ocean of love that exists unexercised in virginity finds its rich expression in the race that childhood will be redeemed from orphanage.

Any one who has thrown away this rich endowment of the human being, has in so doing desecrated or trifled with the health of body and soul. Such an one is unfit for marriage unless and until by repentance, expiation and redemption, the lost potency has been regained.

The preservation of the purity of our youth, their growth from innocence into virtue, is the ideal towards which our thought and practice must tend. It is in the light of this ideal that all our practical measures must be studied.

Strength, Beauty and Love lie enfolded in this sacred human endowment of Purity.

REV. S. S. SEWARD.

PURITY— HOW PRESERVED AMONG THE YOUNG.

By the Rev. S. S. Seward, New York City.

Man is born neither good nor evil. His mind is not like the printed page, which must always bear the impress of what is stamped upon it, and which cannot be changed for better or worse without destroying its identity; but like a blank page, upon which he may, under God write such characters as he chooses, whether pure or impure. Although the sexual instinct is strong, and when once aroused difficult of restraint, it is as much under our control, with the Divine aid and the use of wise methods, as any of the other appetites of the body. If this is not so, there is no remedy for the evil, and "we are of all men most miserable." If it is so, our task is simple—to discover the remedy and to apply it.

In order to preserve the purity of the young, and in this way of the race, we must begin in the earliest infancy. Every mother should use the utmost precaution to make sure that her child, be it boy or girl, does not handle himself. This care should begin as soon as his hands are free. Even at that early age there is a certain pleasurable sensation connected with this habit, that may seduce the child, if I may use so strong a term, without any instruction from others or sin on his part. Sometimes the contamination comes through thoughtless servants, sometimes through innocent playmates; but more frequently it is due to the excitement of the parts through contact with the clothing. But whatever may have been the cause, I can bear testimony, from the confidences that have been reposed in

me in my pastoral capacity, that many an impure and
unhappy life has been begun in this manner. The
mother who does not use every precaution to protect
the little ones committed to her care against this
danger is guilty of criminal neglect. For this
purpose the clothing should be so arranged as to guard
against it, and all causes of irritation avoided. At night
the child should be dressed warmly about the shoulders
and arms, and taught to sleep with its hands outside
the bed clothes. Its mind should be imbued with a
horror of handling itself, and the little hands should be
punished if they do. If it becomes necessary to commit
the child to the care of nurses, or to others than the
mother herself, she should spare no pains to make sure
that no wrong habits are fostered or permitted.

This is the first duty. The next is to guard the
child, as soon as it grows old enough to associate with
other children, against impure suggestions. To this
end the mother should always know where her children
are and with whom they are associating. She should
select their playmates with as much care at this tender
age as she would the society of her grown up daughters.
If any improper conversation has been had she should
be able to discover it. For this purpose she should retain the implicit confidence of her children, and teach
them never to indulge any confidences with others that
they cannot share with her. This done, a few simple
questions at "the mother's hour," when the evening
prayer has been said and the little ones are being tucked
away in their beds, will suffice. If anything wrong has
happened during the day, the innocence and ingenuous-
ness of childhood will not be able to conceal it, and with
a little effort the whole story can be brought out and
the antidote applied. I am sure I need not dwell upon
the importance of this kind of precaution. Many of us
know by experience, and others will not need proof or
illustration, that the most subtle and deadly poison that
is ever infused into the human mind is infused in this

way and at this time. It is the more subtle and deadly because it is received in the innocence of the child's heart and implanted deeply in his nature. In later years he begins to know the nature of his own thoughts, and resents, or at least questions, an evil suggestion. But at this innocent and uninstructed period of its life the child does not "know to choose between good and evil," and imbibes evil suggestions as readily and as deeply as good ones. In this way children of both sexes have been known to teach each other the crime against nature, while it is not to be doubted that their mutual and stolen conferences on these secret and to them occult subjects, are not unaccompanied by that extravagance of the imagination which is characteristic of the childish mind in other respects. It is impossible to over-estimate the deadly nature of the virus that is insinuated in this way, or to measure correctly the pollution that must be repented of in adult life if the victim ever comes into a salvable state. It sets the imagination on fire. It arouses longings and desires that are all the more dangerous because vague and ill-defined. It causes the mind to wander and destroys all fixity of pursuit and purpose. It renders purity of thought out of the question, and oftentimes leads to lewdness of conduct. It takes away the innocence and frankness of the girl as well as of the boy, and produces a kind of false modesty that is painful to witness. It renders a pure and holy love of one of the sex impossible, and brings the man and woman together, even in marriage, on the plane of the flesh instead of the spirit. And yet all this could be guarded against by a little wisdom and self-sacrifice on the part of parents, God helping them; and this I believe to be one of the most important and needed lessons that parents can learn. The marriage relation and the parental instincts were not created merely that children might be born naturally, but spiritually; and parents who neglect to learn all the subtle dangers to which their children are exposed, and

to guard them against them, are derelict in their highest duty.

Thus far I have dealt chiefly with preventive measures. Sooner or later it will be the privilege as well
as the duty of parents not only to provide their children
with means of protection within, but to guard them
against the infusion of wrong notions from without.
For this purpose it will be necessary to give them all
needed and proper instruction on these important and
vital topics.

We cannot say exactly when such instruction should
begin. It is impossible to lay down laws universally
applicable to all. As a general rule, it may be said
that as soon as a child, whether boy or girl, is likely to
be exposed to impure influences of which it is impossible for parents to have any knowledge, or against
which they cannot guard at the time—when, for instance, the child goes to a large school where they cannot choose or control his companions, or has frequent
opportunity for private intercourse with other children
of which they can know nothing—it is time for them
to take him into their confidence, explain to him as
much as he can bear of the nature and use of his sexual
organization, and ask him for his confidence in return.
Nor need there be any difficulty about this. In com-
municating knowledge on this subject it is not necessary
that we should clothe our ideas with obscure figures and
far-fetched illustrations, for fear of contaminating the
minds of children. On the contrary, the air of mystery
may be carried so far as not only to obscure the truth
we wish to impart, but to arouse questions and suggest
conjectures that may produce the evil we are striving to
avoid. The sacred confidences of a mother with the
little one she loves better than her life, cannot easily
lead to wrong. The secret conferences of children with
each other, carried on with a great show of privacy and
many "hushes" and "don't tells," may have such an
effect. "The wicked walk on every side when the vile-

ness in men is exalted." (Psalm xii., 8.) But coming
from a mother actuated by a no less holy purpose than
the salvation of her child from impurity and lust, they
bring with them none but heavenly influences, all of
which will co-operate with her in her holy purpose.
Children are under Divine protection. "Their angels,"
that is the angels who are associated with them, "do
always behold the face," or understand the interior and
most loving purposes of, "the Father in Heaven"
(Matt. xviii., 10); and they are by this means constantly kept in innocent and chaste thoughts, unless unhallowed and filthy ideas and imaginations are infused
by some adverse influence from without. The Lord
and the angels will co-operate with us if we will co-operate with them.

Such being the case the simple story of the egg and
the chick will serve to suggest to them how little children are born; while the fact that with some animals,
like the colt or the calf, the egg is developed within
the mother, and not without, will solve the whole mystery of their origin beyond all childish questions. This
simple story, coming from a father's or a mother's lips,
and accompanied with the sphere of holiness and purity
which, because of its marvellous analogy with spiritual
birth, is associated in the angelic mind with natural
birth, will be the most wonderful story the child has
ever heard. Not the slightest taint of impurity will be
associated with it in his mind. It will be regarded as a
sacred confidence to be shared with his mother alone,
and it will bring his life again into vital union with
hers. If told that he must never talk of these things
with others, and if there is anything that he wishes to
know he must come to those who love him best for the
information, he will respect the admonition; and with
continued care and affection on their part, his parents
may be sure that the impurities that he will inevitably
hear as he grows up will make little or no impression
upon him.

But the time will come, in the case both of the boy and girl, when they will desire to know more. When that time comes the father should take the boys in hand, and the mother the girls. And here again the simple truth of the matter—the fact that the egg, which is formed in the mother, must be impregnated with the germ or seed that is formed in the father, and the latter must be transferred to the former—will best answer the purpose; and this can be told in such a manner by a wise and loving parent as to satisfy the mind without suggesting a thought of excitement or passion. We know that this can be done because we know that it has been done, and because, so far from being impure, there is nothing so exalted and holy as the things connected with conception and birth. Besides this, the need for such instruction as I am now speaking of will not occur to the youthful mind until the rational faculties have begun to be opened; and when this is the case we can appeal to the sense of right and wrong, the powers of self control, and the responsibility to his Maker, which is implanted in the mind of every rational being.

Certain it is that if the child has thus far been guarded against improper habits and impure thoughts, the holy lessons of a parent on such transcendent themes cannot be readily misinterpreted or misapplied; while if he is left to learn what he must learn sooner or later from the tainted lips of playmates and companions, accompanied with many impure suggestions and vain imaginings, the result cannot but be disastrous.

The conclusion then is that two things are requisite in order to preserve the purity of the young; first, that parents should guard their children in infancy and childhood against all contamination; and, second, that they should give them all the information they need as they grow up, and not leave them to gather their knowledge from less trustworthy sources.

But it will be noticed that in explaining these things I have given but the barest outline of what seems to be requisite. I have done this partly because it is all that can be done in the limited time at my disposal, and partly because it is all that would be proper in an assembly like the present; but principally because, after all that can be said, we must rely chiefly on the good sense, delicacy, tact and Christian spirit of the parents themselves. Those who will undertake this task with the right motives, looking to the Lord for guidance, cannot fail of encouraging results. If, however, more information is desired, it can be obtained by reference to any of a number of little books that have been published for this purpose. But such books, excellent as they are, should be used with caution. They should never be placed in the child's hands, but their contents should be filtered through the parents' minds and tinctured with their spirit in order to come to the child with authority and without danger of misconstruction. The minister and physician may instruct the parents what they should teach, but they should not, except in cases of necessity, permit themselves to usurp the parent's office. One of the first lessons we need to learn is that the education of children in these vital respects belongs in the providence of God to parents, and that it is a responsibility they cannot delegate to others. The truth regarding the genesis of life can best come to us through those from whom we derive our life.

Having given an outline of what seems to me the best method of preserving the purity of the young, and by this means that of the race, I trust I may be allowed a few remarks by way of enforcement and stimulation.

1. It should be understood at the outset that the child's mind is perfectly pure in the beginning. It is a tablet prepared for the tool of the engraver, but as yet virgin. The impression, too commonly entertained, that the sexual nature in man involves a kind of moral taint, into which we are all born and from which we cannot escape, is as false as it is degrading. It is an

impression that this Alliance has done much to dissipate during the past year by the publication of its admirable "Medical Declaration Concerning Chastity;" an achievement that would in itself be a sufficient vindication for the existence of the Alliance if it had never done anything else, and the moral force of which it is impossible for us to overestimate. I am firmly convinced that if the children of the rising generation should be fully protected in the way I have indicated against the wrong habits and "evil communications" to which all are exposed, they would grow up perfectly innocent and free from all impure thoughts and desires. I am convinced that this is true of boys as well as of girls; and I am convinced of it, not as a mere matter of theory or speculation, but from facts that have come within my own knowledge and the experience of others. I am convinced that this more than any other passion is a slumbering monster, that needs to be awakened before it becomes dangerous; and that it is awakened, not only by the bad habits into which children innocently fall, but a thousand times more by the vague imaginings that are excited by secret confidences and lewd and obscene conversations. Childhood is the season of germ planting. The Divine injunction not to "despise" one of these little ones was not spoken of them as individual beings only, but of every childish state or experience through which they may pass. Convince men in this skeptical and leprous age that the child's mind is not in itself impure, and that it can be defended against the inroads of pollution from without, and you have done much to secure the end in view. After all, Bob Ingersoll to the contrary notwithstanding, health is more contagious than disease, and life stronger than death.

2. But, on the other hand, it should be equally well understood that *our* children are as liable to fall into these evils as other children. While they are born free from actual taint, they have a strong *tendency* toward it, and have no inherent protection in themselves.

If we happen to belong to the middle or well-to-do classes, the danger is even greater than with the very poor. Our children are more by themselves; they have more opportunity for improper conversation; they are left more to servants, and their appetites are more pampered. The notion that because they are our children, and seem to be innocent and unconscious in the presence of others, they do not need the utmost care and watchfulness, should be guarded against as a temptation of the devil. This applies especially to parents who have escaped the dangers to which others have fallen victims. While we rejoice that there is a heaven, and that the way thither is made so plain that "the wayfaring man though a fool shall not err therein," we must not forget that there is a broad and easy path that leadeth to destruction, as well as a straight and narrow one that leadeth to life.

3. In the third place we must disabuse our minds of all false modesty and shamefacedness with regard to our sexual nature—as a thing never to be spoken of except with bated breath, nor thought of without a sense of shame and guilt. On the contrary, we should learn that because it has the highest end in view—the procreation of the human race and the multiplication of the heavens—and because it is the centre and source of the highest and purest affections of which mankind is capable, it is the noblest endowment with which we are gifted. In its creative power it is nearer the Divine than any other gift of human nature. Instead of apologizing for it, we should be humbly glad, every man for his manhood and every woman for her womanhood. Instead of looking upon it as a kind of necessary evil, we should learn, and should teach our children as soon as they are old enough to understand, that it is not the use but the abuse of our sexual nature that makes us guilty; and that consequently it is our highest duty to consecrate it to the heavenly purpose for the sake of which it was designed. Here again a little wise in-

struction with regard to the Divine origin and high and holy use of marriage will do more to correct the evils of which we complain than any amount of repression and denunciation. Let any young man (or young woman) grow up *minus* the taint of a corrupted imagination and *plus* a true and exalted idea of his manhood through a pure and holy marriage, accompanied by a confident trust in the Lord for light and support, and in his case the battle is more than half won.

4. Again it should be understood that this work of preserving the purity of the young, and finally introducing them under the Divine auspices into a heavenly marriage, is in the line of the Divine Providence, and cannot fail to call forth the Divine approval and aid. Bringing little children into the world and training them for heaven is the highest use we can perform, to which all other pursuits of life are subordinate and intended to contribute. In this work we may be sure of the Divine co-operation. The Lord has not left us alone. "All the angelic powers on high" are on our side, and their influence is continually exerted to strengthen and confirm right ideas as fast as we implant them in the child's mind. It is from the angels who are unconsciously associated with little children that their innocence is derived, and they are in the constant effort to preserve it. If parents would but recognize this truth and take advantage of it with a believing faith, there would be no such thing as failure. "All things are possible to him that believeth."

5. Finally, it follows from all that has been said that this is the most fruitful field in which we can work for the preservation of the purity of the race. It is an old and trite saying that an ounce of prevention is better than a pound of cure. This is doubly true with regard to the social evil. No amount of legislation or regulation can correct it, so long as our children are allowed to grow up with tainted minds and corrupt habits. It is idle for the churches to unite for the pur-

pose of closing houses of public resort, if the young men of what are called the best families are permitted to become the supporters of such places. If we would succeed in the work of reform we must strike at the root of the evil and not at its effects. We must begin in our own homes, and in the secret chambers of our homes – the nursery. What the world needs is a campaign of education on this subject. Every minister should be a true shepherd or leader of his flock in this respect. Every physician should be the protector of the young who come under his influence. Every wise woman, above all, should be the helper of the less wise or less favored. Not merely White Cross movements for the instruction of the young men and maidens of the land should be organized, but golden cross societies for the stimulation of parents and the protection of infants and little children. There should be if possible a universal federation of parents to stamp out not only all glaring and open vice, so that it cannot appear before the eyes of the young, but every secret sin and impure communication among the little ones themselves; and so to enable them to grow up as free from taint in this world as we may imagine those do who have been transplanted in infancy to the other world.

MRS. J. H. KELLOGG.

PURITY AND PARENTAL RESPONSIBILITY.

By Mrs. J. H. Kellogg.

Were there some spot upon this sin-shadowed earth where impurity could not enter, or a time or an age in the life of a child when temptation would not assail him, then might responsibility with impunity lie, as it so often appears to do, with a feather's weight upon the parent's heart. But with vice everywhere prevalent, the parents who hope to keep their children in the path of virtue must be awake to their trust, studying to understand the hundreds of different avenues by which depraving influences and temptations may reach their homes, and striving to increase the safeguards around their children. They must face the fact that their children, like themselves, are by nature sinful and liable to stray into forbidden paths; hence they must endeavor to hedge up the way against evil by right training, by the formation of correct habits and by the environments of a pure home atmosphere.

Few other influences have such power to keep a person in the path of rectitude as that of right home training. Upon parents rests the responsibility of this training. They stand before God as surety for those human beings, made in His likeness, whom He has entrusted to their care. Parents may shrink from this self-assumed responsibility, ignore it, shirk it, try to delegate it to others, but it is still there—they cannot escape it.

To train a child wisely, to develop within him a strength that shall dominate over weakness, to inspire in him such a love for that which is pure and good that evil will be distasteful, is the duty incumbent upon all parents. If, through their mistakes or those of their ancestors, their child has inherited a nature morbidly suceptible to evil, ready to fall into temptation at the slightest provocation, then is their responsibility indeed greatly increased; then what special watchfulness and care are needed to intercept temptation, to build up the wall within at the points were it is weakest, and to so accustom the child to a pure moral atmosphere that he cannot breathe freely in any other. Inherited tendencies may be overcome or greatly modified by proper training; but it should not be neglected till the germs of evil have sprouted and their roots become firmly grounded, and the attempt be then made to crowd them out. The evil should rather be preoccupied with good seed, and thus the mischief-making seeds be prevented from germinating. Says Dr. Talmage: "Before they sow wild oats get them to sow wheat and barley. You will thus fill the measure with good corn, and there will be no more room for husks." Herein lies one of the highest responsibilities of parenthood, to so nourish and cultivate right tendencies that the evil ones will be choked out.

One of the chief reasons why so many homes are saddened by the terrible revelation that a son or a daughter has gone astray lies in the fact that parents do not awaken to their responsibilities early enough in the life of their children. They think, as they watch their little one in its cradle, or guide its first faltering footsteps, that when the child grows older their responsibilities will increase; but if for the present his physical needs are well supplied, and the enjoyment of his waking hours assured, it is all sufficient. All the child's thoughts and tendencies are left to chance during this susceptible period when every word he hears and every act he sees may serve to influence his whole life. In these impressionable years the seeds of both good and evil take deeper root because the child is lacking in the power of resistance which comes with later years. If parents neglect to sow and tend the good seeds at the outset of life, while they are asleep to duty the enemy will come and sow tares and weeds. If these first germs of evil are allowed to take root and unfold, it need scarcely be wondered that in later years rank growths of sin should flourish in the soul and yield their harvest in unchaste lives. The embryo man should be started along the path which the man of mature years ought to tread.

We are so accustomed to associate impurity with some gross breach of moral rectitude, that the early beginnings, the first steps, the little deviations, the trifling words and acts, are overlooked and neglected. The floodgates are closed against the great temptations, but the little drops which go to swell the mighty river of impurity too often fall unheeded; and yet these little things—mere trifles they may appear to be—sum up into a vast column, the total of which is appalling.

The change from virtue to vice is not a sudden one. A long preparatory process goes on in the heart before the individual commits open sin. Parents must study to recognize the first indications of evil, and check them at the outset. This they can only do by maintaining the closest intimacy with their children, by studying to know them and their needs, by keeping in full sympathy with them—in other words, by "living with their children." This sympathetic relation must begin with the very dawn of life, grow with the child, and overspread with loving light his whole existence. The wise parent who establishes such an intimate fellowship with his children will find it one of the strongest barriers against evil that could be erected. It will, however, require much painstaking effort, trouble and self sacrifice on his part to perpetuate such a relation, for it must be continuous, not merely spasmodic, in its nature.

The secret of so many parental failures lies in their unwillingness to sacrifice the love of personal ease and enjoyment, to set aside the demands of society, the

engrossing cares of business, or other of their own selfish ends, for the sake of their children. It is so much
easier to turn the little ones out of doors to hunt up
their own amusements than to give up one's time to
their instruction and diversion; so much less trouble to allow them to select their own companions than to accord
them one's personal companionship, that a danger.
ously large proportion of parents share the sentiments
of a mother who, when asked by a friend concerning the
welfare of her five little ones, replied: "I am so thank-
ful to have them out of the way that I don't trouble myself to find out where they are so long as they come in
for their meals at the proper time and are in in time to go
to bed at night." Yet this mother, a prominent church
member, kept two servants, and was in nowise so hampered as to be unable to give her children watchful
care. One shudders to think of the risk such parents
are carelessly and, perhaps, thoughtlessly taking, particularly when it is remembered that before the child
has reached the age of ten years the parents have done
half they will ever be able to do toward the formation
of its character. With this thought we turn again to
the magnitude of parental responsibility and the importance of early beginnings.

Among those elements of character which, if early
established and firmly rooted, will help to antagonize
vice in later years, is self control. The boy who is
trained in childhood to intelligent self mastery over his
appetites and passions will grow to manhood strong to
resist the blind leading of impulse. Self control is not,
however, an innate instinct, but a quality that must be
cultivated by judicious training ; hence it is a matter
resting largely in the hands of the parents. Much of
the child's inability to govern himself in later years is
due to his mismanagement in infancy. It is so much
easier to give baby what he cries for, to consult his in-
clinations and whims, than to make the effort necessary
to restrain and control him, that parents are very apt to

make the mistake of choosing that which will afford the easiest course at the moment. The little one very soon learns that he is master of the situation, that what he cries for he will get, and so he cries for everything he wants ; if the coveted thing is not immediately forthcoming, he cries the harder. To his mind the act of crying is the effort he must put forth to secure the desired object, and so he increases his efforts in proportion to the delay. He is only doing as best he knows how just what he would be commended for in his struggles to attain success in later years ; but he soon cries so hard that he is unable to stop, and his parents begin to wonder what can have caused their little one to exhibit such " outbursts of temper."

A recent writer upon babyhood asserts that children do not exhibit temper until they have learned to be angry either through seeing signs of ill temper in others or through being unnecessarily thwarted in their natural impulses. The little one was not angry when he began to cry, he was simply putting to use the means he had at command, which from previous experiences he supposed would be effective in bringing about the result he desired ; and when at first his eff rts seemed unavailing he increased them until he became wholly excited and unbalanced. If he is permitted frequently to bring himself into this condition, the habit of uncontrol will soon take possession of him. The oftener he gets into such a state, the easier it is to again lose control of himself. All bad habits as well as all good habits gain force and strength by exercise. Through thoughtless mismanagement parents may thus foster a condition of uncontrol which years of after discipline can never quite correct. A parent who duly appreciates the great work that every human being has to do in attaining self government will assist the process from the very first by every means within his power.

Self control can be made much easier for the child by careful attention to his physical habits, particularly as regards his diet. A child fed largely upon stimulating foods will be likely to have a fiery and excitable disposition. If by careful feeding his physical condition is kept in an unexcitable state, the temptation to give way to irritability is lessened, and self control made more easy. While parents teach their children to do right, they should *make it as difficult as possible* for them to do wrong. Much of the child's ability to control himself is dependent upon his physical condition. The will is under the control of the nerve centres. The will inhibits or restrains the action of the muscles and of the intellectual organs just as other nerve centres restrain the action of the heart. An unhealthy condition of the nerves will therefore lessen the individual's power of self control. Hence every cause productive of an unhealthy or abnormal nervous condition should be sedulously avoided. All hygienic measures, such as good, wholesome food, plenty of sleep, proper clothing, and abundant air and exercise, lend a most salutary influence toward the upbuilding of self control.

One of the helpful measures to be used in early childhood where self control is yet lacking is a daily physical drill. Training in Swedish gymnastics serves a most admirable purpose in this direction; it not only strengthens and invigorates the whole body, thus giving tone to the nervous system, but the variety of exercises at one lesson necessitates close attention and quick voluntary movements, thus disciplining the will in controlling the muscles. Control exercised in one direction aids control in other directions. Every child desires to be strong physically because he sees how much greater enjoyment and usefulness comes to a strong person than to a weak one, and moral strength can be made to seem to him quite as desirable as physical strength. Character influences character, and high ideals of control properly presented to the young mind will greatly aid in the establishment of self government. But let parents bear in mind that "the highest in the child is aroused only by example," and that whatever lessons they desire their children to learn they must themselves first learn.

Although self control is one of the first essentials to be striven for as an anchor for purity in the young life, it is not the only element the parent must seek to establish in the child's character. Impurity is so closely interlinked with other sinful propensities that the only sure immunity from evil comes from the right formation of character in its entirety. Obedience, well learned, lies in the path of self control. The more perfectly the habit of obedience to parents is fixed, the more easy it becomes for the individual to yield to the behests of right and duty.

The child who is taught to respect his own body as the temple of the Holy Spirit, lent him for his temporary use, to be returned pure and undefiled to his Creator, will find it far easier to exercise self control in the use of it.

Self reliance early taught will aid in making the child capable in self entertainment in wholesome and profitable ways. The boy or girl who is wholly dependent upon somebody else for entertainment and happiness, who does not know how to spend a leisure hour profitably, is in great danger. Such an one is easily led into pernicious associations, and may only because of favorable circumstances escape the path of ruin.

Often the danger which besets the pathway of the youth comes through a lack of training in industry; through the neglect of parents to instill into the child's character a love of work for work's sake. The child must be occupied with something; if he is not occupied with good he will be busy with evil. "The idle hour waiting to be employed, idle hands with no occupation, idle and empty mind with nothing to think," these are the great invitations to vice. To the child who has been trained to love work idleness will not be pleasurable. The boy or girl whose time is filled with wholesome occupation will have little desire to loiter upon the street corners, frequent the parks and other public places where temptation so often assails the untaught, pleasure seeking, indolent youth. Let parents reflect that thoughtfulness of mind, stability of character and purity of life are among the natural outgrowths of a training in industry.

Another fountain from which springs the stream of impurity, is the lack of a proper training of the appetite, a failure to teach that its gratification is to be made subservient to right and reasonable ends. The appetite, like all natural instincts, is susceptible to education both in a right and a wrong direction. This fact is often unrecognized, and the child's appetite left to chance development, which, far more frequent than otherwise, leaves him subject to rather than ruler of it. Depraved appetites are frequently inherited, but they are as often created through lack of proper care and training. Purity of heart is a condition quite incompatible with sensual pleasuring of the appetite. Children allowed to eat at all hours, to partake of unwholesome, stimulating food, to overeat, to eat without need simply to please the taste, are thus taught self gratification rather than self control and are almost hopelessly placed under the dominions of their lower natures. A love of appetite established in one direction will be hard to restrain in others.

Not the least among the influences which tend to lead boys astray is the acquirement early in life of a disrespect for womanhood. Laxity of parental discipline is in a great measure responsible for this. The boy who is permitted to trample upon his mother's authority soon loses respect for her and, in time, for her sex. The average boy judges all women by his estimate of his mother and sisters. The discrimination so frequently seen in families in favor of the sons soon leads them to esteem their sisters lightly, and to regard all women as inferior beings. In many households the daughters are taught to wait upon the sons, and to make their own wishes subservient to those of their brothers ; thus these sons grow to manhood with the idea that women's chief mission in the world is to minister to man's convenience and pleasure. Two different standards of morality are the outgrowth of the training in many homes. While the daughters are carefully instructed in the ways of modesty and virtue, the sons, instead of being taught from earliest infancy that God intended them to go through life just as pure as their sisters, are left to come up as they may, with no training whatever, and their first steps on the downward road are condoned by the oft-repeated excuse, "Oh, he is a regular boy," thus making a tacit distinction in the moral standard of the sexes.

One of the greatest responsibilities of the parents lies in the direction of imparting proper knowledge at the proper time. The influences which children are sure to encounter at school, upon the playground, along the streets, and even in their own homes, makes it imperative that they be forearmed against danger by being forewarned. To shield one's children from seeing or hearing evil is a matter of especial importance, since it is true that "by beholding we become changed;" but ignorance is not innocence. Knowledge is power; to be able to discern evil when evil comes unexpectedly is a strong defensive armor against the wiles of Satan. Shield them from contact with evil under every possible circumstance, but fortify them against sin by that knowledge which shall make them in love with truth and in fear of that which is impure and unholy.

The responsibilities devolving upon parents, if they would have their children grow up clean and pure, are indeed almost numberless. All along the way from infancy to maturity, the way is so beset with pitfalls that eternal vigilance is the only price of safety. Parents must seek to cleanse the pathway which their children's feet must tread—to guard their associations, their amusements and their reading—and to barricade every possible avenue leading to evil. They must themselves supply the proper conditions for upward growth; then, through the grace of God, they may hope to witness the development of a noble manhood and a true womanhood upon the foundations thus carefully and securely laid.

MORAL EDUCATION OF THE YOUNG.

By Mary Wood-Allen, M. D.

Perhaps no moment in a woman's life is so full of sacred joy as that in which she looks for the first time into the face of her child. That little helpless bundle of capabilities owes its life to her. From her it has received many of its talents and tendencies. Upon her depends very largely its moral and physical training. Will she prove equal to the demand, is the question that presses upon her with overwhelming force. To the father the same query presents itself, yet in all probability not with the same force, nor in the same way. His mind leaps forward toward practical success in maturity, and sees in fancy the results of the training, rather than the processes by which these results are to to be secured.

Upon both parents, however, rests the responsibility of the right moral training of the child, and neither can shirk the duty, nor lay it off on the shoulders of some one else, without great loss to themselves as well as to the child. Certain phases of moral education they will have no inclination to shirk. They expect to teach honesty, truthfulness, consideration for the rights of others; in fact, all the principles of ordinary business probity. But there is a field of moral training which perhaps they shrink from entering, and that is the domain of sexual morality. While they desire that their children shall grow up virtuous in life and pure in thought, they hesitate about giving specific instruction along these lines. They hope that by guarding them as far as possible from evil companionship they may be able to preserve their innocence until the demands of actual life shall make information a necessity. The

MARY WOOD-ALLEN, M. D.

child who is guarded only by parental watchfulness from the acquisition of evil knowledge, finds that guardianship only too easily evaded, and outside of its pale he is greeted with voluntary proffers of the information so sedulously kept from him by his parents, but clothed, alas! in the garb of vile words and shrouded with a veil of evil mystery which stimulates his imagination and arouses a prurient curiosity to pry still further into the fascinating darkness. In all probability if the same facts which he learns in a guilty and alluring manner, and which conduce to evil thought and conduct, were presented to him by parent or teacher as simple, scientific truths, he would find in them no mysterious charm, but the effect would be rather to strip them of their fascination. This is no mere theory. Experience has proven it to be true.

A father discovered that his little boys were being taught certain physiological facts in regard to animal life in mysterious and secret ways by other boys. Taking the children openly to the place where they had gone secretly, the father explained to them purely and scientifically the matter they were so curious to investigate, and from that moment the crude knowledge of their childish companions lost its charm, and at the same time the simple truth, told with the authority of science and the purity of parental love, destroyed their prurient curiosity. Perhaps few fathers would dare to follow this example, but the result more than justified to this father the wisdom of his course.

In this question of the moral training of children, we must bear in mind the fact that we cannot keep them in ignorance until we have come to the conclusion that they are old enough to be instructed, and we must also remember that their moral training begins in the cradle, and therefore its inception is in our hands. By the habits of life with which we surround the infancy of the child, are laid foundations of moral character. The regularity of hours of sleep or of feeding has more than a physical bearing; it is moral in quality. Felix Adler says that "Regularity is not of itself moral, but it conduces to morality. Rules may not be good, but a life of unregulated impulse is always bad." Those who are taught, or allowed in childhood to yield ever to the demands of the senses, be it only in so small a matter as eating whenever the impulse seizes them, are being weakened in will power, and are thus being unfitted to cope with the stronger temptations of more mature life.

The quality of food has also a bearing upon this question. Foods which, by their stimulating and irritating qualities, produce nutritive disturbances, may also be responsible for local irritations which may lead to the formation of bad habits. Many a child has contracted evil habits simply by an effort to allay a local irritation produced by indigestion and its consequences. The clothing of the child has its influence. By its uncleanliness; by undue pressure from improper construction, or by being outgrown; by its tightness and consequent production of pelvic congestions, it may be the cause of physical habits which, in the beginning, had no moral quality, but which come in time to be decidedly immoral.

This is a phase of the subject which the thoughtful mother will ever bear in mind. She will also not forget that in the sacred boundaries of her own home may exist influences tending in the same direction. From nurses and other servants, or from chance companions whose visits may be brief and infrequent, may be learned direful lessons of evil.

As the child develops in intellect he begins to need something more than a careful guardianship, and should have some direct instruction as to the sacredness of his own body and the need of himself protecting it from evil. This does not involve frightening him with horrible delineations of the results of sin, but by arousing a reverence for his bodily temple that makes him instinctively shrink from the invasion of its sacredness, even in thought.

It is unfortunate that while we are so hesitant in regard to teaching openly the facts of sex, we are unconsciously stimulating sex-consciousness, not only among the older children, but even among the little toddlers who, in all innocence, manifest an innocent fondness for each other. I have in my possession a scrap cut from a newspaper which says, "Cards are out announcing the engagement of Master Willie Scott, aged four, and Miss Mabel Perry, aged six," and these babies are taught to regard each other as lovers and future husband and wife. What comprehension of the dignity of love or sacredness of marriage can they have in maturity, when they have been given these ideas as toys to be played with in their childhood! And this is not the only result of this teaching, but we are laying foundations of immorality and breaking down bulwarks of protection. We are teaching the boys that they may treat girls with familiarity if the girls will permit it, and we are teaching the girls to permit it in childhood, and then later we try to undo this teaching, too often with little effect. Boys and girls also imbibe the idea from our foolish jests that there are no other relations between persons of opposite sex except that of sentimentality, and a condition arises which furnishes one of the most perplexing problems to the teachers of our public schools. These teachers testify that foolish sentimentality pervades the schools, and boys and girls are so constantly engaged in writing love letters, quarreling, making up and holding clandestine meetings, in fact are in such a state of emotional excitement that study is interfered with.

At first this might seem an argument against co-education, but in fact it is not the association in the school room that is at fault, but the suggestion through the jests and teasing of friends at home. The girl in convent or a girls' school, is apt to invest young men with ideal virtues, but the glamour vanishes when she comes to compete with them in practical school life, and this would be still more completely the case were she permitted, outside of school, to associate with them on terms of frank comradeship. While we claim to be exceedingly reticent concerning the fact of sex, holding it to be indelicate to teach scientifically the truths of the body and its powers, we are actually stimulating to a consciousness of sex which embarrasses the association of young people with each other. What we need is by accurate information concerning the peculiar physical endowment of men and women to create a reverence for true manhood and womanhood which forbids the question of sex to intrude itself into all the relations of life, but allows it to remain in retirement until it is called upon in the sacred precincts of the home, to confer the gift of earthly life and so add, not to personal gratification, but to the power, greatness, virtue and glory of the nation and of the race.

The facts of sex can be taught so simply that the child receives the knowledge with as little embarrassment as he does instruction concerning plant life, but the consciousness of sex arising from constant allusions to some mysterious relation between boys and girls must of necessity be accompanied with undue stimulation of the very feelings which we as parents should desire to repress.

The flirtations and loverings of school children are often but the prelude to a deeper intimacy which perhaps ends in shame and ruin. The revelations of immorality which sometimes come to the surface in our public schools, are but the floating straws that indicate the tendency of the deep, strong current which bears them along. When we learn of some child whose sin has found him out, we spring upon him with ferocity and call him a reprobate; when in fact he has been, by our silence and our jests, led to do the evil for which we condemn him, and which condemnation he does not understand but instinctively feels is unjust. And he is right in this feeling.

The child has a right to understand himself in all his functions, and it is but an intuitive knowledge of this right that has led him into the evil for which we desire to punish him. What he needs is not punishment, but proper instruction. I know that there are those who believe that the information concerning himself and the facts and purposes of sex will lead him still more surely into criminal conduct. But facts do not support this theory. If the information incites to evil it is because of its manner of presentation.

Take, for example, the little child who comes to his parents with that intense longing to know concerning himself which is the problem of the philosopher as well as the child. "Whence am I?" he asks. With blushes and confusion the mother bows her head and answers with an evasion, and the little questioner intuitively feels that his coming into the world is surrounded with shame, and it is no wonder that he no longer questions mother, but listens with avidity to the story told by some wiser child-companion, which, in its impure thought, explains to his immature mind the cause of his mother's embarrassment. From that time the thought of fatherhood and motherhood is tainted. There is to him no sanctity in the relation of husband and wife, but he feels that there is something in the home that is hidden from view because too vile to bear open inspection, and it need not be wondered at if later in life love and marriage are only names that cover thoughts of lust and self-gratification.

But, supposing at the time that the innocent child came with his honest query, the mother had taken him in her arms and with holy words had told him of the days when he had been part of her own life, when held in her close and protecting embrace, he had grown with the beating of her heart and been moulded by the touch of her thought, when her love had enfolded him and her prayers had created the tenor of his own thoughts, when through long days she had dreamed of him and worked for him, and prepared for his coming, and finally had gone down into the vale of physical pain, perhaps even to the gates of death, with a brave courage to welcome him to his independent earthly existence, ah! do you not believe that the holiest of feelings would have been aroused in that child's heart, and henceforth to him mother would be the tenderest, holiest word, and love and marriage be symbolic of unselfish loyalty and most sacred responsibility? When the sweet story fell upon the ear of one child, he threw his arms about his mother's neck, exclaiming, "Now, mamma, I know why I love you best of all the world."

Later, in the mind of the little philosopher a query arises which may strike new terror to the heart of the parent not prepared to meet it—the question of the duality of parentage, but even here we need not stand appalled. Through plant-life and lower animal forms a child may learn reverently to think God's thoughts after him, and come to see that only through the plan God has chosen to perpetuate life would it be possible to bind humanity together in bonds that defy time and change, and even death itself; bonds that not only unite human beings to each other, but bind them to the great Creator himself. What force would the words, "Like as a father pitieth his children," or "As one whom his mother comforteth," have to us, if we were not endowed with creative power and the divine prerogative of parentage? Life takes on a new meaning when we realize the dignity of parentage and the "Fatherhood of God" becomes comprehensible to our finite minds through our own yearning over those to whom we have given life.

As the boy and the girl approach the height of maturity, they pass through the mysterious land of the "Teens", at the gateway of which is conferred upon them the gift of creative power. This gift is accompanied with the wondrous unfolding of powers, physical, mental and moral. The body develops into greater beauty and perfection; new avenues of thought are opened and new and strange emotions begin to sway the youth with tremendous force. The whole organization seems to be in a state of revolution, and the result is often shown morally in willfulness, perversity or hysteria, and physically in the appearance of languor, or of inherited tendencies toward some special form of disease. This period may justly be styled a climacteric, which Webster defines as "A critical period in human life in which some great change takes place in the human constitution."

Marion Harland says: "All climacterics are attended with more or less peril. The transition period in religion, in government or in the individual is one which calls for wisest care and vigilance."

Parents usually comprehend that the girl at this period needs especial care and watchfulness, even if they do not give her special instruction; but few parents recognize that the boy needs as much sympathy as the girl—indeed, even more, for the internal forces are stronger and work with greater energy while the temptations from without are more numerous and powerful. One can scarcely wonder that the boy falls into immorality when we recall these few facts, and add to them the fact of his ignorance and the common idea that he is not to be held to the standard of absolute purity which is raised for the girl.

To the boy trained according to ordinary methods, the endowment of virile power means only an added means of personal enjoyment, and he is led to believe that he is most the man who soonest calls into activity the new power. He has never heard of the sacredness of manhood. No one has ever suggested to him that the new forces are his as a trust for future generations; that upon him and his use of his manly power depends any part of the honor, virtue, health, courage and value of the race. In his mind the whole question of sex is covered with a veil to be lifted only by unclean hands, its mysteries to be investigated only with impure thoughts and vulgar glances. Dr. Blackwell asks: "What practical steps can be taken to secure the truer standard of morality which will remodel the education of youth? This weighty question," she adds, "can only receive a complete answer as the intelligence of our age awakens to the fact that the attainment of the principle of sexual morality is the fundamental principle of national growth. The great truth to be recognized is the fact that male as well as female purity is a necessary foundation of progressive human society. The necessity of upholding one moral standard as the aim to be striven for must become a fundamental article of religious faith. Above all, parents must realize the tremendous responsibility which rests upon them to provide for the healthy growth of the principle of sex in their children."

This dictum of the experienced physician indicates that the education of the child *must* begin in the *minds* of the parents. If they accept God's plan for the perpetuation of life as pure and holy, and recognize in it the way by which selfishness is to be banished and love in its truest sense to be made the governing power in every human life, they will perceive that a true understanding of the relations of men and women is one of the most important safeguards of public virtue. We often declare that the stability of the nation rests on the sanctity of the home; but the sanctity of the home rests on the right understanding of what Dr. Blackwell calls the "noble principle of sex;" and this right understanding is only to be obtained by pure, scientific instruction given to the young by their rightful guardians, instead of leaving them to acquire inaccurate, insufficient and unclean information from young companions, whose knowledge has come to them through polluted channels, and is spiced with vulgar witticisms and served in secret.

This duty of parents and teachers we may indeed shirk, but in so doing we lay up "wrath against a day of wrath" for ourselves, our children and the nation. We see how our silence is accompanied with secret vice, with shame, the degradation of manhood, and the ruin of womanhood. We see that with lack of knowledge vice flourishes, or is even legalized, and outraged motherhood and unprotected childhood bear witness to our national degradation. Could frank and scientific instruction be productive of greater evil?

But if our young people were so wisely taught that they would recognize the advent of creative force into their own lives as a sacred trust, to be guarded as jealously and worn as nobly as the diadem of the monarch, we should have a mighty force working toward regeneration through right generation, and we should thereby be storing up a constantly increasing inheritance of righteous tendencies, making each generation stronger, purer and more capable of self control.

This is the path we even now mark out for woman's feet to tread. Why should there be a dark and dangerous by-path in which we imagine young men may walk without condemnation? Have we so little confidence in our sons that we believe them incapable of the highest virtue? Our failure to hold them to the highest standard arises largely from the mistaken opinion that the physiological needs of man abrogate moral law, and the lad is early led to believe that the use of his powers is a test of his manhood. He needs to know that Tennyson expressed scientific truth as well as poetry, when he wrote,

> " My strength is as the strength of ten,
> Because my heart is pure."

An able surgeon has left on record his advice in these words: " The boy has to learn that to his immature frame every sexual indulgence is an unmitigated evil, every illicit pleasure a degradation to be bitterly regretted. It is of vital importance that boys and young men should know the danger of straining an immature power, and that the only safety lies in keeping even the thoughts pure."

A continent life is enforced in rigid training for athletic sports as one of the means of attaining the greatest possible amount of vigor and endurance. This fact observed in ancient times is confirmed by modern experience. It is well known that the early ancestors of our vigorous German race guarded the chastity of their youth until the age of twenty-five years as the true method of increasing their strength, enlarging their stature and enabling them to become the progenitors of a vigorous race.

With right instruction, then, as to the possibility of self control, of the subjugation of passion to the higher faculties, marriage takes on a new aspect, and no longer appears as an opportunity for license but as an opportunity for the development of the strongest powers of self government and the dominance of unselfish love over unreasoning self indulgence.

If there is ever a need of moral training of the young, it is when they are about to enter into that relation which involves not only their own happiness but the possible welfare of future generations. Ought we who have learned, perhaps through sad experience, how our lives, our thoughts, our habits, even in the far away years of youth, have recorded themselves on the tendencies of those who draw their dower of life from us, ought we to keep silence through any false delicacy and allow these our children to make the same blunder, to perpetuate still further our mistake?

I know there are those who believe that instruction along these lines will awaken and arouse prurient curiosity and do harm rather than good. But an observation of years has convinced more than one thoughtful person that pure, reliable knowledge is the surest safe-guard of virtue, and that all topics which have a bear-ing upon the welfare of the young may be safely discussed with them.

Young people are more sensible than we sometimes give them credit for being. They are desirous of knowl-edge, and that is a commendable longing. They would prefer authoritative instruction if it were obtainable, and failing that they take what is so eagerly offered them by the emissaries of vice and feel no shame in so doing. Why should they feel ashamed? Moral con-fusion has met them at the very threshold of responsi-ble life. Sex is an incontrovertable fact; its impulses thrill them, but society gives no absolute standard in regard to it. For the one sex it marks out an unmis-takable path of purity, but for the other it leaves much leeway. True, the boy hears much moral preaching but he sees much immoral practising; so he comes to believe that the sin is not in doing but in being dis-covered. He is not trained out of his childish and ignorant innocence into a wise and manly virtue. His theories of right and wrong are vague; his inexperience will not permit him to reason from cause to effect, and thus understand the consequences of wrong action. Those who could instruct him are silent, and those who proffer information are careful to say nothing that will warn him, and so he stumbles along blindly, swayed by impulse, and, perhaps, by premature use of his im-mature powers, leaves no space between puberty and established virility for storing up vital force; but, ignorant of possible results, finds himself in early man-hood, much to his surprise, a physical wreck, morally contaminated, and suffering under the remorse of his own conscience and the condemnation of those through whose silence he drifted ignorantly into the wrong.

Moral training is not complete also if it does not cover the explanation of the responsibility and dignity of parentage. If the influence of parents upon their chil-

dren began after those children had begun their independent existence it would do to postpone the instruction of parents until then; but we know that even in
childhood the individual in his habits is forming the
characteristics of his maturity. We are beginning also
to understand that at the same time he is creating the
characteristics of his posterity. What harm would there
be in his knowing this while yet he has time to modify
his own life and thus tend to modify the tendencies of
his posterity? What harm would there be in his realizing as fully as possible that the wild oats he sows in his
youth will probably be harvested more abundantly by
his descendents? What harm for the girl to comprehend that her heartless flirtation may make it easy for
her daughter to slip over the boundaries of virtue and
sink in the gulf of shame? What harm that both husband and wife should understand at the very outset of
married life that the momentary feelings of their hearts
at the initial moment of another's life may taint that
life with impulses that shall make it criminal in its
tendencies or impart those upward impulses which shall
give it the characteristics of a regal nature?

Such possibilities are too vast, too full of an overwhelming power to be left to chance; too sacred to be
sullied by evil thoughts, too dignified to be the subject
of jest.

"Love must come," said Mrs. Jameson, "and
Death must come — Love and Death, the Alpha and
Omega of existence, the two points upon which God's
universe turns." Which is fraught with the greater
burden of weal or woe—Love or Death? Death is the
gate of personal future life. Love opens the gate of
individual existence, earthly and eternal, for the generations that follow us and carry on with them the change
our lives have created for them.

The maiden's whispered "yes" we may hear re-
echoed in the stentorian tones of a hundred men who
bear on heart and brain the impress of her obscure life,

her hidden thoughts, long, long years after her body has turned to dust.

O, friends, this subject of moral training is so broad, so high, so deep, so wide that it involves the whole of life. It is found not only in the lessons at the mother's knee, but in the school, the pulpit and the press. It is found in the statute books where laws remove or strengthen the safeguards of virtue. We may keep silence, but myriads of voices are proclaiming truth or falsehood in regard to purity. In city streets or country lanes, in field or forest, in market or court, from printed page or the book of nature the facts of sex are being taught. Shall we turn away in confusion and leave the world of innocent childhood to learn these inevitable lessons from the evil book or impure companions? or shall we, believing in God, proclaim His truths with dignity and purity, not abashed before the pure eyes of our children because the "truth has made us free," and God himself is justified through His works?

REV. J. B. WELTY.

THE NEED OF WHITE CROSS WORK.

BY REV. J. B. WELTY, SECRETARY OF THE WHITE CROSS BRANCH
OF THE PURITY DEPARTMENT OF THE NATIONAL WOMAN'S
CHRISTIAN TEMPERANCE UNION.

The object of the White Cross Branch of the Purity Department of the National W. C. T. U. is clearly defined in article second of the constitution, and is as follows:

"To elevate opinion respecting the nature and claims of morality.

"To maintain the law of purity as equally binding upon men and women.

"To protect women from wrong and degradation.

"To preserve the purity of society.

"To shield the young and weak from temptations to impurity.

"To advocate the highest standard of manhood and womanhood.

"To uphold in their integrity the institutions God has appointed for social relations."

Is there any need for special work along these lines?

There is; and there never was a time in the history of our country when such work was so much needed as now. This is evident from the following considerations:

1. The fundamental institutions appointed of God for social relations and the laws regulating them are to-day boldly assailed, and that at many points.

Marriage between one man and one woman, which is the only foundation for well ordered society, is under discussion and is adversely criticised. By many it is disparaged, underestimated, dishonored, travestied and robbed of its sacred sanctions. We hear it denounced as "a dismal makeshift," "a miserable failure," "a relic of barbarism," an unaccountable custom of a benighted age," "a bond of slavery both for men and women." Freeloveism, with its vagaries, sophistries and sensuous philosophy came in about forty years ago, sowed its seed of social tares and society is now reaping its unclean harvest. According to its dictum "the entire edifice of matrimony is antiquated, unsuitable, unfitted for the intelligent women of the last half of the nineteenth century." The thinking of multitudes concerning marriage has been misdirected, corrupted, poisoned; whilst in practical life this all-important, basic institution is degraded, dragged down to the level of a common business transaction or employed as a mere civil arrangement for love and lust.

Legislation in almost every State in the Union has lent its aid to the abuse and degrading of marriage by the enacting of loose, mischievous, iniquitous divorce laws. Divorce has been made easy, and when divorce is made easy divorces multiply, and that too at an ever increasing ratio. The results are far-reaching, fearful, degrading and corrupting to individuals and to society. Conjugal fidelity is weakened and the sacredness of the marriage vow is violated. Homes that might have been happy are broken up, and children that have a right to parental care and protection are worse than orphaned and turned out upon society. New and unholy alliances are formed by unscripturally divorced persons, and thus the sin of impurity is spread farther and sinks deeper into the life of the people. The very foundations of society are threatened with destruction. It may safely be written down as a law that all trifling with fundamental and approved institutions of society means mischief, social disorder, social danger, social sin and inevitable corruption. Where God's plans and laws for the sexes are not scrupulously honored and jealously guarded there licentiousness is sure to enter, and more and more, in all its horrid forms, will abound.

There is needed to-day in every State and in every community, town and city throughout this broad land an earnest, aggressive, red-hot propaganda of Christian ideas and principles concerning marriage, divorce, the family, the home, and the duties of men and women pertaining thereto. The White Cross means such a propaganda.

2. That White Cross Work is needed is evident from the fact that the double standard of morality is still operative in society. It is well known how that law binds the obligations of purity loosely upon men, but tightly upon women; that it condones in men what it damns in women; that it tolerates the scarlet man but condemns to eternal infamy the scarlet woman. It has been described as

> " A common law by which the poor and weak
> Are trampled under foot of vicious men,
> And loathed forever after by the good."

That unwritten but everywhere present and tyrannous law is wrong, unjust and severely cruel to women. It makes them the hunted game of protected libertines. It is wrong to men for it is a species of license for them to commit nameless crimes against women. It is also a wrong to society for it is a breaking down of the law that God gave for social purity. For the man and for the woman it is written: "Thou shalt not commit adultery."

The double standard means leniency to guilty men, and when lust is treated with leniency virtue is treated with indifference. Tolerance to scarlet men means danger to women—to our sisters and to our daughters.

This invidious law is to be reprobated also because it excludes the guilty woman from an equal chance with the guilty man for repentance and restoration. Before God they have an equal chance to repent and reform and they should have the same equal chance before men.

There must be a mighty campaign of annihilation against this hoary, unjust and wicked law. The cruelty, tyranny, injustice and wrong of it must be portrayed before the people until public opinion is changed and its repeal secured.

3. That there is need for such work as the White Cross proposes is evident from the fact that women do, in many ways, suffer wrong and degradation.

There is discrimination against women in legislation, in business, in commerce, in the trades, in the shops, in civil service, in many schools and colleges and everywhere in matters of work and wages.

Men still arrogate to themselves the legislative function, and this is the prime cause for all unjust and unequal discrimination against women. They that do not have equal rights and privileges in political matters must suffer wrong and submit to limitations in many other places and in many ways. Keep women from the ballot and you debar them from a thousand other rights and make the path of human progress an unequal one. Continue to exclude them from legislative halls and they will be just so long handicapped in every other department of political and industrial life. It is more than we dare expect of human nature that one sex can or will wisely, justly, impartially and fully legislate for the other sex. Men in the past and up to the present time in all their legislation in matters concerning the sexes, have uniformly discriminated against women and no doubt will continue to so discriminate as long as they are the sole law makers. "Because of the hardness of their hearts" it has been so. The best for each, for the men and for the women, for society also, and the State, can be reached only when women as well as men shall have a voice and vote in the making of the laws that govern either or both.

Reward in the matter of wages has ever been and is to-day a grievous wrong against women. Poverty is the enemy of virtue, and women in poverty are doubly tempted. But there will be, there can be, no correction of this crying injustice until women can vote and have their votes counted. There can be no uplift for mankind to the highest and best until womankind is fully emancipated. The sexes must rise together and at equal pace, and with equal political rights, or they shall both flounder together and remain incomplete. Political emancipation, full, free, unhampered, is the only leverage that can raise women from social and industrial damnation. No class of people, not even mothers, wives and daughters, can, in this democratic America, be denied political freedom and not suffer wrong and degradation. It is clear that protection to women—to all women—can be secured only by giving them a part and a voice in making the laws that concern their honor and well-being.

4. The need of White Cross work is made imperative because of the ravages of licentiousness.

Of all the master vices that prey upon and curse American society, or any other for that matter, it is admitted by those in a position to know, that licentiousness is the greatest. It is, more than all others, universal, deep seated and most deadly. It is easily the darkest sin in all the catalogue of sin and shame.

We have evidence that licentiousness to-day, as never before, has assumed the proportions and methods of a trade. It has the form, phases, agencies and machinery of a great, complicated, ramifying business. Its agents travel everywhere; the telegraph and the United States mails transmit intelligence for it; and the railroads, express companies and ships at sea carry its vicious freight. Vile literature in papers, magazines, books and pictures, full of unspeakable abominations, abounds everywhere and is propagating ideas of social nastiness.

The stage, now popular in city and town and village, with its spectacular scenes of love and lust and managed by a hundred thousand men and women, mostly low, lewd and lawless, is vitiating the minds and hearts of thousands, until their sense of the pure and the impure is obliterated.

The saloon, that legal institution of infamy and tyranny, is firing the passions of men and sending them down the scarlet avenues that lead to chambering and wantonness.

We see also that efforts are being made in different places and in high places and even in legislative halls, and with alarming success, to establish professional prostitution in our cities under cover of law and under the control of police force. That means the traffic in and the sale of untold thousands of the young daughters of the people throughout the land. The procurer and procuress already travel, even under the guise of honorable business and sometimes of piety, to hunt for "the precious life." Incredible thousands of our sisters and daughters are sold every decade like cattle in the tolerated shambles of lust. Oh, the fearful ravages of licentiousness! Monstrous, harrowing, and still on the increase! There are now two hundred and thirty thousand (230,000) fallen women in the United States, and that means at least eight times that many fallen men. To supply the demands of passion in men one hundred families must give up a daughter apiece every day in the round year. What a draft this is on homes! What sin and shame and misery and heartaches and remorse and cruelty and murder and death and damnation this means! Think of it! Estimate if you can the fearful cost of this scarlet commerce! And then remember that this unclean, abominable, merciless business is going on now, that it is ever enlarging, spreading, taking in more victims; and there is little or no effort being made to stop it. What if it goes on for another ten or twenty years with the same ratio of increase that has marked it in the last ten or twenty years? "What will the harvest be?"

5. Special effort in purity reform is forced upon us because of the inadequate instruction, or lack of instruction, by parents in their homes, teachers in the schools and pastors in the churches upon the subjects of personal chastity and social purity.

The reticence of parents in these matters is well known. Because of temerity, false modesty, inability, or ignorance of the need of it, they fail to instruct children and young people in positive knowledge concerning sexual relations and duties. For the most part, especially with the boys, their first lessons about sex and reproduction and motherhood and fatherhood are learned from corrupt playmates, unclean innuendo, vile literature, obscene pictures, vulgar stories and unfortunate personal experience. There are some things, some knowledge about ourselves, that must come by teaching, by explanation, by discipline. Important among these are the facts and duties indicated in the Seventh commandment of the Decalogue. Let alone, boys run to the bad and at an incredible early age become impure in thought and often in practice.

In the public schools there is almost a total neglect of all the facts that pertain to sexual functions, relations and duties. Physiology stops short of these most important things and the young are left to inference, or to unfortunate ways for learning what above all they need to know. If we are to believe the testimony of teachers of public schools then we are persuaded that uncleanness and vileness and impurity, in word and in conduct, are fearfully prevalent in them. Dr. J. H. Kellogg gives an instance where a superintendent of city schools made a careful inquiry into the personal habits of four hundred boys between the ages of ten and eighteen, and found but seven in the entire number who claimed to be free from impure practices. Nor is there any guarantee that the matter is going to be corrected, for our school authorities make no manner of provision for instruction in the laws and principles of sexual relations. personal chastity and social purity.

Nor is the pulpit of our times, save in a very few exceptional cases, outspoken in warnings and instruction concerning chastity, the sins of licentiousness, social disorders and dangers and all unholy sexual associations. There are but few preachers that ever preach on the Seventh commandment of the Decalogue; or upon Christ's law of purity; or give an exposition upon his teachings concerning marriage and divorce. If they took up these subjects more frequently they would not so often be caught officiating at the marriages of unlawfully, that is unscripturally, divorced persons.

Ministers are or should be in a special sense the monitors of public morals and the guardians of children and women. Yet how few there are who speak out bold, clear and timely words of warning against the sins of the flesh; and how seldom are sermons preached exposing the wrongs that are perpetrated against womankind; and how silent the pulpits are concerning the legislative crimes in every State of the Union, whereby the sanctity of marriage is destroyed, divorce made easy and promiscuous prostitution encouraged. The simple, sad fact is that the ministers in the churches are not doing the purity work that is needed. They have entered upon an era of silence upon this subject. They do not teach their young men as they need to be taught by their religious guides; they do not boldly and pointedly rebuke the old men of unclean habits; and plain words of counsel are never spoken to the women of the churches. Strange, guilty, dangerous silence! The old preachers and prophets were not like dumb dogs upon these subjects, and the preachers now ought not to be dumb where and when there is needed line upon line, precept upon precept and warning upon warning. Oh, for men like Nathan, who went to guilty David and said, "Thou art the man;" like John the

Baptist, who went to the licentious Herod and told him frankly that he was living with the wrong woman.

In all this I make no charge against the ministry; I simply state a fact—sad, universal, alarming fact.

Somebody should speak out; somebody should tell the truth about these matters. The work must be done and God will find people to do it. If the ministry will not take it up God will raise up men, messengers and workers, from the ranks of the democracy who will take it up.

The W. C. T. U. seeing the ravages of licentiousness, feeling the power of unholy and unjust laws, like that of the double standard, knowing the need of reform and painfully, regretfully conscious of the silence in the churches, have felt constrained to take up the work. They have added to their purity department the White Cross Branch. They bid God-speed to all who are in the same work and extend the hand of co-operation to all workers in this important reform.

6. There is yet one other evidence that White Cross work is needed that should be mentioned in this place. It is the fact of the indifference, false modesty, cowardice and ignorance among the best people of the land concerning the nature, extent, power, threat and actual mischief of licentiousness.

To-day, as of old, it must be said: " My people perish for lack of knowledge. They do not know as they ought to know their dangers and their duties. The great Apostle to the Gentiles, seeing the people in sin and in ignorance, went to them, "warning every man and teaching every man that he might present every man perfect in Christ Jesus." Warning and teaching are the two important things needed to-day in purity work. To be well taught is to be well warned. Information here is social salvation. " To be forewarned is to be forearmed." The people, and especially the young people and the young men, need the teaching and they need the warning, and for this the White Cross is here.

It seeks to arouse such a noble, beautiful chivalry as will lead every man to treat every other man's mother as he wants his own mother treated; to treat every other man's wife as he wants his own wife treated; to treat every other man's sister as he wants his own sister treated; to treat every other man's daughter as he wants his own daughter treated.

CHASTITY AND HEALTH

By J. H. KELLOGG, M. D., BATTLE CREEK, MICH.

That a most important relation exists between chastity and health is a fact too obvious to require formal demonstration.   That there is a natural as well as a divine law, if such a distinction can be made, prohibiting unchastity, is shown by the terrible penalties which are inflicted for violation of the law of purity, which, from a physical standpoint, far exceed in severity those which follow the infraction of any other physical or moral law.   Men have sought, by every artifice imaginable, to avoid these penalties.   One of the most specious of these is embodied in the so called Con_ tagious Disease Act, requiring medical inspection of prostitutes, which has been for many years in operation in Continental Europe and India, and which has repeatedly been proposed in legislative halls in this country; but, thanks to the efforts of this Association, through its officers and kindred influences, such legislation has thus far found no substantial foothold on American soil.

There is probably no country in which the provisions of this Contagious Disease Act have been so thoroughly carried out as in Germany; nevertheless, the commission appointed by the Society of Medicine of Berlin, with Professor Virchow as president, recently reported, as the result of an investigation, that both prostitution and venereal diseases were found to be rapidly increasing in Berlin.   For example, the number of regular prostitutes, recognized as such by the police, was, in 1886, 3,006.   The number had increased in 1891 to 4,364, an increase of almost 50 per cent.   This

J. H. KELLOGG, M. D.

represents, however, but a small proportion of the women actually engaged in prostitution, as 16,000 women are annually arrested for plying their vocation upon the streets in Berlin, and it is known that a great number of women live lives of prostitution clandestinely, so that the committee estimate the total number of prostitutes in Berlin at 40,000 to 50,000.

Some idea of the number of persons who are annually infected by venereal disease may be gained from the fact that the committee reported nearly 80,000 cases as having been treated at two hospitals alone in Berlin between 1880 and 1889. The fact was also mentioned by the committee that a great number of cases were doubtless not included in this category. They quote the estimate of Blaschko, that one in every nine or ten of the male population of Berlin has been infected with syphilis.

A most convincing evidence of the utter inefficiency of the inspection service in preventing the spread of venereal disease, was shown by the fact developed by the committee, that the naked-eye inspection, which has been universally relied upon, detects less than one in five of the cases of gonorrhœa, to say nothing of syphilis. By making a bacteriological examination of each case, the proportion of prostitutes found to be suffering from gonorrhœa was increased from nine per cent. to fifty per cent.

The conclusions drawn by the committee as to the proper action to be taken under the circumstances seem to be quite absurd. Instead of recommending the abandoning of the unwise attempt to make vice safe, by enabling the criminal to escape the penalty which nature inflicts for the transgression of moral and natural law in relation to purity, they recommend a more rigid investigation, suggesting that the examination should be made twice a week instead of weekly, and that a bacteriological examination should be made in every case. They also recommend that special hospitals and dispensaries shall be provided for persons suffering from venereal disorders, where they may be treated at the public expense, and thus enabled to return as quickly as possible to their base and immoral business.

What a horrible spectacle is this to contemplate in the midst of our boasted civilization! A vast outfit of laboratories and hospitals, an army of physicians, nurses, pharmacists, clerks, etc , all devoting their lives to the fostering and encouraging of a business which depends wholly for its existence upon the violation of the laws of God and man! If the moral sense of society, especially of politicians—and we fear the same must also be said to a considerable extent of the medical profession— were not blunted to a most astonishing degree, the only remedy which would be suggested for this gigantic evil would be its absolute prohibition and extermination by means of severe penalties and a faithful administration of the law. What can be said of the inconsistency of which nearly every civilized community is guilty, shown in the maintenance of laws rendering prostitution and licentiousness a crime, while at the same time this deadly traffic is winked at, and not infrequently protected and encouraged!

We commend these facts to the consideration of those who are anxious to introduce into this country laws for the regulation and inspection of prostitutes.

The infection of one-tenth of the entire male population of a great city like Berlin with so horrible a constitutional malady as syphilis, means race deterioration at a most terrific rate, and yet this estimate is, probably, none too large, for even a larger estimate has been made in relation to Vienna, Paris and some other continental cities; and eminent specialists do not hesitate to place New York upon an even footing with Berlin. We say race deterioration, for the reason that the evil consequences of vice are not to be studied alone in the vicious, but may be traced with equal distinctness in the progeny of the unchaste. Vice of every sort, but most of all sexual vice, places an indelible mark upon its victims. The progeny of the impure are not only the subjects of special ailments, which have been traced directly to the various specific infections communicable through unchastity, but they are also subject to general constitutional feebleness, weakness of will, lack of mental, moral and physical stamina, with little resistance to disease and a proneness to structural degenerations of various sorts. Largely—I think I may say chiefly—through the influence of impurity, a vast multitude of persons, who might properly be termed the disinherited, are to be found in our modern society. This great mass of unfortunates is augmented annually by a numberless host of recruits.

A philosopher has said, "It is the greatest of all human felicities to be well born." It is yearly becoming more and more apparent that an increasing proportion of human beings are badly born. In every large city are to be found thousands who belong to what are known as the vicious, the criminal, or the indigent or pauper classes. For the most part these persons are born into the condition in which they are destined to spend their lives, and are little more responsible for the unhappy situation in which they find themselves than are the deaf and dumb and blind, or those who are in other respects congenitally deformed. The only difference between the infirmities from which these persons suffer and those with which the crippled, the blind or the deaf are afflicted, is that their physical deficiencies are less conspicuous; they are, nevertheless, as real. For the most part their deformities consist in bad or abnormal construction of the brain, although a minute examination will reveal, in the majority of persons belonging to these inferior classes, external deformities of a very pronounced character.

That these weaknesses and abnormalities of body and mind are perpetuated by heredity, is no longer a question upon which there is any difference of opinion.

It is as clearly settled that mental and moral characteristics are inherited as that the color of the hair and eyes, or other physical characteristics, are thus derived. It is equally true, although the fact is often forgotten, that the resemblance of the internal structures of the child to those of his parents is as close as the likeness which can be traced in the external features. Heredity is a force which operates in the most thoroughgoing manner. Every human being is the product of a principle which has been taking careful notes of the lives and habits, the neglects, the excesses and the abuses of every crime against the body through all the generations from Adam down to the individual man in question. The living man or woman is simply the material representation, the focus, or vortex, so to speak, of the myriad of influences which have been operating from the earliest ages of man's history down to the moment of inspection.

Man's physical, mental and moral character is as much a matter of heredity as is the capital of wealth with which he starts out in life. The man who lives the life of a spendthrift and dies bankrupt leaves his children penniless. Sometimes it takes a series of generations to consume completely the accumulated earnings of preceding generations. So it is with bodily and mental health. The complete mental and physical bankruptcy which lands a man in the insane asylum or an almshouse infirmary, may be simply the results of two or three generations of sins against the body and the soul on the part of the profligate ancestors. "The fathers have eaten sour grapes, and the children's teeth are set on edge."

The world looks with disdain upon the money spendthrift. The man who recklessly squanders the family inheritance and leaves his children penniless, is regarded by the world as little short of a criminal, a thief, a robber. What does society say about the man who, by a process exactly identical, disinherits his children of the most valuable of all possessions—soundness of body and mind? Society ignores the sins of this class of criminals, never asking a man to consider the consequences of his course of life upon his possible progeny, but allows him to squander, without questioning his right, the constitutions of his unborn children, in open violation of the law by which nature has protected the well being of the human race.

Through this almost universal ignoring of the duty devolving upon every human being to preserve intact, as far as possible, the natural powers transmitted to him from his ancestors, and by training and painstaking development make the most of them, we find the human race deteriorating in physical stamina, and a rapidly growing multitude of "disinherited" individuals who are born into physical, mental and moral bankruptcy. It is high time that society gave more serious attention to this great class of bankrupts by heredity, from which springs the greater share of crimes and criminals, cranks, lunatics, fanatics and imbeciles.

The wonderful investigations made by Hertwig and others into the method of cell growth, multiplication, and especially the vital activities connected with reproduction, have thrown a flood of light upon the problem of heredity which has a very interesting bearing upon this question. These investigations show that in the process of reproduction both parents actually enter into the formation of the new individual, and in so real a manner that a man may be actually said to live in his son, heredity securing a physical immortality for the individual as well as for the race.

In the marvelous process of *karyo kinesis*, which has been especially studied in the fecundated ova of various species of fishes, and other inferior animals, it is seen that in the process of reproduction each animal in each sex contributes an imperfect cell, which, by uniting with an analogous cell from an animal of the same species, but of the opposite sex, becomes a complete cell, representing the characteristics of the two individuals.

Bouchard, the distinguished French physiologist, has recently shown that the character of these cells, as well as of all other cells within the body of an animal, depends upon the influence of certain subtle substances in the fluids of the individual, which, although so small in amount that they have, until recently, evaded the closest scrutiny of the physiologist and the chemist, are, nevertheless, so potent in their influence upon the animal organism that they practically control every function from the first step of nutrition in the digestion of the food to the final process of assimilation in the conversion of food elements into tissue.

Bouchard has called especial attention to the influence of these substances upon heredity, both through the influence which they may exert upon the activities of the sexual glands and through their absorption from the mother's blood during fœtal life. The marvelous control which these potent substances exercise over all the nutritive processes was first discovered by the late Professor Brown-Sequard, an American born physician, who achieved the highest honors which could be bestowed upon him by the physicians and scientists of France because of the numerous remarkable additions which he has made to physiological science, as the result of the long painstaking researches to which he devoted his life. Dr. Brown-Sequard was the first to point out the fact that certain structures within the animal body give rise to these peculiar substances to which he gave the name "internal secretions." The supra-renal capsules of the kidney, the thyroid gland and other structures, together with the sexual glands, he mentioned as being the seat of important secretory processes whereby a marvelous control was exercised over all the processes of life. So called ductless glands have been a mystery until now.

When last in Paris, a few years ago, I had the pleasure of renewing the acquaintance of this distinguished man, which, as a student in medicine, I had enjoyed more than twenty years ago, and while assisting him in his laboratory in a special research in which he was then engaged upon this subject, I listened with amazement—and I must confess with some incredulity—to the novel theories which he expounded. These theories, after producing something of a sensation at first, were later made the butt of much ridicule and sarcastic criticism, but as Bouchard, Roger, d'Arsonval and others have taken up the investigation which the eminent savant laid down with his life a year or two ago, his views had not only been largely confirmed, but, following the same line of inquiry, other equally interesting facts have been developed.

Dr. Brown-Sequard stated to the writer that he had been convinced for more than twenty years that certain glands in the body produced secretions which, being absorbed and circulated in the blood, influence the nutrition and development of the body in a remarkable way. His later researches and the researches of his associates, d'Arsonval and others who were engaged with him in this interesting work, have shown the correctness of this theory and have demonstrated many remarkably interesting facts. For example, it is now known that the removal of the thyroid gland from the body of an animal will produce death by the development of a peculiar form of disease, but if an extract of thyroid gland, made by macerating the gland in water, is injected into the body of the animal from time to time, the injurious effects ordinarily resulting from the removal of the gland do not appear. It has been found also that if a thyroid gland, or a portion of a thyroid gland, be introduced into some other part of the body of an animal from which the gland has been removed, the animal recovers from the injury inflicted by the removal of the gland. The supra-renal capsules of the kidney, the spleen, the lymphatic glands, and the pancreas, have each their peculiar internal secretions, which influence and modify nutrition in various ways. For example, the internal secretion of the pancreas is a peculiar ferment, by the aid of which the body is able to burn up or oxidize the sugar introduced with the food. When the pancreas becomes diseased and ceases to furnish this ferment the sugar is not utilized and appears in the urine, producing diabetes. The internal secretions of the lymphatic glands and the spleen exercise a special influence over the formation of blood capsules. The internal secretions of other parts have for their function the destruction or antidoting of certain poisons which are produced within the body or which are introduced from without in the food. Dogs from which the thymus glands had been removed, died if fed upon a meat diet, but if fed upon a diet of bread and milk remained in health.

The eminent Claude Bernard had some inkling of these remarkable physiological effects, and had prepared extracts of muscles, glands and other tissues. Experiments which have since been made by Brown-Sequard and his pupils show that every tissue produces certain substances which, circulating in the blood, modify every other tissue, thus producing unity and harmony in the development of the various organs of the body, independent of the nervous system and explaining what has heretofore been one of the greatest mysteries of animal physiology.

One of the most striking of all the observations made by Brown-Sequard was the fact that the secretion of the sexual glands is possessed of most remarkable physiological properties. For example, Dr Brown-Sequard stated to the writer and published to the world the fact that in experiments made upon himself he found a notable increase in strength by the simple hypodermic injection of an infusion freshly made from the sexual glands of a rabbit. He observed not only an increase of muscular strength, but of general vigor and vitality. His observations have been confirmed in a vast number of cases, although the careless method employed in the testing of the theory by many experimenters led to so many negative results that no practical therapeutic use has ever been made of the discovery in this country.

Dr. Brown-Sequard's first experiments were made upon himself. At the advanced age of eighty years I found him hard at work all day in his laboratory, although previous to the beginning of his experiments he had been barely able to work a few hours in the forenoon. He experienced not only a notable increase of muscular force, but also of intellectual vigor. He had previously been greatly troubled with inactivity of the bowels, making the use of purgatives necessary. Since using the injections, both mechanical and medicinal means for aiding the bowels were entirely unnecessary.

It was not claimed that the organic changes of old age can be modified by this means, but that the vital activities of the body are marvelously quickened by the introduction of this vital fluid obtained from the sexual glands; neither was it claimed that the effects were permanent, it being necessary to repeat the injections every few days.

The bearing of these discoveries upon sexual hygiene is, however, very obvious and highly important. The investigations of Brown-Sequard and the subsequent investigations of Bouchard and others, have shown that the sexual glands are useful, not only as a means of race perpetuation, but for the physical well being of the individual through the vital stimulus exercised by them, through the influence of their peculiar secretion upon the processes of development and nutrition. In view of this fact it is evident that so far as the individual is concerned, physical benefit is to be looked for, not in the loss of the secretion of the sexual glands, but in its retention and appropriation. In other words, reproduction is accomplished at the sacrifice of individual interests, a law which prevails throughout the whole organic world, being in some instances so pronounced that the development of progeny is accomplished only through the death of one or both parents.

These discoveries afford a thoroughly satisfactory and scientific explanation of two facts which heretofore have rested solely upon the basis of observation and experience:

1. The fact that continence is favorable to physical vigor.

2. That sexual intemperance is productive of exhaustion and debility to a most extraordinary degree.

The influence of the sexual glands upon development has been understood from very early ages. The influence of the removal of these glands in the equine or bovine race is well known. The proudly arched neck, the graceful roundness of trunk and limbs, the magnificent courage and vigor of the stallion, are not found in the mutilated animal. The massive head and horns, the flashing eye, the terrible majesty of the bull, are never encountered in the castrated animal of the same species, the meek-eyed ox. The difference in size, appearance and character, which exist between the horse and the stallion, between the ox and the bull, are purely the result of the loss of the magic influence of the secretion of the sexual glands as a stimulus to development and a regulator of the nutritive processes.

The removal of the sexual glands before puberty, or the failure of their development from any cause, gives rise to similar difference in the human male. We encountered a year ago an interesting example of this fact. A young man between twenty and twenty-five years of age presented himself at my office for examination with reference to a condition which he supposed might be remedied by a surgical operation. On examination, I found no evidence whatever of the presence of the sexual glands in the usual location, and learned from the young man that he had been informed that the

glands had remained in the abdomen, having failed to
descend at the proper period before birth. Upon careful examination I became satisfied that the glands were
present in only a rudimentary state. On further investigation I found that the young man presented many
evidences of the influence of these glands upon development. His hips were broad and his thigh large like
those of a young woman, while his shoulders were narrow. The difference between the breadth of the
shoulders and hips was only half what it should be. The
sternum was proportionately short, as in women. There
was an entire absence of beard and other external evidences of development, the external genital organs being infantile in appearance. Notwithstanding the
feminine appearance presented by the young man in
many respects, the legs and arms were long, as in men,
and the case was evidently not of the mixed but of the
neuter type.

The loss of the influence of the sexual glands results in the production of an effeminate man, while the
removal of these glands in a young woman who has not
reached the age of puberty produces a mannish woman.
It appears then that the influence of the sexual glands
is to develop in man manly characteristics, or those special features which contribute to make up manhood;
while the sexual glands of woman produce in her those
qualities and characteristics which are especially womanly.

Within the last twenty years, in dealing profession-
ally with some ten or twelve thousand cases of men who
have been, in various ways and various degrees, transgressors of the law of chastity, I have particularly noted
the frequency of effeminacy in appearance as a characteristic of those cases in which habits of sexual indulgence had been begun before puberty and practiced to
a considerable extent during the developmental period,
showing that the excessive loss of the activity of the
sexual glands in a normally developed person produces

results analogous to those which follow the extirpation of the glands.

In view of these facts we can readily understand why the acute observation of the trainers of the Greek athletes led them to require, as one of the conditions most essential to the development of the highest degree of physical vigor, absolute continence—not simply temperance, which is all that is expected by most trainers at the present time. The conditions of Greek society were certainly less favorable to purity and continence than are those of to-day; yet so great was the ambition of the Greek to win a prize in the Olympian games that he willingly exercised the great self control necessary under the peculiar circumstances under which he lived. Plato, in his " Laws," makes one of his characters say: " So then they, to obtain victory in wrestling and running, thus abstained; and shall our children be unable to persevere for a far nobler victory?"—a statement approved by the apostle Paul in I Cor., 9:25-27, when he says, "Now they do it to obtain a corruptible crown; but we an incorruptible . . . . . But I keep under my body, and bring it into subjection."

The compensation sought by the Greek for the restraint of his animal propensities was to become a stronger and more vigorous animal; and in this he was not disappointed, for Plato mentions a number of celebrated athletes, among others, Astylos and Diopompos, whose bodies were "much lustier" than others. Having practiced total continence during their training, they had much stronger and more vigorous bodies than others who had not subjected themselves to the same restraints.

The doctrine that continence is unfavorable to health, if true, supplies a very strong argument for the maintenance of a harlot class for the benefit of soldiers and sailors, who, for the most part, cannot marry. This doctrine is indeed the stronghold of the apologists for prostitution and of the advocates of laws regulating vice. The considerations already offered seem amply sufficient to show the fallacy of this doctrine; nevertheless, I will offer a few additional items of evidence, including the testimony of a number of eminent physicians.

Dr. James Henderson, a physician in Shanghai, China, writing in refutation of the idea that continence is more difficult or dangerous in tropical countries than in temperate climates on account of peculiar climatic conditions, says: "I have seen many suffer severely, destroying their health, happiness, and life by following the promptings of their unbridled passions. Need I say that I have never seen a man suffer from keeping himself pure?"

In the course of my own professional experience, I can truthfully say that I have never met with a single instance in which disease of any kind was present as the result of a pure or continent life. On the other hand, I have seen the most horrible results from the unlawful and unprofessional advice sometimes given by physicians to young men, suggesting unchastity as being essential for the relief of some physical weakness, though I have never met with a single case in which the slightest benefit had been derived from following such advice. My observations with reference to the character of those who give professional advice of this sort have long ago led me to the belief that, as a rule, only those who have themselves been impure to such an extent that they were bereft of their ability to judge properly of the influence of a pure and continent life are capable of giving such unwise and immoral advice.

Acton, an eminent London physician, declares that the claim that disease results from continence "is a device of the unchaste, a lame excuse for their own incontinence unfounded on any physiological law." The same writer adds: "The admitted fact that continence is frequently productive of distress, is often a struggle hard to be borne, still harder to be completely victorious in, is not to be at all regarded as an argument that it is an evil."

These statements are amply confirmed by common experience with animals, especially in continental Europe, where the castration of working animals is practiced only to a very small extent. The experience of many most distinguished men must also be quoted in confirmation of these statements. Among such men may be mentioned Sir Isaac Newton, Kant, Paschal, Michael Angelo, St. Augustine, and many others of the early Catholic Fathers who were among the ablest and most learned men of their time, and in fact, of all time, and who led continent lives. The majority of these men lived to a very great age, retaining to the last their wonderful mental powers.

The exorbitant demands of the sexual appetite encountered among civilized people are not the result of a normal instinct, but are due to the incitements of an abnormally stimulating diet, the seductions of prurient literature and so called art. and the temptations of impure associations.

The relation of diet to impurity is one which is far too little considered. Certain senses are given us to add to our pleasure, as well as for the practical, almost indispensable use they are to us. For instance, the sense of sight is not only useful, but enables us to drink in beauty without stint and receive no harm thereby. The same is true of music and other harmonies, which may come to us through the sense of hearing. But the sense of taste was given us to distinguish between wholesome and unwholesome foods, and cannot be used for merely sensual gratification without debasing it and making it a gross and harmful thing. An education which demands special enjoyment or pleasure through the sense of taste is wholly artificial; it brings us down to the animal plane, or below it, rather; for the instincts of the brute creation teaches it to eat to live.

There can be no doubt that unwholesome food, especially such stimulating articles as spices and other condiments, and the excessive use of flesh food, pastry, and highly-seasoned viands, is one of the most active causes of impurity in modern times. The early Romans, who fed upon the simple fruits of the earth, were as chaste in morals as abstemious in diet; but, under the degrading influence of a luxurious and stimulating dietary, the Roman emperors developed a degree of moral turpitude that astonished and disgusted even the heathen world in which they lived. The great monarchies which once ruled the world became immoral and corrupt only when their citizens became wealthy and adopted luxurious modes of life. Simplicity in diet, dress, and in all the habits of life, is most conducive to virtue.

The same principle applies in relation to sexual gratification as to the gratification of the sense of taste. The sexual function is double in its purpose: first, the sexual organs are always active, even when not excited to such a degree as to obtrude their activity upon the consciousness, as they supply the body with a needed vital stimulus and regulator; secondly, they furnish the only means by which the physical immortality of the individual in the perpetuation of the race may be accomplished. In neither of these important functions is the personal gratification of the individual the primary consideration. The exercise of the sexual function with a purely selfish purpose would seem to be as much a debasement of the sacred function in which man approaches most nearly to the creative power of which he is the image, as is eating for the mere gratification of the palate a debasement and prostitution of the appetite and the sense of taste.

Evil association is often the avenue through which the father of lies and iniquity leads his victim down to ruin. A moral contagion is abroad in the world. The troops of boys of all ages, from five to twenty, seen upon the streets of every city, sitting on the curbstones, loitering about the corners, gathering here and there in little knots from which the ears of passers-by may easily catch words and phrases which bring the blush to virtue's cheek, are evidence that parents are by no means generally awake to the danger which lies in evil companionship. Many boys, especially in the cities, are allowed, after they reach the age of ten or twelve years, to select their own associates; and it is generally the case that the association most easily formed is with some foul-minded youth, who is only too anxious to impart to an innocent lad the evil knowledge which he has in like manner gained from some other boy-missionary of evil.

Growing up thus, with an abnormally developed sexual appetite, it is not strange that young men very readily imbibe current notions respecting the hygienic necessity for incontinence, and that they find in their own experience an apparent evidence of the correctness of this most pernicious doctrine. It is, therefore, highly important that a warning voice should be raised, and with no weak or uncertain sound, against this immoral and incontinent teaching. If the young man finds a continent life extraordinarily difficult or a cause of suffering, he should be informed that the apparent necessity is purely an artificial and an abnormal one, and is either the result of a sensuous imagination or of morbid conditions which require medical treatment, and which will be certain to be aggravated rather than alleviated by the gratification of the desires. The young man should be taught so to order his habits of life, his diet, his regimen, his exercise, that he may be enabled to maintain self mastery. Plato calls attention to the fact that the man who reaches a high degree of physical vigor as the result of severe training, finds the control of the sexual appetite a much less severe task than does the man who neglects muscular activity.

The value of a simple diet and active muscular exercise in subduing abnormal animal propensities, the writer has proved in hundreds of cases in which his prescription has been carried out by young men seeking relief from the thralldom of clamorous desires.

My purpose in this paper has been to show, from purely physiological considerations, that unchastity can be, under no circumstances, either necessary or justifiable; that science and religion, the teaching of nature and of the decalogue, are in accord; that chastity, not incontinence, is the law of nature. The considerations which have been brought forward I think amply justify me in the assertion that chastity is not only consistent with the highest health under all circumstances, but that it is one of the conditions essential to the attainment and maintenance of the highest degree of physical and mental vigor.

JOHN J. CORNELL.

REMARKS OF JOHN J. CORNELL.

John J. Cornell, of Baltimore, said that while his work had been mainly regarding the suppression of intemperance in the use of and traffic in intoxicants, he had not been unmindful of the enormity of its twin evil, the existence of the social vice, and he was in hearty sympathy and accord with the object of the present Congress. He felt that this great evil, if it did not have its origin in the use of intoxicants, was largely fostered and sustained by them; and while he recognized the necessity of organized opposition to these evils and hailed it as an omen of an advancing public sentiment, he yet realized the need of a dependence upon the revelation of the Divine Spirit, to which, if one would listen and be obedient, it would lead him into such a life as would free him from the commission of these as well as other evils.

C. W. WATCH.

SIXTH SESSION.

SOCIAL PURITY WORK IN CANADA.

BY REV. C. W. WATCH.

We must know the conditions to understand the work. Our land is one of vast areas, stretching from ocean to ocean and from the lakes to the Pole, in all about three and a half millions square miles. A land not of perpetual snows, but rich with resources. We are not over crowded with people: our population is about five millions. Montreal, our largest city, has nearly a quarter of a million, and besides this we have about fifty cities and towns, with populations of from five thousand to two hundred thousand. We are somewhat mixed as to our nationality; over a million of our people are French Canadian, speaking the French language. Canadians are steady going, making progress slow but sure. An opinion as to the moral sentiment of our people might be formed by the temperance votes recently taken. When asked to express themselves as to the prohibition of the liquor traffic, four Provinces out of seven, representing a population of nearly three millions, said, by a majority of nearly 133,000 at the polls, that they favored prohibition; and another Province, of over 300,000 people, declared by the unanimous vote of their Legislature that they also were prepared for it. So that, doubtless, did the whole Dominion speak at the ballot box, it would declare with a majority of 100,000 in favor of prohibition. Thus perhaps we are morally no worse, and, it may be, we are a little better, than some other nations, but we certaiuly are not as good as we ought to be.

Then again there are conditions which the workers in other lands have to meet from which happily we are spared. The regulation of prostitution and vice is unknown to us; not but some may desire it, and in a few cities districting may be winked at. Yet recently, when the Chief of Police of Montreal expressed himself in favor of supervision and districting, the better element of the city protested with emphasis, and nothing more has been heard of it. Though we have one garrison town—Halifax—the C. D. Acts would be impossible in Canada. To know of such a system would result in our people loathing it. We have no struggle over uncertain or lax divorce laws. We have neither a divorce court nor law, except in one of the smaller Provinces. To procure a divorce with us requires a special Act of Parliament in each case. The result is that for the past ten years there have been only forty-eight applications for divorce, forty of which have been granted, or about one divorce for every six or seven thousand marriages consummated. Even those who by establishing a residence in any other country may secure a separation, it is a question if our laws affecting bigamy are not sufficient to reach them, should a marriage be consummated again within the Dominion.

As to our laws, in regard to age of consent we are below the standard, sixteen being the age. It is criminal to seduce under promise of marriage up to the age of eighteen, but the male is not responsible under the age of twenty-one. An effort is being made to raise the age of consent and to make it a criminal offence to seduce under promise of marriage in the case of a female not more than twenty-one years of age, and in the case of a male from the age of eighteen. But the difficulty arises just here from the indifference of our representatives in Parliament to this class of legislation. Rape is punishable by either death or life imprisonment. Illicit relations with girls under fourteen is punishable by life imprisonment and whipping. Another advantage we have is the exclusion from our mails of indecent literature and pictures, under heavy penalties. We refuse admission into our country, or sale among our people, of the *Police Gazette*, or any such papers. In all matters of legislation we are much indebted to Mr. John Charlton, who is our leader in Parliament on social purity questions. Notwithstanding our advantages the social evil exists, disorderly houses in some places are tolerated, and too often the periodic raiding and regulation fine are looked upon or understood as a license. One birth in every seventy-nine or eighty is an illegitimate birth. There is an apathy of sentiment on the part of a large portion of the general public, and a lack of high principles cn the part of another considerable portion, and so we have with us in social life the unequal standard of morals for the sexes and too often the same conditions as other peoples for making girlhood an easy prey for vile men.

Purity work is the outcome of Christian philanthropy. The churches may be wofully ignorant of their responsibility touching the low age of consent and of the wrong there is in an unequal standard for the sexes, yet it is ever the Christian sentiment of the country which is seeking to educate the public conscience, awaken a public interest, and sustains those institutions and helpers who are lovingly engaged in the work of rescue and prevention. There is not a city and scarcely a town of any size but are found homes and workers in women and child saving. Among the Indians of our country the gross immoralities of other days are impossible now, and it is the missionaries, male and female, of all the churches, who by their teaching and life have brought about the change. On the Pacific Coast the Methodist Missionary Society and the W. C. T. U. have Refuges for the saving of Chinese girls, brought into the country from seven to fourteen years of age, altogether for immoral purposes, and marvelous are the stories of rescue and conversion.

THE NATIONAL PURITY CONGRESS.

In speaking of the educational phase of our purity work, that our Press is fairly clean can be truthfully said, but just now a moral protest is being heard, and it requires yet that it be made more emphatic against the details of vice and scandal and crime published to gratify the prurient mind. We take pride in our public school system and think that no country can boast of teachers purer in life and example than can we. Temperance and hygiene are taught in our schools. We carefully guard the separation of the sexes in the playground, still we find both teachers and parents lamentably slow to believe the dangerous possibilities from the teaching of vile practices of boys to boys and sometimes of girls to girls, or if they realize it they are certainly slow to meet the danger with honest teaching and exposure. We have but few White Cross societies as such, but we have White Cross and Social Purity committees working in other organizations. The W. C. T. U., by its literature, by its standards of living and everywhere by the consistency of its members in living up to its standards, is an educational strength to us. No matter who frowns upon them they seem determined to hold out until peace, purity and prohibition are secured for all. The Royal Templars, a body of advanced prohibitionists, are, under Provincial Superintendents, keeping the White Cross movement before its membership, and by a special department in its organ, having a circulation of 25,000, going to all parts of the Dominion, they are keeping the social purity movement before the people. The Y. M. C. A. and other young people's Christian societies are not one whit behind in purity work their fellow workers in other lands.

We cannot speak of our work without identifying with it that undertaken in the interest of prevention and rescue. These homes are in nearly all our cities and are carried on after the same manner and with the same object as the Florence Crittenton and other rescue missions. To mention two or three will be sufficient to in-

dicate what is being done by all. The W. C. T. U.
have homes for shelter and rescue in Halifax—a garrison town—with all those conditions existing which go to
make the work both more difficult and urgent, and in
Quebec, Montreal, Winnipeg and in the cities of the
Pacific Coast. Where we find these workers without
homes under their own immediate supervision, we still
meet their members on all boards and committees for
the helping of their unfortunate sisters. In Quebec
Province, the population being largely Catholic, the
Protestant missions can accomplish but little. Yet here
we find earnest educational work being done by many
priests in that church, while the various sisterhoods
strive faithfully to save and reclaim the fallen of her
women. In Montreal "The Woman's and Children's
Protective Society" not only undertakes rescue work
but also that of inquiry and prosecution. Ill treated
and neglected wives and children come within their
sphere of operation, and over three hundred cases
passed through their hands last year. In Toronto,
among other agencies, we have "The Haven and Prison
Gate Mission," dealing with as many as 700 or 800 cases
every year, not by any means all fallen women; many
of these are women addicted to drink, and who would
probably become impure, and many other poor girls
who seek and receive shelter as well as inspiration to a
better life. The last workers to enter this field are
those of the Salvation Army. Their rescue work was
inaugurated eight or nine years ago, and now they have
eight homes in as many cities. A shelter for women
with a nursery attached, and also a shelter for children.
During the past year 514 girls have been received into
these homes; of these only 38 were known to have defi-
nitely gone back to vice, while a very large portion of
the remainder were sent to situations, changed in their
right minds. Three hundred and thirty-six children
passed through the Children's Shelter. The Women's
Shelter supplied 4,945 beds and 3,681 meals. One sad

feature of all this rescue work is that no matter how many homes are established, nor how many are saved by their influence, still they are continually kept filled. The cause remains, the wrong is with us, and while rescue work is essential and Christly, we are convinced that education and legislation is even more so.

In the city of Toronto, in connection with its police, there is a work done in the interest of purity unique in police methods. Toronto is a city of 200,000. It has only 150 saloons strictly closed on the Sabbath, and no street cars run on the Lord's day. But there is one de-partment of police work of special interest to purity workers. It is known as the morality department, and is placed in charge of one of the most experienced officers, a Christian gentleman of influence in the city and country, Staff Inspector Archibald. This depart-ment was inaugurated in February, 1886. The duties given to this officer and his staff are "To enforce laws relating to the sale of liquors illicitly and houses of ill fame and assignation; to suppress gambling, lotteries and prize fighting; to regulate baby farming establish-ments; to prosecute for indecent exposure, cruelty to women, children or animals, desecration of the Sabbath, immorality of all kinds, and generally to deal with all cases of a domestic nature requiring police intervention." At the time of the appointment it was said that in the city were about fifty houses of ill fame and equally as many disorderly houses. While to-day we do not deny that there is prostitution, no doubt there are houses where fornication is carried on, yet there is not a known house of ill fame that can keep its establishment open as such. The women that persist are of the lowest grade and gravitate between the court room, jail and street with not more than an average of twenty days upon the street. But the best part of this officer's work is not heard in court nor seen in print. He is the friend of the girl who desires to reform; he is the counsellor of the ill treated wife, the deserted child and the troubled mother. Any or all of these in need may turn to his office. It is often more like the office of a city mission than a police office. The Christian agencies in the city work in harmony with the Inspector. He may be feared, perhaps hated, by the determinedly vile and vicious, but he is respected and trusted by those who, appreciating counsel, would without him suffer greater ruin and misery. In this respect we believe the police methods of Toronto have shown how at one and the same time the law can be made a "terror to evil doers and a praise to those who do well."

What is our situation to-day? Our people are perhaps as moral as any other people, but we feel the indifference of our legislators and also of a large part of our people to the importance of a proper age of consent and to the one standard of morals. Our work for the present must be largely educational. The public conscience has to be reached. The youth have to be taught. "The White Life for two" has to be insisted upon. We may, perhaps, lead others in the matter of prohibition. We are ready to learn from others in methods of work for social purity.

M. L. HOLBROOK

ALCOHOL AND CHASTITY.

By M. L. HOLBROOK, M. D.

In presenting what I have to say on the subject of this paper I will be very brief and not try to go over all the ground that might be traversed. Any one who is interested in the subject can easily do this. The Bible and many historical and temperance works, and even the common observations of most persons, tell the story of shame caused by strong drink. What I desire to say will be presented in another way than this subject is usually discussed, but I hope not on this account less useful.

It is now generally admitted by scientists that man has come to his present state by a process called Evolution, that is, development from lower forms to higher ones, or from simple forms to more complex ones. In this process of evolution there has been added new functions and new powers as they were required by the necessities of his life and his environment. And it is one of the fundamental laws of being that newly acquired traits are not so firmly fixed or established in the nature of man as the older or first acquired ones.

It is believed by our phsychologists that one of the last acquirements of man is the power of self control.

Let us stop a moment to inquire what self control is and how useful it has been and can be to us. If we study animals and low organisms we may see that the power to control their own acts is wanting or nearly so. Let any one observe for an hour under his microscope living micro organisms, and what will he behold ? Endless movement, perfectly meaningless to him. They rush along the line of least resistance without the slightest control of their acts. It is an automatic movement.

With insects it is the same. Does the silk worm say, now I will make a cocoon and undergo my transformations in it, or, I will not make one, but go and enjoy myself in some other way? Nothing of the sort. It makes it under the law of its instinct without any volition of its own. When the time comes it *must spin* it whether it will or no. The reflex actions of its complicated nervous system compel it to do this just as surely as the laws of gravity acting on a ball unsupported in the air forces it back to the earth. It cannot say, " I will not, but I will do something else."

Do the bees or the butterflies plan out and control their movements as they go from flower to flower? Do they stop to reflect before they visit a blossom, or say, we will gather no more nectar to-day? No, they are guided by an instinct—see them fly through the air, now this way, now that. They have manifestly no power of controlling their own lives, or directing their own ways.

When it comes to higher animals, the horse, the dog, the bull and cow, there may be slight intimations of self mastery, but they are slight indeed.

With man, however, the case is different. He has had a story or several of them added to his intellect. It takes in a wider range, a larger view. *Man has developed the power of self control. He takes charge of his own life* and his own conduct. He is able to say, I will do this, for it is wise; I will not do that, for it is unwise. Even though his desires prompt him to do one thing, he can by this inhibitory power given by self control, hold himself back and do something far different, something actually disagreeable, painful. He can even plan out a course of action which will continue for years and hold himself up to it during a long life. With most successful men and women, in whatever field, this is the case. We can hardly estimate how very valuable it has been for them to do this. We get some notion of the use of this new power by comparing a man whose whole life has been aimed at the accomplishment of some noble work and the one who has no aim, but is carried about by the whims and caprices of the hour. Can any animal take its life under control as man can? No, not even the highest ape and hardly the lowest man.

I said in the beginning this power of self control has been one of the last acquired by man and that it has not been so firmly fixed in his nature as some other of his faculties, as that of the desire for food, for air, for procreation. It is not constant as these desires are in the healthy individual. Many persons have it in a low degree, and by just so much come short of having the full stature of men and women; they yield to their likes and dislikes, their whims and caprices, their passions and temptations, even when their best judgment tells them that it is not wise to do so. The inebriate is a good illustration. He does not control his appetite for drink, often cannot. The glutton is another. Our insane asylums are full of men and women who have lost all control over their own minds and they think and act wildly, disorderly, unreasonably.

The sexual impulses are less under our control than they should be, often even in those who otherwise live well ordered lives. These impulses are very important and will be so as long as reproduction of the race must go on. The greatest good as well as the greatest evils results from them. There is no use in denying this. But as the evolution of man goes on, these impulses should and must more and more come under self control. If social purity is ever to make any headway this new power in man's character, new comparatively only, must have a far larger influence on his sexual life. Without probably looking at it from this point of view, this is what the organization convened here is for, to induce men and women to place their sexual nature under the guidance of reason, of conscience, of hygiene.

Now, if I am right in what I have said, anything that makes it harder, or impossible to keep a mastery over one's own nature, is a positive evil, and it is here the relation of what I have said to the use of alcohol comes in. Do alcoholic drinks increase or diminish man's self control over any part of his nature? If they increase it, then they are in this respect a positive good. If any food or drinks can be discovered which will make man more his own master than he now is we may cease half of our efforts for reform and try to induce people to take them. Nor would it be difficult even though they might be unpalatable. But no such food or drink has been or is likely to be discovered, and as related to alcoholic drinks, they always and invariably act reversely and lessen the inhibitory power of man over his acts. If his powers in this direction are great when sober, they grow less and less the more alcohol he puts into his blood. If his powers are small in this respect a little alcohol upsets them and control is gone till nature removes the poison from his blood.

We have abundant evidence of this in that class of inebriates which are found in asylums and institutions for their treatment. If they had not lost self mastery, they would not have put themselves under the care of another to guide them back to health of body and mind.

Let me now enumerate some of the simple facts which go to show that alcohol destroys self mastery. I will take first the muscular system. In health and in the prime of life the voluntary muscles of a man whose body has had proper training are corelated into one movement of almost ideal perfection. Take a gymnast, a sleight of hand performer, a dancer, as extreme illustrations. Take even a skilled wood chopper in some of our Western forests. How perfectly the muscles of each obey the dictates of the brain. But how is it when the dancer, the gymnast, the axman are intoxicated? The power of control is lost in proportion to the degree of intoxication. No longer do the muscles obey his will, but the person reels, staggers, or falls helpless on the ground. Many of us no doubt have had slight experience of the power of alcohol to take away self control of the muscles when it has been used only medicinally and in very small quantities. For this reason it is a dangerous remedy for any one with a weak will and a tendency to evil.

The same thing happens to the mind. Under alcoholic influence the brain begins to think awry. It cannot think straight, clear. The judgment becomes warped, the intellect clouded. A man under liquor once said to me: "Do you see that horrid creature coming down from the stars with a load of snakes, throwing them left and right about the room?" It was a case of *delirium tremens*. His brain was no longer his own, it ran wild like an engine in full motion and no engineer to guide it.

Who of us would knowingly trust our lives on a railway train with an intemperate engineer? We know his judgment cannot be depended on to bring us safely to our journey's end. Many a battle has been lost, many a ship sunk, because the colonel or captain had lost control of his brain through drink.

Shakespeare tells the whole story when he says:

"Drink, and speak parrot, and squabble, and swagger, and swear, and discourse fustian with one's own shadow."

In the effect of alcohol on the moral nature, we find the same result of its taking away man's power over his own acts. Seneca said, ages ago: "Men will do many things in their drink they are ashamed of when sober. It emboldens men to do all sorts of mischief. It irritates wickedness. It was in a drunken fit that Alexander slew Clytus. It makes him who is insolent, prouder; him who was fierce, more cruel. It takes away shame. The tongue trips, the head turns round."

I have thus by degrees led up to the final point, the effect of alcohol on chastity. The sexual impulse as already stated, is one of the most powerful in man. It is necessary that it should be strong, but it is equally necessary that it should be under right guidance. There are no checks to its abuse in human beings as there are in the lower animals. Its wrong action must be prevented by self mastery, guidance. In the normal man, if he knows the benefits to health and happiness which result from chastity, he will take this part of his nature under the dominion of his reason and his better judgment. But the experience of the ages shows that intemperance, drink, alcohol has so lessened the inhibitory power which is slowly growing up in man and which distinguishes him from all lower animals, that this is impossible. Under its influence he drops back to a primal state, yes, worse than a primal state, and gives way to his impulses, whatever they may be—the very worst thing, it seems to me, that can happen to a human creature. He now becomes degenerate.

I could give abundant testimony that the use of alcoholic drinks is a cause of unchastity of no slight significance. Take it away and our houses of prostitution would have removed from them a chief prop to their activity. With the reign of universal temperance its worst forms will, I believe, disappear, and whatever of it that remained could, without doubt, be easily managed by the right kind of education, and a knowledge well grounded into our natures that happiness is the result of obedience to the laws of life and that misery comes from disobedience to the same.

THE PURE IN HEART.

BY HANNAH HALLOWELL CLOTHIER.

" Blessed are the pure in heart, for they shall see God," was the promise of the Master nearly nineteen centuries ago. Practical as His teachings ever were, it must be that this truth, as all others, He intended to apply directly to our daily lives. Not only in the far distant future are we to be called " blessed " and are we "to see God," but *now*, in the golden present, on this earth. We shall see and feel Him in all life around us, in the eyes of our fellow men as in their best efforts and undertakings. The waving of the most delicate flower in the lightest zephyr, as the prostration of the oak in the hurricane, speak to us of the Great Invisible Power of the universe, if only our hearts are pure. Just as a blur on the pane of glass affects the whole aspect of the view beyond, just so the slightest blemish on our hearts affects life for us; its glory is either revealed or hidden through the condition in which we keep our own hearts.

What is purity of heart ? Does it belong always to those whose lives receive praise before men, always to those whose actions resound the world over, always to those whom we call Christians? Sad to say it does not. Sadder still that it seems possible for men to live upright lives before their fellow men, and yet upon their hearts bear the scars and taints of guilt. Saddest of all that they should wish it to be thought they are living for God, when really they are living only for the opinions of men.

Purity of heart belongs to those who are pure, not only in the sight of men, but pure in the sight of God; to those who stand in such relationship to Him that their inmost natures could be laid bare in His sight; to those whose every motive as well as every action works in harmony with His will. There is no hardship in it all; the flower does not find it a cross to bloom, nor do the "pure in heart" find it a cross to feel, think and act under the Father's loving control. Light and darkness cannot dwell together; neither can the Spirit of God take its abode within a heart quickening ungodly feelings, impure thoughts, questionable habits, or wrong actions of any kind. There are many other attributes of our nature which might be mentioned, but I will call your especial attention to those above named, and briefly consider them in turn.

First, feelings. Here the word is used in a broad sense, signifying the state of emotions, under which head fall all the human desires and passions of the heart. Let us query. Are these given to us by nature? Do they lie entirely beyond our control? A very large part of our being they do indeed seem to be; but, before passing judgment as to their origin, let us examine closely and see what may be their quality. If they are those which tender and soften the human life, which express only the spirit of the soul, we need not fear them; they have found their proper places, and will go toward deepening and enhancing life's truest joys and happiness. If, however, they are those which seize us so strongly that they cause our lives to rise and fall, fluctuating in an alarming manner, at one time inspiring us to noble things, at another leading us to destruction, then are they dangerous, and then must we admit that we have no right to call them gifts from God which we are powerless to master. Let us rather bravely say that they have been misdirected, or, perhaps, not directed at all; that we have trusted our lives to an uncertain guide, and that in the future we shall fix our eye on a more steady power, which is able not only to oppose all barriers to its growth, but even to replace them by true aspirations and ambitions, which crave only that which is holy. May we give no depth of earth to the seeds of base feelings and desires, and they will not long remain a part of our being; even without our knowledge the chaff will be separated from the wheat.

Second, thoughts. How is it with them? Too often the mind is considered a sea whereon thoughts drift to and fro, like the vessel with no one at the helm, tossed here and there in storm and tempest, till, perchance, it becomes wrecked upon the rocks, all the while we stand as eye witnesses on the shore, helpless to aid. It is our thoughts that mould our characters. Can it be that they were intended to wander where they will, our lives partaking of all the rubbish which they encounter along the way? Perhaps we say that they come to us unawares. It is not the *coming* which is always the sin, but the being found unawares. We should have our minds under such control that at the very dawn of evil thinking we could turn it into other channels. Martin Luther said that he could not prevent the birds of the air from flying over his head, but he could prevent them from making their nests in his hair. We *can* prevent thoughts from taking their abode with us, if we so decide.

Third, habits and actions. In these days, when such poisonous trash is being circulated in our midst, it has become a stern necessity to guard well one's reading. It is not difficult for those of experience who know the danger to escape the evil, but there are the young under their care, and those beyond the warmth radiating from their own hearth, with whom the bond of common brotherhood closely links them, who are incapable of judging for themselves, and whose innocent, pure hearts are being stung by the fatal serpent. Though unharmed by it ourselves, may we remember that we are our "brother's keepers." We need only stop at some of the news stands in our large cities to realize in a mild degree this evil.

Our pleasures: where do we seek them? In the midst of those things which only result in lowering the ideal standard of purity? It is dangerous ground when the biased reasoning tries to entice us to engage in pleasures which we feel can never harm us, but which all the while are harming others. Our purity should never be so challenged. Beware, lest at a moment we know not we ourselves become tempted.

How much depends upon the company with whom we associate. There is a law of attraction which brings those of like tastes and ideals together, and our characters may often be roughly estimated from the company we keep. The more we seek those of refinement and culture, the more easy shall we find it to grow toward our highest ideals, and the less shall temptations hold us. Our social intercourse should be beneficial to ourselves and to our neighbors, and we should realize the influence surrounding our lives which goes forth to help or hinder another's progress.

In conversation, light and mirthful though it may be, and seem of little importance one way or the other what is said, there are often seeds sown in some one's heart for good or ill. A little word, a look, or, perhaps, a shrug of the shoulders, bearing an uncertain meaning, which we deem unnoticed, our neighbor catches, and its influence we can scarcely estimate. Low jesting, and everything which, if analyzed, would bring shame to the company, should be utterly discountenanced.

Men and boys, in your conversations at the club or in your own rooms, do you speak of things which your wives and mothers should not hear? Women and maidens, is your chastity ever tainted by conversing upon subjects with which you have no right to deal? May we all think sacredly of this matter, and realize its great importance.

May it be our aim to keep our conversation fitting for the angels of heaven to hear.

Who are there amongst us who have not found, in mingling with one another, the truest blessing which results from life and love? I refer to that relation of friendship with our fellow men, through whom, as Emerson expresses it, "all things take nobler form and look beyond the earth;" that close union, sealed by God's own hand, which makes all life the sweeter and softer, because it binds soul to soul in that love which "braveth all things, believeth all things, hopeth all things, endureth all things," and in which we see our friends as they are. This divine gift is one which has come down through the ages, being realized by those who have received and made the most out of life, and is open now, as always, without distinction, to those of all ages *in* both sexes and *between* both sexes. Would that the world could drop the belief that this union cannot exist, and is not advisable between man and woman, boy and girl. An earnest appeal goes forth to put aside this wrong attitude toward life, which has too long turned the world upside down and created abnormal relations between the sexes. May the boys and girls be taught to *let* their souls flow freely to and from each other, taught that they are necessary to each other's lives for their truest and highest development. The girl or woman with her gentleness will bring much to sweeten the active business life of the boy or man, and, in return, the boy or man will open to the girl or woman avenues previously closed in her experience. Did this relationship exist between young people, the happiness from the marriage bond would be assured, because it would be an outcome of a true, helpful service of soul to soul, instead of a mere excited fascination, upon which so many life unions are based, and which is often soon over, burning to ashes in the midst of the responsibilities of life.

There is much that could be said on the subject, but time for little.

As a tribute to her memory I would here speak of a lovely young girl, now passed onward, who had been taught to and did realize the possibilities of beautiful, helpful friendships with those of her opposite sex. Her marriage even did not put an end to them, and after her early death two young men, calling on her mother, with tears in their eyes and on bended knees, gave testimony to what the daughter had been to them, saying that they had never spent an evening in that parlor in company with her and gone away without feeling purified.

Who would bear the sin of taking away these friendships from "the pure in heart," and who would not strive to keep his and her heart pure in order to enjoy them?

From the sweetest thing which life has to give, we shall turn to our last topic, *work*. It may lie in the study of science, it may lie in the artist's studio, or in the service of adding to the volumes of literature; it may lie in the professional or business world, it may even lie in the more quiet walks of life within our own small family circle, ministering to the needs and pleasures of our loved ones. Wherever it be, the field will bear a harvest to those who follow the inward calling of the Master—to those who seek the work which is in the plan for them, to those who, unspotted from the taints of impurity, see God face to face. Work then becomes a joyful service wherein the heart is kept pure by reading the hidden truths as they are revealed.

Summing up in a few words we find that the spiritual ever governing the physical is the law which our lives should follow—the Christ spirit within restraining our feelings when they incline to rule us, making our desires at one with the Father's and bringing every thought into captivity to the obedience thereof. Then will all the fruits of the garden grow and ripen in their proper places, and in partaking of them life's actions will prove only those upon which the Father's blessing rests. The true and beautiful alone is countenanced—only that literature which elevates the soul, only those pleasures which are godly and healthful, only the company which stands for refinement, only that work which reflects honor.

The world is yearning for these "living temples" of the Lord who have heard and realize the glad tidings and are willing to tell them unto others. Not only in the far East, among the heathen nations; not only in the so called slums of the cities, among the lower classes; but, alas, in what is known as "respectable" society, among the higher classes, is there a glaring need for earnest missionaries—"the pure in heart," who clearly and plainly reflect the image of Him in whose likeness we are made. These are in His sight the "blessed" ones of whom the Master spoke. Armed with the breastplate of purity no occasion or circumstance could cause even the suggestion of evil. The immorality of the world they may realize, of the dark sins of their fellow-men they may be conscious, but no plague shall come nigh their dwellings, because they have made the Most High their habitation.

MARY TRAVILLA.

OUR DIVINE POSSIBILITIES.

By Mary Travilla.

In the paper just read our friend says, " Thoughts mould our characters." How these words touch a keynote in our mind and heart? For we know that when we come unto the full realization that "the essence of righteousness is right thinking," and thought always seeks embodiment then in consciousness a new earth and a new heaven is ours. And to all that are upward bound this message must have a deeper, richer significance. "Whatsoever things are pure, whatsoever things are lovely, whatsoever things are of good report, think on these things." When this command is strictly obeyed right action is the natural consequence.

If wrong thought will pull down and destroy, true thought will build up and harmonize. We grant that past thought has limited us in all directions, but by and through the operations of the Divine spirit of truth and progress we behold the dawn of a new era of thinking and living. These words, "Blessed are the pure in heart," fall upon us this golden autumn afternoon like a sweet blessing, with a truer meaning and a clearer perception than ever before. We see men more and more *freed* from the "chrysalis of self and arising on the wings of faith and enlightened knowledge," knowing that all the spiritual forces in the universe are working for good.

When we recognize the necessity of "individual thinking and individual effort for individual attainment then will we endeavor to rouse and stimulate to renewed action the eternal individuality latent in every soul."

This query arises within me: Do we accept the truth of this statement that there is the eternal individuality latent in every soul? This incident comes forcibly to my mind: One beautiful afternoon, while riding in the cars of the city of Brotherly Love, feeling in harmony with the inner melodies and in touch with the beauty of nature, a woman seated herself opposite to me and at once a blur came over the harmonious picture of my thought as I gazed upon the mass of flesh and beheld the repulsive countenance which gave forth no signs of light and love, only darkness and error reflected there. As I felt the truth of this Divine law, "As a man thinketh in his heart so is he," so from the radiation of her daily thinking and living I caught the influence and it told its own story. It was of a woman advanced in years, living off of the profits of crime, responsible in a large measure for the downfall and degradation of the young. Then there arose feelings within me that amounted almost to hatred for that woman, not only for the *sin* but for the *sinner*, and with these burning thoughts I longed to have the *right* to give expression to them.

Then from the inner side of my real life and across the silence of my heart I heard these words, "Oh, child, child, where is thy professed faith *now*, in the eternal individuality, latent in every soul? That Divine spark of love and purity thee has ever felt exists there, no matter how low in the scale of life a child is found, nor how the pictured side of their lives reveals unspoken horrors; here now is a practical test for thee." Then it seemed as if a mighty rush of love came on me, and I was enabled in the rest of the journey to behold not *only now* the distorted side of that woman, but to feel that back and through all the sin and its reflection that Divine pure self was there. God's love never fails and ever expects and *knows* that sometime, somewhere in the eternal plan, the consciousness of every soul will awaken.

Here individual thinking and effort were demanded, not alone for selfish individual attainment, but because there was a growing recognition that when we fall into line with the Divine laws of order and harmony, co-operating therewith according to our growth and understanding, we are helping to clear the darkened, impure, mental atmosphere, and bring forth into manifestation more of light; results may be very slow. "What is that to thee, follow thou Me."

God is tangible, quickening love. We must *ourselves* be conscious of this Divine love and purity before we can see it in others.

"May the boy and girl be taught to let their souls flow freely to and fro from each other, taught that they are necessary to each others lives for their truest and highest development." Then, again, "Who are there amongst us who have not found in mingling with one another the truest blessing which results from life and love?" When these words fell upon my ears how they touched the inner chord of my being, seeing the golden possibilities folded up within them. Think for a moment what it would mean if we were always willing to look for the best in our friends, knowing it is there whether they manifest it or not, feeling we can speak with frankness and freedom from heart to heart. Words not always essential, but by an intuition a silent language is understood, new powers are awakened by this truth and confidence in one another.

"Truth demands true living; no swift condemning of the evil nor the good should pass thy heart or lips. Stop thy evil thinking; speak of the pure and perfect, of the beautiful and true." As an illustration of the power of these words we give this *true* incident. A mother visits a teacher in a secular school, and tells her this story: "My boy does not stay home from school because I need him, but because he is playing truant, and associating with boys that are leading him away from the right path. I am so worried and fearful for the future. My husband is cross and out of heart. Nothing but trouble and disappointment is mine. Now, what *shall* I do?"

"Are you willing to follow faithfully for a week this advice?" she replied. "I will." "Every morning take a half hour from your work, find a quiet spot in your home, then enter into the silence of your heart. Think *only* of the mother-love you have for your boy. Dwell on the truth and beauty in his character, the pure and lovely, seeing him *free* from all error, refusing to think about his wrong doing in that God given silence. *Then* for your husband. Oh! dwell tenderly upon the early days of your love and marriage, seeing *now* the true nobility of his manhood awakening to his real self, then giving unto you all that the heart craves for and that which belongs to you. When they come home meet them with a smile and kiss, a new trust and hope in your heart, born out of that daily silence. Scold or upbraid them not, but steadily expect the best. Come to me the end of the week and tell me what success is yours."

She came, and with a new light in her eyes and a lightness in her step it told its own story of renewed hope and courage, with a complete change.

The great, noble hearted, beloved friend to all, Phillips Brooks, has said, "No man can do much for others who is not much himself." By his glorious life and example he has verified the truth of this statement. Being lifted up himself he drew all men unto him.

When we think of these noble men and women who are to-day giving their lives and service to the uplifting of humanity, helping them to find their true kingship, the Christ within, our heart overflows with thankfulness for these willing messengers. Those who have borne the heat and burden—the early pioneers of this great movement—must rejoice for the promise and hope of the future.

"Love and life go hand in hand, like the sunshine and the sun—love the sun, and life the shine. 'Tis love will break the bonds of wickedness and cruel condemnation."

MRS. ISABEL WING LAKE.

GRADED HOMES.

By Mrs. Isabel Wing Lake, of Chicago.

With such an interwoven network of impurity as there is about us, it would almost seem as if any one wolfish pitfall taken alone were enough to engulf the young of our cities if it were not bridged at once, and yet knowing as I do that this awful iniquity cannot be stamped out at will by persuasion or force, I feel we should move upon it with the utmost discretion and keenest justice. Whether to strike at the heart and reason that death at the extremities must of necessity ensue or approach it from the outskirts and work into the centre, placing sentinels at every outpost, is the point for discussion. I do not consider that I can at all benefit the handling of the subject, for I never knew so little about the remedy as since I have these many years studied the cause of this modern leprosy and its deadly results. Three things I *do* know. The sorrow, the suffering is here. Christ can and does redeem and He has commissioned me to work to this end. What is the best method to pursue ?

I cannot longer visit these poor, misguided girls in their scarlet haunts, and not know that when I tell them of my Jesus, I can show them His power to meet their every need. They should at once get away from their surroundings, old companions and temptations to sin. Alas ! too often it is impossible to find the open door for them to step into, a pure shelter, with loving and tender care. I herewith submit this plan of Seven Graded Homes, where there may be an opportunity for every class of sinning women to return if they will, to purer, truer, better things. I appeal to every true hearted woman, every man of nobility and justice, as to the wisdom of erecting a settlement of this kind on one plat of ground or scattered in the suburbs some distance one from the other.

PLAN OF GRADED HOMES.

LARGE DIFFICULTIES REQUIRE LARGE REMEDIES. — We plan to erect seven buildings, large and roomy, at a cost of $200,000. This undertaking is built upon two principles—*preventive* and *redemptive*.

1. OAK COTTAGE.—This building is to accommodate 100 girls, a dormitory of 25 cots and 30 sleeping rooms, and will cost $6,000.

Purpose.—This is to be a temporary home for pure women, those who in the desperate competition of life, friendless, alone and unprotected, can find no employment and who need a place of refuge until an industrial door opens to them. All the fearful needs involved in this proposition cannot be portrayed here. Instruction will be given in this building in Bible study and methods of mission work in the field of labor we represent. One thing can be safely said, this cottage will be no abode for the idle, as there will be in connection with each home some known industry.

2. MAPLE LODGE.—Will be a refuge for the betrayed girls; she who by being suddenly snared through drugs, deception or ignorance, cries out to us from her despair for sheltering protection. It is not to be that we, who with a stauncher craft and better pilotage, have weathered the wild storms of life, coming safely through, can refuse to heed the signals of distress from those who have made shipwreck. They cling still to the rigging, and plead to be taken off before a merciless sea pounds them into a total wreck. The industrial department will furnish employment to those physically capacitated so that they can pay, feel they are of service in the home until other employment can be found. This building and its equipments will accommodate 100 girls, and will cost about $6,000.

3. ELM NOOK.—A haven for rescued women and girls. Into this home will be gathered those who in their delirium have left home with one they felt they loved, under promise of marriage or some other deception, have been swept into the abyss, not knowing how to climb out, have gone down deeper and deeper into the mire. They swim against the tide to the great ship in which we float, and cry up to us out of the deep—Let down the lifeboat or we die.

This great building will only cost some one an annual sacrifice of $700 in interest money, or a total investment of but $10.000.

We do believe there are those who, looking at an income of $700 a year, derived from a good investment, would prefer to reinvest this sum in the institution that will provide a way of escape for these suffering ones. Cost, $10,000.

4. MOTHER'S MEMORIAL CHAPEL.—In the centre of our equipment will be the chapel to be built only by the gifts of the mothers of our land, or by gifts in memory of devoted mothers from grateful sons and daughters to pay back their debt of gratitude. Surely it will be a holy place with ever open doors to the great Father heart of God. Cost, $10,000.

5. THE NEST—FOR OUR BABIES.—We can make no statement that will describe this cradle over which the mother heart of this organization will brood. While the unwavering principle must be to keep mother and child together, still many will come under our care that need our efforts, that we may benefit the homeless child and the childless home.

The nest must be newly feathered, that these little ones, tossed helplessly on the great tide of human life, may move upward toward a home and purity of life, rather than down into the abode of crime and vice. Will this building that will shelter 200 of these little ones until they can find homes be too expensive if it cost $4,000 ?

6. THE HOSPITAL.—Like a great house of mercy, every brick laid and each cot spread by generous impulses, this noble building will help untold multitudes.

1st Wing.—The convalescing shop girl may recuperate here, and this wing of the hospital will stand between the city hospital and the city brothel to intercept the flow of a great stream of human life that dashes down over this cataract.

2nd Wing.—That great army—slaves of drink or inebriates of any nature—thinking to suicide thought, or quiet the torture of physical pain, they stand at our door—chained women—waiting for a liquor or opium cure or a drunkard's grave.

3rd Wing.—MATERNITY CASES.—Forsaken, poverty pinched and forlorn. This ward will protect the mothers for a time. Rob the average midwife of a suffering victim, stop the discharge in two days or two weeks after confinement to desolate rooms, save the little one, giving it opportunities for health and happiness as God intended, and drive the procuress elsewhere for girls, when we save the child mother from her grasp. Can money be invested for eternity in a more telling, far-reaching way?

4th Wing. — CONTAGIOUS DISEASES. — Sheltering many who would, if thrown broadcast through our city, ruin untold numbers. The hospital will be built with four wings, the body of which will accommodate ordinary diseases.

7. DINING HALL.—A two story building carrying all the culinary equipments. Cost, $3,000.

THE BEEHIVE.

A.—In this side settlement can be a sewing room for some line of fancy work, or otherwise, some light labor for those unable temporarily to perform arduous work.

B.—A paper box factory.

C.—Steam laundry.

D.—Conservatory for winter roses, vegetables, &c.

E.—Raising of chickens and all industries that a woman can engage in.

1st—Class in Physical Culture, Indian clubs, &c.

2nd—Class in Cooking.

3rd—Class in General Nurse Work or Kitchen Garten.

4th—Class in Kinder Garten.

5th—Class in Dressmaking.

6th—Class in Stenography and Telegraphy.

7th—Class in Typesetting.

8th—Class in Book Binding.

9th—Class in Photography and Retouching.

10th—Class in Designing and Carving.

11th—Class in Bookkeeping.

Help us help the helpless.

B. O. FLOWER.

SOME CAUSES OF PRESENT DAY IMMORAL ITY AND SUGGESTIONS AS TO PRACTICAL REMEDIES.

————

By B. O. Flower, Editor of The Arena.

In the brief space assigned me, it would be impossible to touch upon the numerous complex and often subtle causes of present day immorality. I shall, therefore, only briefly notice a few of these wellsprings of death which impress me as being fundamental in character. These I would classify as follows:

I. Prostitution within the marriage bond, or a disregard of the sacred right of the wife and child.

II. Prostitution without the marriage relation.

III. The influence of the liquor traffic.

IV. Unjust social conditions.

V. The lack of knowledge and the absence of high ideals in the mind.

VI. The popular acceptation of the pernicious idea of the "double standard of morals," which in effect pollutes youth, leads to legislation fostering lust, and in other ways proves a positive barrier to moral progress.

I. Prostitution Within the Marriage Bond.— I place prostitution within the marriage bond, involving the sacred rights of the wife and the child, and the obligation to posterity which this evil comprehends, at the opening of this discussion, because through ignorance and thoughtlessness, perhaps, as much as to the supremacy of passion over man's sense of justice above the voice of conscience, wifehood is being debased, childhood is being poisoned, and the society of to-morrow is being corrupted, and this evil will continue to exert a baleful influence until knowledge is forced upon the attention of men and women, and a strenuous appeal is made to the conscience of men in behalf of the wife and the unborn. To me it appears that this phase of the question is of paramount importance, because it embraces the powerful though subtle complex and inter-blending influences of heredity prenatal, and, to a great degree, postnatal causes, as they relate to the oncoming generation, no less than the disregard for sound and wholesome morality, necessarily injurious in influence to the thought world and physical condition of the wife and mother. So long as passion sways reason, and people recklessly or thoughtlessly call little ones into the world, we will find a large percentage of the oncoming generation children of lust rather than welcome offsprings of love. They come into the world so strongly endowed with passional instincts that the balance wheel of reason is powerless to control them, and even the solemn voice of conscience fails to arrest them when the sensual nature is aroused.

I hold that until we recognize that woman has the right of her body, and until parents are made to feel that the bringing of an unwelcome child into the world is a major crime, the work of social redemption will necessarily progress at a lame and halting gait inasmuch as we will have allowed one of the greatest feeders of immorality to remain in operation, and though, like the man Christian beheld in "Pilgrim's Progress," who continued to throw water on a fire only to see it burn the brighter, our work will be largely disappointing, because the fires of sensualism will be constantly fed from an untouched reservoir of death, precisely as in the case in "Pilgrim's Progress" the flame was constantly nourished by one behind the furnace who poured oil on the fire. We must educate and agitate, we must appeal to the conscience of the people, we must demand in the name of the individual, of the nation and of civilization, that the child of the future shall be *well born.*

307

II. Prostitution Without the Marriage Bond. —I have no sympathy with the threadbare, and, in my opinion, thoroughly vicious plea, which urges that prostitution always has existed, always will exist, and, therefore, the best thing is to license and place it under the supervision of medical officials. This that an evil has ever existed and must, therefore, always prevail, has been the slogan of the children of night in every battle for the abolition of giant evils which man has waged in the history of civilization. The overthrow of chattel slavery, and, indeed, every victory for humanity, has been won in face of this plea of a soul deadening materialism, which ignores the very principles of human progress, and seems to find in man nothing beyond the animal. I know the claims which are advanced. We are assured that by licensing this evil it can be confined within certain bounds, and that wives and children will stand a better chance of escaping the most loathsome of diseases frequently contracted by married men who patronize houses of ill fame. The premises on which these assumptions are based are false, and the conclusions deducted are no less erroneous, which will be seen by a careful survey of the subject. We are assured that by licensing prostitution we can restrict the evil to certain locations, and better restrain it. Let us see. We will suppose a certain colony of moral lepers is districted off in one of our large cities. No one is allowed to live there and ply her trade unless she has a clean bill of health from the examining officer. Here is special security granted by government to the adulterous among the married men or the licentiously disposed among the unmarried, but there is no protection afforded the prostitutes which might shield them against those whose blood is poisoned with the virus of the most loathsome diseases. Hence, with each recurring week, numbers of those unfortunates would be refused a certificate, provided the officers observed their oath, and, consequently, be legally prohibited from plying their trade. These unfortunates would rapidly multiply, as they have multiplied in Paris and other cities, where the cause of sound morality has been surrendered to sensual supremacy and a shortsighted expediency, and in time they would necessarily find lodgment within the poorer and more wretched parts of the city. Having no other possible means of earning a livelihood, with society constituted as it is at the present time, they would be driven to plying their loathsome trade in a clandestine manner, and thus the virus of disease would rapidly be disseminated among the working classes and the exiles of society, while the licensed colony would be weekly recruited from above so as to fill the quota required to gratify the rapidly increasing traffic in vice. Any law which would license prostitution might well be entitled *a law for encouraging adultery and licentiousness.* And just here let me point out another fact which must be borne in mind. There is unquestionably a large number of unmarried men who are restrained from patronizing houses of prostitution from fear of one of two things: (1) that the houses may be raided by the police and they dragged before the court, and thus be disgraced, if not ruined in their social standing; (2) they are restrained from fear of contracting disease; but once license these houses and you relieve both these restrictive influences, with the result that prostitution would not only be increased and the demand for healthy girls be greatly augmented, but also it would inevitably increase the percentage of sexual maniacs among the generations of to-morrow; for fathers thus polluted from continual carnivals of lust and the accompanying dissipation would necessarily, according to the inexorable law of heredity, transmit, in a large number of cases, an almost insatiable passion to their children. Moreover, the evil effects upon the young men would be immeasurable. There are thousands upon thousands of boys and youths who are thoughtless, and, to a degree, reckless. They cannot be said to have "come to themselves " as yet; but they have a wholesome dread of contracting a disease as terrible and loathsome as leprosy, and this fear unquestionably oftentimes restrains them until they come to that time in life when moral responsibilities appeal to them. Now, had the sensual gained supremacy before this maturity of soul life, they would have been weakened in body, brain and spirit— too weak in many instances to heed the warning voice of conscience.

Moreover, we must remember the futility which has attended the iniquitous attempts at licensing prostitution. Dr. Arthur K. Stone, in a thoughtful address recently delivered before the Boston Society for Medical Improvement, gave some admirable facts collated from recent authorities along this line. He called attention to the fact that "the Prefect of Police in Paris admitted to Dr. Lassar, of Berlin, who had been sent by the German government to investigate the methods of control in Paris, that there were fully *one hundred thousand prostitutes in Paris*," although this estimate simply included women who had no regular means of support except their ill famed profession. Some very significant facts in relation to the claim that licensing prostitution would be in the interest of health are also given. The eminent German physician, Dr. Blaschko, of Berlin, stated, in the course of a very thoughtful paper, that "from the standpoint of public hygiene no benefit was received whatever from the control as then practiced. In Paris Dr. Vidal, of the Hospital St. Louis, which is the centre of skin diseases of all Paris and France, states that the number of syphilitic patients is daily increasing. Professor Leon le Fort, of the Hospital du Midi, and Professor Fournier and Dr. Mauriac all express the same views." "Dr. Passavant, of Paris, is quoted as saying that out of every hundred inscribed women thirty-five to fifty per cent. have venereal disease. Dr. Fiaux shows that in Belgium in 1881-1889, one half of the inmates of the licensed houses had to be sent to the hos-

pitals for treatment with venereal disease, of whom
about fifty per cent. were syphilitic." These facts are
exceedingly important, going far toward confuting the
strongest and most plausible claims which have been advanced in favor of licensing prostitution. Dr. Stone
also refers to the eminent French Minister, Guyot, who
has made an extensive study of this subject, and has
written an able work on prostitution. This savant has
reached the conclusion that abolition is the proper thing.
He urges that "prostitution is a moral and personal
question, and there is no good reason why it should be
recognized by protecting law." Had I space I should like
to notice this question from the humanitarian point of
view, pointing out its essential inhumanity, and showing
how intimately it is connected with the old idea that
woman's rights and interests are thoroughly secondary
to man's; but I deem it far more important at the
present time to point out some facts which may prove
helpful in the pending conflict which I believe to be
inevitable. The voice which calls for the licensing of
prostitution issues from the black cave of sensual
materialism, and insults every divine impulse in man.

III. THE INFLUENCE OF STRONG DRINK.—A gentleman recently insisted that if the liquor traffic could be
swept from our civilization, the tap root of prostitution
would be severed. But I am not prepared to accept
such a sweeping statement ; nevertheless, I am profoundly convinced that the abolition of the sale of intoxicants as beverages would result in an almost inconceiv-
able diminution in all the train of evils which spring
from immorality as well as crime; and in this connection
I desire to quote a recent utterance of the eminent
French physician, Dr. Motet, made in the Academy of
Medicine. In discussing the influence of strong drink
upon humanity, he affirmed that "the prison statistics
show that fifty-three per cent. of the murderers, fifty-
seven per cent of the incendiaries, seventy per cent. of
the beggars and tramps, fifty-three per cent. of those

convicted for crimes against morality, and ninety per cent. of the men committed for assault are the victims of alcoholism." A great number of prostitutes who have been rescued have declared that the life they led would have been impossible were it not for constant stimulation afforded by wine and liquor; and it is a known fact that libertines, as a rule, resort largely to alcoholic stimulants to fire their passions. That with the banishment of the saloon, prostitution and all kindred phases of immorality would be greatly reduced, is a fact about which there can be no question. But how to attain this desirable end in face of the enormous power wielded by the liquor interest, organized as it is, and representing vast wealth, with its iron grasp on the great political parties, and its influence more or less obvious upon the press and the pulpit, is a problem which calls for the serious attention of thoughtful people, especially when we remember the slow progress— if we may so term the record—of recent years made by prohibition. To me it appears as though the liquor power was becoming more firmly intrenched with each succeeding election, while the growth of temperance sentiment does not indicate that awakening of the general conscience which must speedily take place if the liquor interest is to be checked in its attempt to control and subvert the government. Therefore, I believe that all thoughtful reformers should give serious attention to two proposed remedies which have been recently advanced, and which would unquestionably destroy "the rum power in politics," a result absolutely necessary, in my judgment, before prohibition can be rendered possible. These proposed remedies are (1) the State control of the liquor traffic *without profits ;* (2) the Gottenburg plan, modified to suit our social and political conditions, and shorn of any profits above a minimum interest on the money invested. In each case I would insist that all additional money accruing from the sales of liquor be used in educating and disseminating a knowledge of the evils of alcohol upon the human system, upon the brain and moral nature, and upon society in general, 'and in the establishment of homes for the cure of those who are already confirmed inebriates. These propositions, I say, merit the attention of thoughtful temperance people, because they are steps that are distinctly in the direction of prohibition. I should under no circumstances favor the governmental control of the liquor traffic if the profits went to the reduction of taxes, as that would tend to fasten the system *permanently* upon the government. Still, with the proper safeguard thrown around the State control, or the Scandinavian system properly modified so as to eliminate all features which might tend to make it permanent, the result could not fail, in my judgment to destroy the liquor power as an organized evil, and after its destruction the triumph of temperance would be assured. I believe that the adoption of one of these plans by temperance workers would result in bringing about efficient prohibition many generations earlier than it would be possible to effect it if we continue to pursue our present course, and since the liquor traffic is a large factor in producing immorality this question certainly challenges the consideration of all persons interested in social purity.

IV. UNJUST SOCIAL CONDITIONS.—Wherever we find the slums of cities annually enlarging their borders and poverty becoming diffused on the one hand and great wealth being rapidly concentrated on the other, it matters not whether it be through inheritance, unearned increment, or any other form of special privilege, or through gambling, we will find a condition which produces immorality at the nadir and zenith of society, and from these extremes the poison rises from beneath and percolates from above until it infects civilization throughout all its ramifications. In precisely the proportion that a people disregard the Golden Rule, ignore justice and substitute a baleful artificiality for sturdy simplicity, immorality increases. Extreme wealth produces too frequently indolence, high living, the indulgence in wines and liquors, all of which tend to deaden the conscience and stimulate the sensual in man's nature, while the poor, huddled together in overcrowded tenements, lose to a great extent that refinement and modesty so necessary to the development of virtue, and the multitudes of poor girls who are forced to make a living and who are underpaid, too frequently find themselves at the mercy of their employers or are driven through insufficient wages to add to their earnings by yielding to the demands of the men who possess means or influence. All this acts as a poison upon society, subtle in its workings it may be, but none the less fatal to any civilization which is so blinded by selfishness as to silence the demands of justice, ignore reason and conscience for expediency or policy. It is, therefore, clearly the duty of all social reformers to work for the establishment of an equality of opportunities or the enthronement of altruism where greed and selfism now prevail.

V. THE LACK OF KNOWLEDGE AND THE ABSENCE OF HIGH IDEALS IN THE MIND.—There is a profound truth in the old scriptural saying, "As a man thinketh in his heart, so is he." The imagination is the garden of destiny and the ideals it receives and holds, together with the influence of heredity and prenatal causes largely determines whether the child is to become an honor or a disgrace to himself and to society. It is difficult to estimate the influence of ideals upon the young during the formative period when the mind is still plastic. A great mistake, however, has been made by well meaning but shortsighted people, who, fearing the dissemination of wholesome and necessary knowledge, have not only attempted to enforce the old time idea of silence in regard to the diffusion of physiological facts of utmost importance but have gone so far as to persecute high minded persons who manifestly have been actuated only by the highest possible impulses. These would be censors frequently so confuse the pure with the impure and essential knowledge with evil or pernicious concepts that a guilty silence which is passed current for modesty continues to foster that ignorance, which is a bulwark of lust and which is diametrically opposed to the sturdy morality born of wholesome knowledge. I hold that it is the duty of parents and teachers to instruct their children in regard to the sacred functions of the sexual organism and the holy character of the responsibility devolving on them. This done let the children be shown how vile a thing it is to debase that which is sacred and holy. Let in the light of knowledge, warn them of the pitfalls, and then show them that it is their sacred duty to keep their mind filled with the highest, purest and holiest ideals. They must be shown that those who revel in low imaginings debase their whole nature, weaken their conscience, enervate their mind and sap the vitality of the physical nature, while on the other hand those who dwell in the higher realms of love and spirituality soon triumph over the sensual propensities and come into the enjoyment of the loftiest pleasures known to man, the pleasure which flows from enjoyment of spirituality. If the parents or trusted teacher, however, is silent or equivocates when approached by the child upon the delicate questions under consideration, he soon learns from base and unworthy sources half truths vilely put which color all the thought images with sensualism. Knowledge and a free discussion of a wholesome character is essential to the highest morality, but great emphasis should always be placed on encouraging and cultivating the purest thoughts and noblest ideals. In this connection I wish to say a word in regard to the danger of shortsighted, arbitrary or partisan action of postal authorities, or those who assume to guard public morals, in regard to the disseminating of literature supposed to come under the postal law, because I believe in some instances the cause of sound morality has been greatly retarded by unwarranted action which, to say the least, outraged the fundamentals of justice and seemed to take on the aspect of persecution based on personal or political spite or religious intolerance. I have time for but one illustration, but it will serve to emphasize the point I wish to make. Rev. Joshua Caldwell, the editor of the *Christian Life*, a man whom from all I can gather is noble minded, single hearted and engrossed with a desire to elevate civilization by purifying morals at the fountain head, in one of the issues of his paper published a sermon by a Congregationalist clerygyman dealing with marital purity. While this discourse would probably prove unwelcome to many men who, while prostituting their wives, are loud in their protestations for social purity, it was nevertheless a noble plea by a Christian clergyman for higher moral concepts in the marital relation, a sermon which, in my judgment, should be read by every married couple in the land. Some time after this the Rev. Caldwell criticised the postal department and some persons who had been particularly active in persecuting men who were single hearted and were striving to elevate morals but who had possibly come within the letter of the law by the employment of coarse and repulsive terms. Then it was that the editor of the *Christian Life* was arrested. He plead in vain for clemency at the hands of his persecutors—it was alleged that the sermon he had printed *eleven months before was obscene.* Now it is a fundamental principle of law that the intent of the accused should be taken into account, but this wholesome and almost universally recognized demand of justice was entirely ignored by the postal authorities and the censors of morals who were implicated in this case, though such ignoring of essential justice was inevitably prejudical to sound morality. When the case came up for adjudication it was promptly dismissed by the court as not coming within the meaning of the law, but for five months this poor clergyman had suffered the awful suspense which a refined nature of this character would necessarily undergo not knowing what the outcome of the case might be. He was also compelled to spend his little all in legal expenses in order to save him from the fate of a felon, although his only offence (?) was a sincere endeavor to elevate the standard of morals and a frank criticism of the action of our would be censors of public morals. This poor man had no redress for the wrongs done him or for the financial injury he sustained, while certainly the cause of morality, no less than the fundamental principles of justice, suffered a positive injury through the ill advised and arbitrary action of those concerned in the case. I have cited this illustration to show how dangerous it is to entrust the momentous problems of morality to persons who are lacking in that broad and judicial quality of mind which lifts a man above petty, personal spite, partisan bias, or the unreasoning prejudice of dogma and creed. I am thoroughly convinced that the cause of morality has, in some instances, been greatly retarded during recent years by the indiscriminate action of those in authority, and the probability is that unless a more judicial, just and discriminating spirit is exhibited in the future there will be one of those tremendous reactions in public sentiment which will prove unfortunate in another way for the cause of social purity. It is absolutely necessary that a wholesome dissemination of knowledge regarding the sexual functions and the dangers which beset the young should accompany the insistence of high, noble and inspiring ideals if sturdy morality is to take the place of that vicious mock modesty which shrinks from the august duty devolving upon all high minded parents and teachers, and which comprehends the instructions in sexual morality. *Purity through knowledge, not innocence through ignorance*, is the supreme demand of to-day, and with that knowedge let us sow the mind with the seeds of lofty spirituality, ever placing before the young the highest ideals.

VI. THE DOUBLE STANDARD OF MORALS is another fundamental cause of present day immorality. Generations after generations of men indulging in licentiousness as a recognized prerogative of their sex, forgetting that they tincture their offsprings with the poison which colors their thought world and courses through their veins, and that their daughters, as well as their sons, must necessarily in time become morally enervated, is responsible for much of the immorality which flourishes on all sides to-day. It is from this false though popular dictum, that is known as the double standard of morals, which furnishes the cases upon which the vicious "wild oat theory" rests, and we find our young men poisoning their imaginations, polluting their souls, enervating their will power and corrupting their blood by wild debauchery and unrestrained licentiousness, after which, with the sanction of conventional society, they marry virtuous girls and curse civilization with morally tainted progeny. This same thoroughly immoral idea is also responsible for legislation fostering lust, such for example as the Age of Consent laws, and for the lack of adequate statutory punishment for the betrayal and seduction of the ignorant and innocent. I am perfectly aware of the sophistry which is advanced to support this wellspring of death, but like the pleas urged in advocacy of other evils which are essentially unjust or immoral, it rests for its support upon prejudice and passion instead of reason, progress and the right. We must demand one standard of morals and that a "white life for two."

These are some of the principal or fundamental causes of immorality against which it is important that we direct our united energies, for I am convinced that there are hard battles to be fought in the near future. The forces of corruption are firmly entrenched and are alarmed; they will resort to all resources at their command and not infrequently will assume the livery of conventional morality to prevent the progress of purity.

But the powers of light are with us, the conscience of civilization is becoming awakened, and I believe that we are entering on an era of moral regeneration which will not only save our civilization but lift humanity to a nobler plane than man has hitherto occupied.

THE RELATION OF THE PRESS AND THE STAGE TO PURITY.

By Josiah W. Leeds, of Philadelphia.

I have often wondered at the singular inconsistency of a great many people in condemning woman's appearance in public as a preacher of the Gospel of salvation, while at the same time welcoming her upon the theatre boards to disport in immodest attire for their entertainment. Yet it is only within the last two centuries—in other words, since the time of the dissolute Charles the Second, of England, and Louis the Fourteenth, of France—that the public's sense of propriety has so far weakened as to tolerate this degrading innovation of woman's appearance as a stage dancer and actress.

Some years ago I asked the nominee for Mayor of a large city, in view of the scandal arising because of certain impure stage spectacles which had recently been given, whether he would not be willing (his election being assured) to refuse licenses to the theatre and opera companies which presented the ballet. He replied, in effect, that the ballet was now a tolerated or recognized performance in connection with the amusements of all civilized countries, and he did not feel that he could with propriety set himself against the practice. A little later I noticed his name published as director of a theatre in the city of which he was Chief Magistrate, and hence felt sure that he would stand very firmly by the unencouraging opinion that he had privately expressed to me.

In India and the Orient generally it is only those women who have lost their good name who will consent to appear as actresses or dancers upon a public stage. In Dr. Butler's "Land of the Veda" I find a paragraph of information with appropriate comment upon this matter, which I here introduce. He says, in referring to the Nautch Girls:

"No man in India would allow his wife or daughter to dance, and as to dancing with another man, he would forsake her forever as a woman lost to virtue and modesty if she were to attempt it. In their observation of white women there is nothing that so much perplexes them as the fact that fathers and husbands will permit their wives and daughters to indulge in promiscuous dancing. No argument will convince them that the act is such as a virtuous female should practice, or that its tendency is not licentious. The prevalence of the practice in 'Christian' nations makes our holy religion—which they suppose must allow it—to be abhorred by many of them, and often it is cast in the teeth of our missionaries when preaching to them. But what would these heathens say could they enter our opera houses and theatres, and see the shocking exposure of their persons which our public women there present before mixed assemblies! Yet they would be ten times more astonished that ladies of virtue and reputation should be found there, accompanied by their daughters, to witness the sight, and that, too, in the presence of the other sex! But then, they are only heathens, and don't appreciate the high accomplishments of Christian civilization! Still, Heaven grant that the future Church of India may ever retain at least this item of the prejudices of their forefathers!"

So far, Dr. Butler, whose testimony and whose arraignment of this stumbling product of our civilization was very lately strongly reinforced by the unflattering criticisms of Nasrulla Khan, the rather unwelcome Afghan visitor to England. So shocked was he at what he deemed the disreputable reception apparel of the London society ladies, that when he finally overcame his hesitancy and entered the drawing room, he declined to take in to supper the titled lady assigned to his care because she was in decolleté dress.

And whence do these fashions that so please the world generally, originate? "The Paris stage," said a recent writer in speaking of some of the much affected styles of female attire, "is the originator of fashions in the female dress. The costumes of the actresses in the Comedie Francaise are those usually copied by the society leaders of Paris, and when these ladies adopt a style the whole world follows suit."

It may be remembered by some that a few years ago a certain American Opera Company or National Opera Company (I believe it was known by both of these names) visited successively the large cities of the Union, bringing out a pretentious but very immoral class of spectacular pieces, and becoming notoriously advertised on that account. The managers of the Company, however, made out to overshoot the mark of indecency, its would-be patrons apparently being ashamed to be seen visiting so admittedly vile a show, so that the concern was forced after a short career either to wind up its affairs or to seek for patronage upon a somewhat less shameless basis. Let it here be observed that there are those rated high up in society who scruple not to attend a place of diversion where the character of the entertainment is sensuous and highly demoralizing, provided there is an abundance of respectability to keep them company and in countenance, and to stand by them in condoning the evil. When the fact of the badness becomes notorious, and it may appear in "bad form" to attend, considerations of mere expediency may then operate with sufficient strength to keep a considerable percentage of these pleasure seekers away. But self respect, force of example, loyalty to the Holy One, and bearing His cross, do not seem to be taken seriously into the account.

Now, when this ill famed National Opera Company moved upon Philadelphia in the Winter of 1886-7, and heralded its demoralizing entertainments as about to be given at the Academy of Music, the writer of this paper believed it his duty to call the attention of the several Monday morning ministers' meetings to the coming of the plague, and to ask their co-operation in withstanding its spread. They all took action. Some of the newspapers were not overmuch pleased at this interference. A reporter of one of the papers, however, had admitted that the spectacle was "sensuous and debasing," and that the posturing, etc., of the dancers in their immodest, scant attire, was "simply revolting." Yet the leading editorial in another morning paper alluded to the representation as " a graceful and pleasing exhibition, and not at all immoral in its nature and tendencies, as Mr. Leeds imagined," and advised that he and the ministers should view for themselves the entertainment complained of. This advice was not followed; instead, the editor was confronted with his contemporary's very damaging admission of the immoral character of the play.

With the exception of the *Journal of Commerce*, of New York, founded years ago by the philanthropic Arthur Tappan, under the conditions that it issue no edition on the first day of the week, and print no playhouse advertisements, I do not know of any daily paper in our cities that does not issue the invitations to those seductive resorts. Of one paper reputed amongst the best (and such, I am free to say, it is), I can certify that it nevertheless has printed year by year the advertisements of theatres which make a specialty of bringing out sensuous plays or spectacles. The *Mail and Express*, of New York, is, in the main, a good paper, and it assumes to be run on a Scripture basis of carefulness, but when I read awhile ago its Bible text for the day— it was that passage of Paul's Epistle to Timothy admonishing to "flee youthful lusts "— while at the same time the paper contained special notice of a spectacular stage representation at which were to be troops of bewitching young ballet dancers, I could but feel that the best of books had been contemned, and the way had been indicated toward indulgence in those "hurtful lusts which drown men in destruction and perdition."

Neither of the papers above referred to publishes a Sunday edition, but those that do this devote large space, as we know, in the issues for that day, to theatre news and to stage gossip and scandal. The advertising is well paid for; it constitutes a perennial source of income to the papers' proprietors, and it will hardly be given up for a mere scruple—not even for the scruple of the editor, who may find it difficult at times to reconcile such advertising with his moral advice to the readers. The eminent London preacher, Newman Hall, recently said: "I know a gentleman who was the editor of one of our leading daily papers, a goodly man. He resigned. I asked him why. He told me it was because of the continual advertisements of the theatres, and the favorable comment always made by the theatrical critic. He could not stop the advertisements as editor, and therefore he gave up a very lofty and lucrative position because of the character of the theatres, and the way they were advertised and praised in the London newspapers."

"My father in his youth," Dr. Hall further says, "frequently acted at theatres, and when he became a Christian his whole soul revolted against the theatre as he had known it. He then became the proprietor of the best country newspaper in Kent, [but] would not advertise the theatrical companies which came to Maidstone. It was a great sacrifice, for the theatres pay very well."

Obviously the stage is well entrenched behind and well protected by the daily papers—the popular magazines, likewise, being in large degree its valuable supporters. In the latter connection I recall that one day last Summer, while waiting at the house of a clergyman for the latter to appear, I looked through three of the magazines of the day that were on the parlor centretable, and they each contained an article about favorite actresses, copiously illustrated, and in many cases sensuously so. It must be acknowledged that in many clergymen's congregations a large proportion of the members or communicants patronize the playhouse. Applicable just here is the query of the prophet of old to unfaithful Israel: "And now what hast thou to do in the way of Egypt, to drink the waters of Sihor? or what has thou to do in the way of Assyria, to drink the waters of the river?"

One of the most convincing statements that I ever read in proof of the position that the theatre is not a safe school of morals, was furnished by an article upon "Divorces of the Stage," written by a theatre goer who had given a great deal of attention to the domestic life of actors and actresses. Actuated by the wish to contribute a very readable sketch, and yet not to appear to decry the profession, he apologizes for his subject with the remark, "Don't think that I belie the profession. I'll give you the cold, hard facts to prove that almost every actress of note of the day has been separated or divorced from a some-time lord and master. Tragediennes, comediennes, ingenues, soubrettes, chorus girls, ballerine—few have escaped the contagious unconnubial conditions of stage life. It has always been thus." Then follow confirmatory facts concerning about one hundred and twenty actresses of note of the several classes above given. That was a truthful comment certainly of the *Pittsburg Gazette*, that "as a furnisher of grists to the divorce mill nothing has yet been discovered equal to the stage."

Mary Anderson has lately told the world that it was the happiest day of her life when she quit the stage forever. "The best thing," says Madame Janauschek, "for a young girl to do, no matter how great she expects to become, is to keep away from the theatre, and do anything but go upon the stage. This is what I tell them all." Indeed, it was but a little while ago that she told the people of Baltimore that the key to success on the stage at present was notoriety, no matter how in-famously gained "Coarseness and sensuality," she said, "seem to be the views of our nineteenth century life. The prize ring supplies the stage with its male stars, and the divorce court supplies it with its female stars." And Frances Kemble sorrowfully wrote of the occupation: "A business which is incessant excitement and factitious emotion seems to me unworthy of man; a business which is public exhibition is unworthy of a woman."

While woman continues, as at present, that same unworthy business of dancing and disporting upon the public stage, the feeders of impure pictorial representations will thrive and their product increase.

It is the pictures of actresses and ballet dancers immodestly attired or postured, that form the staple supply of the cigarette manufacturers' pictorial advertising. One mother wrote me, with anguish, of finding such a picture in her boy's jacket that she had taken up to repair, yet such pictures are handed out, sent out, or exposed in show windows, by the million, to the corrupting of other mothers' boys. Again, it is generally the pictures of actresses and ballet dancers that contaminate the pages of a great deal of the illustrated periodical literature of the day. Still further, it is the same class of lewd pictorial representations that appear as advertisement posters of the theatres, and call forth constant protest all the land over because of their libels upon decency and pure womanhood.

Let every one claiming to be Christian or claiming to be church member cease to thirst for the dark and polluted waters of this Egypt and this Assyria, let them stay away from every debasing entertainment even though it be brought out on the boards of an Academy of Music, and I am sure that the cause of purity will witness a wonderful uplift, while paganism will no longer confound a corrupted civilization with the pure precepts and practice of the Christian religion.

DEBORAH C. LEEDS,

WHO READ TO THE CONGRESS THE PAPER BY JOSIAH
W. LEEDS.

SOCIAL PURITY—ITS RELATION TO THE DEPENDENT CLASSES.

By Mrs. Frances E. W. Harper, Philadelphia.

Friends, I need not tell you that I belong to a race which more than thirty years ago stood on the threshold of a new era. A homeless race to be gathered into homes, a legally unmarried race to be taught the sacredness of the marriage relation, and learn to plant around their firesides their strongest batteries against the sins that degrade and the vices that demoralize. It has been said that

> " The precious things of life lie all around our feet,
> It is the distant and the dim that we are sick to greet."

And I hold that no woman loves social purity as it deserves to be loved if she only cares for the purity of her daughters and not her sons; for the purity of the young girl sheltered in the warm clasp of her arms, and not for the servant girl beneath the shadow of her home. In your homes to-day are women in whose arms your babes are nestling, who are holding up their baby footsteps on your pavements, and who are leaving the impress of their hands upon your children during the impressible and formative period of their young lives; and when the degradation of one class is a menace to the peace and welfare of the other, no mistress of a home should be morally indifferent to the safety of any inmate beneath her roof, however humble her position may be. As crime has neither sex nor color, so its prevention and remedies should not be hampered by either race or sex limitations. Sometime since in one of the slums of our city I found a woman who had drifted downward. I went to a midnight Mission and asked if a colored girl

could be admitted, and was answered "no;" and yet I
do not think there was a Charity in our city that talked
more religion in its advertisement than this one. At
another time I went to that same Mission with a degraded white girl whom I had found with one or more
colored persons; for her the door was opened and a
ready admittance given. Black and white could sin
together, but they could not be rescued in that home
together. It was as if two women were caught in the
quicksands, and the deadly sands were creeping up to
their lips, while other women stood on the shore with
lifelines in their hands; to one they threw out their
ropes of deliverance, but for the other there was not one
strand of salvation. In rescuing the perishing we need
a religion which is a living power, and not a spent force.
A religion clear sighted enough to look beneath the darkened skin and see the human soul all written over with
the handmarks of Divinity and the common claims of
humanity, which recognizes in every one who steps on
the threshold of life, the child of the King. While in
these days of religious unrest, criticism and investigation some are ready to relegate the story of the Annun-
ciation to the limbo of myth and fiction, but there is a
lesson in the story which could not be received aright
into the world's great heart without making life higher,
better and more grandly significant. Has not every
prospective mother a right to ask for the overshadowing
of the same Spirit, and has not that Spirit been promised as freely as we give good gifts to our children; and
what is the use of believing in one incarnation if we
do not believe that the same Spirit may be inborn
into every soul that is open to receive it? Had all the
mothers of the present generation, when a new life was
throbbing beneath their hearts, sought and dwelt beneath the overshadowing of the Holy Spirit, would it
have been possible for slavery to have crushed us with
its crimes, or intemperance degraded us by its vices?
Would the social evil still have power to send to our

streets women whose laughter is sadder than their tears, and over whose wasted lives death draws the curtain of the grave and silently hides their sin and shame? Oh, Christian women of America, God commits into your hands great privileges and glorious opportunities. It is for you to instruct the ignorant, warn the wayward and guide the inexperienced. To write upon the hearts of those who live within the range of your influence thoughts that you will not blush to see read in the light of eternity and printed amid the archives of heaven, that the young may throw them as bulwarks around their lives and bind them as amulets around their hearts, that when they tread amid the snares and dangers of life the voices from home may linger around their hearts like angels of guidance around their steps. What mother would permit her child to enter any section of a city where the diptheria or cholera might be raging? But are there not immoral conditions in all our large cities "worse than fever, plague, and palsy and madness all combined," and yet are there not many mothers who fail to warn their children against the danger of gathering the flowers of sin that blossom around the borders of hell, and of impressing upon them the intrinsic value and true nobility of a life which shall be a moral and spiritual force, a life hid with Christ in God amid the sin, the sorrows and disorders of earth?

MISS JESSIE A. ACKERMANN.

PLAN OF WORK ALONG SOCIAL PURITY LINES.

By Miss Jessie A. Ackermann.

In this humanitarian, philanthropic age, when so many men and women are giving their best thoughts to the elevation of humanity and the redemption of the world; when new methods of endeavor are being devised and the needs of the human race better understood, it is little wonder that the Purity movement is engaging the attention of some of the foremost reformers of our day. The sentiment that now exists concerning the standard of purity for man and woman is one that has been handed down to us as a legacy from the dark ages. The code of morals given to Moses, but long before graven upon the human heart, has too often been interpreted as a special command for woman and the violation of those laws regarded as sin only when offended against by woman. With this sentiment pervading all conditions of society, those who would be reformers indeed must enter upon systematic effort to overthrow a false idea concerning the relative position of man and woman to the great question of Purity and build up a new standard based upon justice to our sex, by educating the public up to the great thought of " *A pure life for two.*" To do this successfully new methods must be devised and a wide departure from the usual lines of reform entered upon. In all reforms in all ages, special effort has been directed to the masses, and little, if any, thoughts given to the classes, who really stand in as great need of work along these lines as the large numbers whom we are wont to call "the common people."

In the first place I am convinced, from an observation extending to every land and twice round the world, that the standard of purity among the rich is no higher than among the poor, the only difference being the former are entrenched behind the mighty fortifications of wealth, where the only sin is in being found out. The neglected rich are left to educate their own consciences and form their own standards of purity. Braver than any who have fought or died for principle must the man or woman be who will make a departure from the beaten lines of reform and enter upon a mission to the neglected rich by trying to set up among them the new standard of "a pure life for two."

All reforms that must be brought about by the education of public sentiment are of necessity of slow growth, for we are prone to cling to the ideas of our forefathers and walk in their ways. From time immemorial we have read of fallen and outcast women, forms of speech used only in reference to our sex. To my mind the time has now come when we should apply the same term to sinful man, and not only apply the same term but brand them with the same infamy with which similar sins mark woman, and refer to them in the same phraseology in which we speak of erring woman. Mark man as an outcast and call him so. Let society grant no license of conduct to man that it does not recognize in woman, and for all violation of the laws of God by him send him, fallen and an outcast, from our homes as we have always done woman.

The greatest weakness of rescue work in the past has been its onesidedness. It has busied itself in reclaiming women, while men have been passed by. Woman has always been regarded as the principal offender. The two great exceptions are found in the law of God, who, amid the thunderings of Sinai, gave the "thou shalt not" to man as well as woman, and in the action of our Lord, who refused to sanction the

333

stoning of the woman taken in adultery when no pro-
posal was made to punish the guilty partner.

We hail with joy and gladness a measure passed
some time since in England, a clause providing in connection with the prosecution of the keepers of the
houses of ill repute, for the punishment of men found
there, and it is hoped the principle there introduced will
have a telling effect upon legislation in other lands.

Why not begin missions to fallen men? Why not
enter the houses of shame and try to rescue the men
first? Why not build rescue homes for men? Why not
form rescue bands and station them at well known
houses of ill repute in large cities to begin a mighty
effort in the interest of outcast men? What is the
Church doing for outcast men? Did Christ come only
to save woman? Have Christians no duty toward de-
bauched and degraded men? Save the fallen men and
there will be no such a thing in all the land as an impure woman. If the energy and money put into rescue
work for women could be for one year directed toward
fallen men a wholesome public sentiment would be
created that would count immeasurably in the onward
march of this mighty movement. How I plead for
outcast, neglected, fallen men. No one to help them
up nor to tell them how utterly lost they are, and few
realizing what unfit companions these polluted creatures
are for pure women. The great cry of the hour, indeed, the demand, should be a mission to fallen men.
The only work of this kind on record so far as I know
is carried on by an officer of high rank in the army in
Holland. Imbued with the courage of the Cross, inspired by the Captain of his Salvation, this brave man
with a band of earnest workers starts out into the market places of vice with the object of rescuing men.
Night after night in full dress uniform he confronts the
soldiers before they enter these pitfalls and entreats
them to turn from the haunts of shame. So well has he
succeeded that many houses of ill repute have been

closed. The only possible way to bring about a better day for women, when they will one and all possess the choicest gift of pure and unsullied life, is to begin with men and try to elevate them to the standard of a better manhood.

In connection with this a thought comes to me that I urge upon the consideration of all who may chance to read these lines. I speak now in defence of innocent children, long ago branded by custom. A sweet, beautiful child born into this world along the same lines of law on which every other child has come, the only legitimate lines prescribed by nature, but born out of wedlock, has been stamped as illegitimate, when as a matter of fact the only illegitimate factor is the father. Upon the brow of innocence must rest the stigma that rightfully should rest on the father. Let us wipe out of our vocabulary the term illegitimate child; there can be no such thing. Let us begin to talk about illegitimate fathers, and treat them as such. Then to the pure and good, the true and brave, the leaders of fashion and the trainers of the young, goes out a plea for help. A great feature toward reform will be to arouse in the heart of woman a sense of woman's loyalty to woman. Ladies of society are in a great measure to blame for the pitiless manner in which erring woman is crushed to the earth. The very sin that bars her from society, from the home and hearthstone, the sin that locks and bolts the door against her, too often forms a passport through the portals of society for offending man. His base life is viewed in the light of "sowing his wild oats," and without even the virtue of a penitent heart he is received on an equal footing with pure women. Let every woman give men to understand that for purity in herself she exacts the same in them; that no license is allowed because of sex; that the eternal laws of God that change not are alike binding upon men and women Take that stand and men will soon be just what woman demands of them.

CHILD SAVING AND PROSTITUTION.

By Hon. Elbridge T. Gerry.

The consideration of juvenile prostitution, its causes, extent, repression and cure, is one of the most interesting branches of child-saving work. And yet there is something in it so essentially painful, so abhorrent to purity and decency, so loathsome in its details, that the philanthropist shudders when in the cause of morality and Religion he is compelled to touch the subject. For when we consider that little children are the most beautiful images of God's Own Purity; that they enter this world in absolute ignorance of the meaning of the sexual relation; that their development depends very largely on the atmosphere by which they are surrounded in early years; and that too often their growth in vice is due to the ignorance attending their condition of innocence, we are almost tempted to exclaim, in the query addressed to the Master of old, "Does the child sin, or its parents, that it is born blind?" Then, on the other hand, side by side with ignorance, which proverbially is the parent of vice, comes what is still worse—*partial* knowledge; for on the subject of the sexual relation by children, partial knowledge is almost as bad if not equally as strong a factor as ignorance, in the creation and encouragement of vice. The child who is ignorant discovers, either accidentally by itself or by information imparted from others, the existence of physical powers given it for a specific purpose when it arrives at maturity. The child, on the other hand, that receives an erroneous impression on the subject from others of its age or perhaps older, is apt in either event to end in the same result—either the commission of secret vice or premature

336

HON. ELBRIDGE T. GERRY.

indulgence in sexual excess. In either case the factor is ignorance or imperfect knowledge, coupled with the existence of the child in a vitiated atmosphere; and it is worth while to pay a few moments' attention to these two factors, in order to get at the root of the evil.

And first on the subject of *ignorance*. The uneducated masses are frequently very slow to impart to the children a correct knowledge of the purpose and the meaning of the sexual relation. Left in ignorance, secret vice is almost certain to ensue; and in the Societies for the prevention of cruelty to children, where medical examinations are frequent in cases of outrage, or in determining the physical condition of children found in dens of vice, the number of those who practice secret vice is found to be something perfectly appalling, especially among the female sex. And on questioning the unhappy little victims, in almost every case this practice is found to be due to some local physical irritation, is followed in ignorance of its danger or its results, and almost certainly when so followed results in prostitution at an early age. Again and again, as the career of these little innocents—for such they were at the commencement—shows, this steady growth towards the final fall originated from causes of which they were perfectly ignorant. And in hundreds of these cases, the neglect of parents to properly inform their children at a very early age, of the object and the meaning of the sexual relation, has produced this fatal and deadly result.

Then again as to *partial information*. Very many well-meaning parents seem to imagine that any real statement of the facts is apt to create erotic ideas in the mind of the child and perhaps enlighten it on subjects where it should be kept ignorant. And hence either an untrue answer is given to questions very properly put by the child to its parent; or, as is frequently the case, when the information is applied for by the child elsewhere, the vicious or ignorant evade the questions, thereby stimulating its curiosity, or else make answer in a form which simply produces directly the reverse of the truth itself if properly stated. Then the mind of the child begins to act upon the information received, for the Devil is always ready to suggest thoughts of impurity to the young or old, but especially to the young. Then the child begins to communicate its ideas to others older than itself, and is soon confirmed in those views; and lastly follows in natural sequence the desire, the gratification and the result.

There is one very important factor in child prostitution which it would be well for the philanthropist of this age to consider. I refer to the inevitable result among those who are not simply wretchedly poor, but who by reason of the size of their families are compelled to herd together in one room, with the certain result of a sacrifice of feelings of decency and modesty. Until the laws of the State regulating the use of the tenement houses shall provide specifically the number of each sex permitted to occupy the same room, and absolutely preclude all members of a family, of both sexes, herding together in the manner which is now practiced in large cities as matter of necessity and not from choice, the ruin of the children will still continue. Because if a child is placed in a condition in which it cannot shut its eyes or ears to matters which are going on resulting from the marital relations of its parents, or from physical contact with the persons of other members of its own family of the opposite sex, it is idle to suppose that its own innate sense of decency will not suffer by the contamination. The laws in this respect should be stringent. Decency should be preserved, even although the result be to engender additional expense. Parents and children should not be permitted to be grouped together, when the latter become of a certain age, in the same bedroom and beds. And the restrictions should be concise, definite and such as can be understood and enforced.

The three grounds mentioned practically embrace the sources and causes of the evil, because they include contamination by information, contamination by observation and contamination from ignorance. Next is to be considered the *extent* of the evil.

Few have the remotest idea of the enormous extent to which sexual vice exists among children at the present time in this country. I use the word "sexual vice" as including both self-abuse and prostitution, the former being known as the solitary, and the latter as the social, evil; both equally soul and body destroying in their result. The one necessarily leads to the other, and the other becomes apparent only when it is discovered. Nothing but the vigilance of parents and guardians can detect the solitary vice, and hence statistics are very difficult to obtain, excepting where the one vice leads up to the other. But in the other case, the figures show a frightful prevalence at the present time of juvenile prostitution. True, under the stringent laws which have been enacted in the various States of our Union, at the instance of Societies for the prevention of cruelty to children, those who utilize little children for the simple gratification of lust are made to suffer a felon's imprisonment; and while the effect has been to practically denude the brothels of youthful victims, still the vice exists, more especially among the lower classes, to a degree hardly credible in this civilized country. A large number of the brothels at the present time are replenished by juvenile prostitutes rather than by those who have fallen but once; and as the average life of the professional prostitute is but five years, it is appalling to think of the holocaust of victims thus immolated for the purposes of lust. That the disease is spreading is unquestioned, and indeed is not to be wondered at when the present large component part of the American People consisting of the foreign element imported from all parts of the world is considered. Until educated to pay a proper regard to the morals of their children, little improvement can be looked for among these classes. The parents of the lower classes abroad do not trouble themselves much about the matter, and as they do not concern themselves about it to the extent they should, it is not at all surprising that the children suffer as the result of their indifference, inattention or ignorance. Hence what is needed at the present time, more than anything else, is the arousing of the minds of parents of the middle and lower classes to their responsibility. Those interested in the cause of purity should speak in no uncertain language on the subject. The evil should be fully and thoroughly explained to parents, so that they will see the result of their apathy and indifference; and when this is done the first step will have been taken in the right direction for the rescue of children from child-vice.

Then again, another difficulty is the neglect of Religion. The apathy on religious subjects too often exhibited by parents to their children deprives the child of the light of Religion, and it gropes in the darkness of this world with the same uncertainty as a mature person in a dark room. Its ideas of objects are distorted, it has nothing to hold it to the cause of purity— for morality is not Religion, neither is it purity; and the absence of Religion is almost invariably followed by the prevalence of immorality; and infidelity on the part of the parent invariably leads to immorality on the part of the child. The two go hand in hand; they cannot be severed; they are congenial. Indifference to the one begets indulgence in the other. And hence it is that those who work in the cause of purity are compelled to recognize the fact that only an adherence and loyalty to the GOD of Purity can continue the reflection of that purity in the soul of the human race of His creation.

Now parents too often consider that their religious duties to their children are entirely fulfilled when they send them either to the Church or to Sunday School, and having done this, the matter of personal religion does not seem to be any more their concern. The result of this is, the children get simply a perfunctory knowledge of religious duties; because while the general subject of purity is undoubtedly inculcated in a general way by both those means of religious instruction, at the same time in the large majority of cases only a parent can personally instill into the mind of the child those ideas of purity which are so essential for the formation of its character in after life. Again the foe of ignorance steps in, and the ignorance of the parent as to precisely what should be taught the child very often indeed results in the child learning absolutely nothing on the subject of Religion, especially in connection with the subject of personal purity. However pure the parent herself may be, she hesitates about conveying information to the child, and in a vague sort of way supposes that if the child is kept in ignorance it will necessarily grow up pure. This is well worthy the attention of this Convention to consider, because it strikes at the root of the entire matter. The greatest safeguard that a child can possibly have is a pure, religious parent. The greatest blessing that such a parent can render her child is to inculcate in it at the earliest possible age those ideas of purity which the child should be taught to revere, and the horror of impurity from which the child should be taught to shrink. The sin of impurity is one which cannot be parleyed with. The thought suggested must at once be repressed. The story with a double meaning is not to be applauded, but the ears stopped which otherwise would listen to it; else the touch with the pitch defiles the childish mind; then follows recurrence of the thought, then the evil suggestion, then the opportunity, then the fall. There is an ancient Spanish proverb that the Devil often lurks behind the Cross, and too often even in the Sunday School corrupting influences are resorted to with the young, by their companions, resulting in the ruin of the child. More than one such case has come to the knowledge of the writer.

One of the saddest was that of a wretch who utilized his acquaintance with a very young girl in
the Sunday School to accomplish her ruin. And
again it is suggested that it is of the utmost
importance that parents should not be simply
awakened but aroused most thoroughly to a
sense of the danger of their little ones from
not being taught what to shun and how to
shun it.

The foul stream of prostitution is fed by countless
springs, each pouring in its vile contribution of poison,
from as many different sources. In other words, youthful prostitution is frequently due to specific surroundings which lead to the result; and it may not be out of
place to consider a few of these, as showing the primary
causes producing specific results and inevitably leading
to the ruin of the child.

Now in the first place, strange as it may seem, one
of the most prolific sources of child prostitution are the
schools. Not simply the public schools where miscellaneous acquaintances are formed, but too often schools
where confiding parents place their children in the hope
that they will be educated properly and under the best
of circumstances. And yet one single girl will frequently corrupt a dozen, and you have only to listen to
the reports of that excellent man, Anthony Comstock,
the fearless champion and enforcer of the laws for the
protection of social purity, to learn how his Society for
the Suppression of Vice has unearthed the poison in some
of the best and most respectable educational institutions
in this country, to the horror and dismay of the
reputable persons who supposed that they were con-
ducting the same in a manner impervious to even the
suggestion of impurity. I will not dwell on the details
of this factor, but allude to it as only showing how
deadly and how masked are the avenues which lead to
child ruin.

And closely akin to the schools are the factories.
True, the law at the present time does in this respect to

a certain degree limit the age of employment of children in factories, but the immorality which prevails there is utterly beyond belief. Not only is the opportunity great for one child to corrupt another, but the facilities for such corruption are very extended. Indeed, a careful examination of many of the larger brothels in New York City will show the fact that the factories are looked upon almost, so to speak, as mills from which are ground out the material out of which youthful prostitutes are made. It is quite true that in our large cities, where there are few factories, the evil is not so apparent; but in country towns and in factory towns, as they are called, throughout the entire land, it will be found not only that the temptations are numerous, but that the falls are concurrent in number with the temptations. Vanity, love of dress, desire to make money easily—all these elements in the childish mind blunt the sense of purity. The Tempter soon comes, in one way or the other, and whichever the allurement, the result is the same.

Another source, and unfortunately a very fruitful one, of youthful prostitution is the Stage. I do not refer here to what is known as the legitimate drama, where children are incidentally only employed in a theatre where the audiences are reputable, where every care is taken to prevent anything like immoral influences, and decency is preserved, like order, as essential to the reputation of the theatre. But the atmosphere of the theatre is by no means the most conducive to youthful morality, and most pernicious are the exhibitions known as the "leg" drama. Again, the insane propensities which now seems to exist almost universally among modern playwrights, illustrating forcibly their paucity of ideas, to exalt children in plays as conspicuous characters, especially on the variety stage, where the continual encore of their supposed youthful talents simply flatters their vanity, and encourages them on the downward path. It is absurd to say that the mother pays attention to the child's morals and guards carefully over the same. The mother does little if anything of the kind. If the mother is herself on the stage, too often she is occupied with her own stage business; and whether on or off, her own vanity is flattered and her pecuniary resources increased by the exhibition of her youthful prodigy. Imitating, as it unconsciously does, the exposure, the grimaces, the suggestive attitude and accents of those older in the business, before the child becomes a woman it loses all idea of purity, and simply step by step descends to the point where temptation offers and there is no motive for resistance. The transition from an infant prodigy to a young ballet girl and thence to a "living picture," is but brief. When the last is produced, there is nothing left but personal pollution. Even recently efforts have been made to introduce children very extensively in this living picture craze, but the vigilance and determined resistance of the Societies, instituted for their protection, stamped it out. If any one were to talk for half an hour with these wretched little children who love the glare and glitter of the footlights, and who fancy that they are going to become, as they express it, heads of troupes and stars in the profession, and who too often fill early graves from impaired health, caused by exposure to draughts and overwork, they would learn better than pen can describe how potent a factor is the illegitimate drama of to-day in the luring of children from the paths of purity.

Then there is another spring of impurity, known but to few, and that is the utilization of young girls, often long before they have become women, as nude models for artists. Abroad, in the cities of Europe, the artists' models are selected on account of their physical symmetry and not necessarily for their beauty of face. In almost every case they are fully developed women, in age running from seventeen to twenty-five years, and almost invariably the mistress of some one of their employers. They avoid dissipation because that necessarily ruins the figure and diminishes their marketable value. They are not common, in the sense of being purchasable at will by any one, but on the contrary occupy their illicit relations as a matter of choice. A child model is almost a thing unknown. On the other hand, in this country, and notably in some of our great cities, there is hardly an artist's studio where the so called lover of art does not hire young children to pose nude in order to enable him to cultivate his studies of art in nature. Not very long since the attention of The New York Society for the Prevention of Cruelty to Children was invited to a school of well known and reputable artists where children were hired again and again for the express purpose of so exhibiting themselves, and with the consent of their parents, who could see no harm in it. Several of these models described to the writer exactly what they were expected to do for their money. The children are stripped absolutely nude and placed like jointed dolls in every conceivable pose. And when it is considered that the students who viewed and studied the details of their anatomy were men of various ages, and that these exposures were constant, it may well be understood what the blighting effect must have been and was upon these unfortunate little children who were obliged by their parents to make money in this way because, as the latter expressed it, "they saw no harm in it." To the credit of the school be it said, that on the President calling the attention of its directors and teachers to the matter, the request of the Society was complied with and children under the prohibited age are no longer permitted to be so utilized.

Then again, the utilization of children, especially very young girls, in peddling, under the pretext of selling newspapers, flowers and the like, has for years been a prolific source of supply to the stream. This the efforts of our Societies for the prevention of cruelty have practically stamped out in our great cities; but it crops out every now and then, more particularly among the foreign element, where the children are driven out in the streets by their parents to beg or steal, or make money in any way, and to obtain it or starve if they come home without it.

And lastly but not least, are the picnics, dance halls, dime museums and other places where an apparent attraction is held out, and one child goes with another child either to see the curiosities, to enjoy the dance, or possibly because somebody else is going; and there, parental vigilance being relaxed, vicious acquaintances are made, opportunities are offered, and the result follows.

And yet with all these elements conspiring to drag down the unhappy children of to-day, still the result of the enforcement of legislation shows that while the vice has not been eradicated, it certainly has been stemmed. America is not yet as bad as Europe. We have some respect for law in this country. And if those who are not ashamed to avow themselves as advocates of purity persist in a vigorous demand not only for laws for the protection of the young, but for their enforcement, they will find, as the history of the past has shown, that lives may yet be saved, vice prevented and children rescued; and that whatever may be the popular uproar at times against what are called the cast-iron methods of preserving personal purity, yet after all, Purity does and will prevail in the end. It is earnestly hoped that this present Conference will vigorously discuss this matter, and in no uncertain terms suggest wise and effective methods to preserve the purity of the young and rescue the unhappy little victims of sexual vice.

A word as to the horrible life itself. When the child prostitute becomes a professional it is either from ignorance of the final end, shame and dread to return to the parental roof, or vanity in being able to make money rapidly in an easy way. Rarely does the element of sexual passion enter into the case. Disease from ignorance of proper physical cleanliness usually in some form assails the poor little victim early in her career. Before long the demon of drink gets in his fatal work either to drown remorse or to stimulate the physical exhaustion which is incidental to the life. And the end comes soon—five years is the average limit, and another soul is numbered with the lost. Truly child prostitution is a sight over which both men and angels may well weep; and there can be no subject more worthy of consideration by the lovers of purity than the pitiful appeal of helpless, degraded childhood from such a life and such a death. Surely this Conference will consider it.

PROF. ELI M. LAMB.

PRESIDENT BALTIMORE BRANCH AMERICAN PURITY ALLIANCE,
BY WHOM MR. GERRY'S PAPER WAS READ TO THE
CONGRESS.

EQUAL SUFFRAGE AS RELATED TO THE PURITY MOVEMENT.

BY MARIANA W. CHAPMAN.

It is a matter of some difficulty for an ardent believer in the moral force of woman suffrage to take hold of a proposition which it seems to her puerile to dispute, and present for it an argument worthy the attention of thinking people; but, with the chance that there may be a few within hearing of my voice to whom the solution is not affirmative, I venture to trespass upon your time. Primarily it is admissible to suppose that whoever uses a ballot will use it to protect themselves; and while men and women rise or fall together, woman is unquestionably the greater sufferer in the social evil. It is, therefore, no stretch of logic to infer that she will labor more indefatigably to arrest its progress when her choice in the matter of laws and lawgivers counts at the ballot box. If any one desires to know how women would vote in this direction, he has his object lesson in the late history of a Kentucky campaign, where the record of a Kentucky Congressman came to the knowllege of the women of the State, and they determined that Kentucky should not be so dishonored in the Congress of the United States. No deposit of a piece of white paper counted for them; they had only their voices, and their pens, and their strength, but they arose in their might and sent forth their protest. Throwing aside the reserve which it is hard for a woman to drop, they traveled, they held meetings, they had barbecues, they urged, they warned, they besought the men of Kentucky to stand for the honor of the State, and the

MRS. MARIANA W. CHAPMAN.
PRESIDENT BROOKLYN, N. Y., WOMAN'S CLUB.

men of Kentucky answered them nobly, and bravely and well. But why, dear brothers, should it have been so much harder for them than for you to work this righteousness? I tell you truly such men cannot go into our Legislatures when the women of this country have the ballot in their hands.

Joseph Cook says: "Woman's vote would be to the vices in our great cities what the lightning is to the oak." We hear it declared even by temperance advocates that the woman's vote will not help that cause. Why, then, do we find always and under all circumstances, wherever there is a movement for woman suffrage, the solidly united opposition of the saloon element? Alice Blackwell says "it is because the children of darkness are wiser than the children of light." Most of you have read details of the traffic in young girls carried on in the mining and lumber camps of the Virginia mountains. Can we think this would continue if the women of Virginia had an authoritative voice in its Legislature? The women of Virginia are not behind the women of Kentucky in moral atmosphere, which is true of the women of every other State. The man or woman who thinks otherwise insults our American womanhood. It is significant that the first bill ever introduced by a woman into a State Legislature was one for the protection of young girls. In California, when a bill licensing social evil was about to pass, under the plea of its imperative necessity to public health, some California women succeeded in having another introduced which made the same provisions for all participants, and was clearly more consistent with the professed purpose. The result was the one desired — neither passed.

Those who have read "Drummond's Ascent of Man" will remember that he places in the mother the root of the struggle for the life of others. He considers it the seed of all the altruism the world has ever known. We can depend upon human nature to repeat

itself; and think you the time will ever come when
mothers in general will not struggle for the best surroundings for their sons and daughters? A God-given
instinct will not desert the womanly nature. No man
changeth the laws of the universe. Over and over
again men who are opponents of woman's enfranchisement have said, "But there are so many bad women
who will vote," and we have answered, "We will take
care of the bad women if you will take care of the bad
men." The very large proportion of these profligate
women or victims are under voting age, if we may rely
upon the statistics of those who have given the subject
careful attention, and who declare their average term of
life to be five years. The small proportion of those
past this age, if voting, would be instantly out of sight
in the other overwhelming majority of American womanhood. I once asked an English woman "whether this
class troubled them at the polls in England." She said,
"Oh, no; they never come. I only wish they might,
for then they would come a little nearer to us, and we
could help them." Some of our opposers claim that
women would not use this power, but Wyoming records
show that there nine-tenths of the women vote and only
eight-tenths of the men. And De Witt Talmage wrote
from New Zealand: "I hereby report to the American
ladies now moving for the right of suffrage that New
Zealand is clear ahead of them, and that the experiment
has been made here successfully. Instead of the ballot
box degrading woman, woman is here elevating the
ballot box. . . . It is often said in America that if
women had the right to vote they would not exercise
it. For the refutation of that theory I put the fact that
in the last election in New Zealand, of 109,000 women
who registered 90,000 have voted, while of the 193,000
men who registered only 129,000 have voted. This
ratio shows that women are more anxious to vote
than men." Another authority in that country, J. W.
Copithorne, says: "The fears of the liquor interest were

justified, for the vote of women was cast almost solidly against it, and a Parliament favorable to anti-liquor legislation was chosen. The women also looked carefully to the personal character of the candidates, and voted accordingly, so that it was shown that their influence was a purifying one in politics." Repeated experiences of this kind will be our best object lessons, and the best element of humanity will in time perceive the helpful factor at their doors.

There is always a certain amount of helplessness attendant upon a disfranchised element, and the further that element is away from power the greater the calamity. Not long ago an educated Hindoo woman said, "My prayer and supplication are, 'O, God, let no more women be born in India.'" One easily divines the reason for such prayers. A year ago a correspondent of the *London Methodist Times* said, "The conception of morality existing in Indian society is of the most unhappy character." They have no word in their language to express the chastity of men. Three Brahman gentlemen had written a handbook for boys' schools, and one part of it was upon honesty, truthfulness and chastity. One of our ministers asked them what word they had used for the last. They mentioned a Tamil word, and he said, "But that does not refer to men at all. What have you stated in this section?" They replied that they "had urged upon the boys the importance of teaching their sisters and wives to lead pure lives, but it had never occurred to them to suggest purity for the boys themselves."

Wherever the gulf is greatest between the manhood and womanhood of any people, you have the lowest moral condition of the human race. Where daughters are bought and sold, and women look through masks and blinds and ignorance at the outside world, you have an enforced motherhood, with its sequel in sons who are to-day burning, plundering and assaulting women and children in Armenia. It is truth beyond cavil, and as old as the garden of Eden, that they whom God has joined together no man should put asunder, whether it be in school, church or State.

If there be those who hold that we are together in the best way now, we say, "No, a thousand times no;" not until we can make the laws of this country as stringent upon men in the social world as they are upon women, not until the polling places are open to us in the same simple way as the street cars, or any public hall where men and women go together, not until legislation can feel directly the force of the woman thought. We shall not equal the knowledge of men in finance, in commerce and great business enterprises, but we shall know what kind of schools we want for our girls and boys, we shall know whether we want saloons, whether we will have other dens of iniquity, and what kind of men or women we want for lawmakers. We are not afraid of the polling places of America because we believe in our American manhood and, with Henry Ward Beecher, "that if any venture to molest the crowd will swallow him up as the whale swallowed Jonah!" George William Curtis said: "The sphere of the family is not the sole sphere either of men or women. They are not only parents, they are human beings; they are also members of the State, and from the very equality of the parental function, which perpetuates the State, they are equally interested in its welfare. Has the mother less concern than the father in the laws that regulate the great social temptations which everywhere yawn for their children; or in the general policy of the Government which they are summoned to support?" And further: "If women do not care about the question, it is high time that they did, both for themselves and for men. The spirit of society cannot be just nor the laws equitable so long as half of the population are politically paralyzed."

And here we strike the keynote of the thought which must come to the women of every country before their enfranchisement can be secured. Women *must* care and increasingly they do. Thought of the national welfare belongs to an advanced motherhood. A woman unfit to vote is a woman unfit to be a mother. How shall she teach what does not enter her perceptions or her interests? If intelligent in outside matters she sees easily that society surrounds her daughters with a protection not extended to her sons, whose young manhood may be lured into gilded halls aflame with gilded vice. Happy are they if strong in the precious security that comes from the absorption of a mother's moral strength in early life! Who is worthy of motherhood if she throw not the whole of her best possessions into the impressible nature of the dear young hearts about her, which are the most sacred links that bind her to the Father's work. Verily, "if ye have not done unto the least of these, ye have not done it unto Me."

But when the nursery work is done and the mother heart follows these tall young men and women across the threshold to the outer world, the law steps in and says, "Hold! you have nothing to do in these arrangements; your opinions shall not count here, you shall be of no authority in the State.' One alarmist says: "It might bring a union of Church and State," and cites the strong influence of a Catholic priesthood; but no class of women in America is taught to hold a higher standard of purity than the women of the Catholic Church.

We will venture to say that they will increase the proportion of that church whose heads are not muddled with liquor or clouded with tobacco smoke, and will, therefore, help to make a clearer thinking, wiser and more prudent majority.

But the majority of women in this country is of other faiths and not likely to be governed by clerical influence in their political views. Women who are self supporting can easily perceive the disadvantage involved in their disfranchisement. The wage earning woman needs more power to protect herself from unjust discrimination, to demand equal pay for equal work, to choose lawmakers who will make her as safe from injury as the woman of the household. No class appeals to us so strongly as the great army of wage earning girls, who need all the help their older sisters can throw about them, and for whom we could do more as an enfranchised power.

We should ask it then, not only for the sake of preserving social purity throughout this working world, but in the name of justice, one of the highest and holiest attributes of a perfect life.

So, at least, we have long been accustomed to regard it, though a leading daily of New York stated some weeks ago, in an editorial, that "at an earlier day in the history of the republic abstract justice counted for a great deal," but that "at the present time practical results outweigh every other consideration." This may be a correct statement in regard to the present general trend of thought, but if the righteousness of justice in daily dealing is no longer one of the verities which are eternal, we declare virtually that present practical results make principles for ordinary use. Most of us would prefer to believe that the ten commandments are still in force as the foundation of a solid white tower of truth which is slowly building, the stones of which, after much rubbing and wearing and trial by fire, go in at last to stay, with the temple rising always toward the shining light of heaven. Even with the belief that practical results will demonstrate the force of our argument for suffrage without distinction of sex, we must see that there is a larger view which has its influence among the people and its sequence in the increasing desire to furnish equal opportunities for the education of children morally, mentally and physically. The simple direct thought of people thus strengthened and enlightened will lead toward the clearer perception of justice; and though there will never be wanting those whose intellect will bring forth that serpentine reasoning of old which resulted in "Cursed be Canaan," the great majority will be so permeated with the larger light that an enfranchised womanhood will be the part not only of righteousness but of *expediency*.

Even the fallen woman herself will quickly perceive the shallow sophistry of so enlightened a philosopher as Prof. Lecky when he calls her a priestess of society and a preserver of home life. No twisted logic will make her other, in her own eyes, than the victim of the insatiate greed of this Moloch of humanity.

However people may dispute about the virtue of vicarious suffering, they will never stand for the virtue of vicarious sinning. But, inasmuch as all reform comes through the Divine power moving in the hearts of men with its outward expression in the world's work, I beseech you, brothers and sisters, to let no opportunity pass that may help to place with the weaker half of humanity the power of protection that lies in the ballot. It is a principle for which strong men have given their lives and suffered untold martyrdoms.

It does not change its virtue when a woman holds out her hands and asks leave to help you to the higher life

DR. EMILY BLACKWELL.

DR. EMILY BLACKWELL'S ADDRESS APPEARS ON PAGES 72-80.

ADDRESS BY MRS. MARY T. BURT,

PRESIDENT NEW YORK STATE W. C. T. U.

The hour is so late that it seems almost presump-
tuous for me to claim the attention of the audience for
even the briefest time, but my interest in the work for
which this Congress is convened, and profound pleasure
in its success, is my excuse for yielding to the invitation
of your presiding officer, so kindly given, to address
you. It is not often that laborers in moral vineyards are
privileged to see results, but surely the President of this
society must feel that his years of patient and devoted
labor are in a measure rewarded when he looks upon
this assembly of men and women, who, in their representative capacity, voice the sentiments and the wishes
of the best elements of the country on the great question of purity. And what advance the work has made!
What friends it has called to its aid! A few years ago
densest darkness surrounded the question. Prejudice
had built a wall about it that only those whose souls had
been deeply touched with the needs of the work cared
to scale. That which you discuss here, and to which
the press gives respectful attention and widest circulation could not have been so publicly spoken then.
There were a few devoted men and women who realized
that when you put your finger on the purity nerve of
the human body you touched the spot that sensitized
the whole system. And what was true of the individual
life was true of the civil life as well. But truth works
its way and sheds its light through strongest prejudice
and doubt, and the agitation for purity during the past
few years has taken shape and definiteness in the societies organized throughout the country to promulgate the
Gospel of Purity—to proclaim one standard of morals
for men and women; to wage war upon all forms of im-

MRS. MARY T. BURT.

purity; in literature, in art, in the press, upon the stage, whenever and wherever its deadly presence is seen or felt, and to arraign with strongest protest the "Age of Consent" laws which now blot the statute books of the nation.

In New York we feel we have made great progress the past winter in raising the "age of consent" from sixteen to eighteen years. The Empire State is one of the five States to take this advanced step this year, and while we rejoice that this age limit has been reached in New York for the protection of young girls, we feel that friends of purity should not rest satisfied until the State fixes the same age for the protection of the person that it does for the purse, which is twenty-one years; and then, because we believe the "age of consent" laws are degrading to manhood, we would have them abolished forever. I take this opportunity of expressing to your President my appreciation of the suggestions and kind helpfulness received from him in my purity work for the New York State W. C. T. U. It was the Society for the Prevention of State Regulation of Vice, of which Mr. Powell was president, succeeding the revered Mrs. Abby Hopper Gibbons, that first drew attention to the shocking "age of consent" laws in the various States; and when the bill raising the age from ten to sixteen years was pending in the Legislature of New York, Mrs. Gibbons, then in her eightieth year, went to Albany and plead before the legislative committees for its success. It is such devotion and such labors we are reaping the fruit of to-day. To me this Congress is a joyous harbinger of what the future holds for this great work. The banner of purity which is set up here stands for a "white life for two," and encircles with its folds the unprotected girlhood of the nation. The truths it bears are vital truths, and before its onward march impurity will flee away. The heart and conscience of the people will be reached, and in proper time, as the individual life becomes purified and exalted, will the national life take upon itself the same attributes and weave into the body politic the principles and truths for which this Congress stands.

Frances E. W. Harper.

MRS. HARPER'S ADDRESS APPEARS ON PAGES 328-30.

LETTER FROM MRS. C. T. COLE.

MT. PLEASANT, IOWA, Oct. 11, 1895.

DEAR FELLOW WORKERS FOR PURITY:

With deepest regret that I cannot be with you in person, as I shall be in spirit during the days of your sessions in Baltimore, I ask myself, in case I were with you in the Congress assembled, with what message would I fill the few moments which might be granted to me?

One point I would urge upon the leaders in this movement is to seek to impress upon all workers whom they may enlist the importance of looking at this subject—impurity in all its phases— and the remedies proposed, in *the large*, in so far as possible *from above.* It seems to me we are immensely helped by looking backward as well as forward, by tracing this sinuous evil through the history of the race, and comparatively in different ages and stages of civilization. We are thus guided in probing down to its taproot, and the sources from which this root draws its nourishment. Thus shall we be prepared to work wisely and well with less of wasted zeal.

Another point I should like to emphasize is that of individual responsibility in the great work before us of creating sentiment for the one standard of purity for all God's children. This is positive work, exceedingly difficult, long deemed impossible—work that now calls for every loving heart and loyal hand because the task of removing the old, false, blasphemous Double Standard and planting for all time the Divine standard of purity of heart and thought and life as the only condition of seeing God—is herculean. But, friends and fellow workers, do we not know that this work brings "its own exceeding great reward," because so evidently a part of the Eternal Power and Purpose that "makes for righteousness?"

One more thought seems to us of deep importance in this present stage of the purity movement, viz.: that in all the attempts to separate religion and morality we recognize the fact that a truly religious life is impossible without personal purity—purity not only of the external life, "known and read of all men," but purity of heart, and of the thought, and "the imagination of the thought of the heart." Hitherto there has seemed to be no general comprehension of this deep, vital feature of Christianity. Too much stress has been laid upon external observances, forms and ceremonies—the "anise and mint and cummin" of religion—and too little upon this essential, indispensable feature. The inspiring tread of the marching hosts of young people toward the field of Christian work is not without its dangers as notably evident by the painful Durant trial now in progress in San Francisco.

As workers in this white harvest field we find too many, in pulpit and pew, who need to have a vision like that of Paul at Damascus, to see what God calls them to do. A single sentence from Mrs. Butler's letter as published in the October *Philanthropist*, is in point: "A good man, a spiritual man, a pastor and teacher, lately confessed, after a successful ministry to souls, that when brought face to face with this question with which we are dealing, he felt—and God showed him—that he needed to be reconverted."

Still one more caution should be extended to all workers: it is not to allow attention and effort to be so entirely directed to any special features of this hideous, omnipresent evil until hope, and faith, and courage shrivel and perish in its loathsome atmosphere. Rather let us strive to maintain the attitude of the archangel, with the dragon writhing beneath his firmly planted

MRS. C. T. COLE.

foot, his two edged sword poised for death dealing blows, but his face turned sunward, serene, though tremulous. So let us but glance down at the dragon while we keep our faces turned toward the Son of Righteousness—the Beauty of Holiness—thus keeping ourselves in harmony with the great uplift toward nobler living.

And now let me add a sentence to bear testimony to my deep appreciation of the work of the *Philanthropist*, quiet, unpretentious, like the clear water of a mountain rivulet coming to us from the heights. Will not this Congress devise ways and means for sending this water, so full of tonic, to every part of our land? And the *Arena*, and its stalwart editor, who seems to us a very Sir Gallahad in this conflict with darkness and impurity. And among its contributors we think first of Helen Gardener, not only for what her keen pen and earnest brain have already accomplished, but for the evident fund of reserved force to which we look with hope and expectation for still grander work in the future.

God grant that this Congress may prove a "Mount of Vision" to many who have not yet felt any sense of responsibility in this great rising tide for purity, and that its stimulus may be felt in every hamlet in our land.

Yours Ever in the Work,

C. T. COLE.

PROF. JAS. STUART, M. P.

HONORARY SECRETARY INTERNATIONAL FEDERATION FOR THE
ABOLITION OF STATE REGULATION OF VICE.

FLORENCE CRITTENTON MISSION RESCUE WORK.

REMARKS BY MRS. A. L. PRINDLE, MATRON OF FLORENCE CRITTENTON MISSION.

DEAR FRIENDS:

I am here to day to represent the twenty-one Florence Crittenton Missions for mothers' girls.

The people of God in all ages have been slow to learn His blessed will and wonderful love for the poor outcast, friendless, homeless, unpitied and unloved erring woman.

Every other class of sinners known in all the earth has been looked after by the Church of God, save her, who has had *no* helper, no place for repentance, though she has sought it diligently with tears. The Church has been very deficient, as many of you know, in looking after these lost ones and giving them help. Let the Church of God cover her face with shame and cry out in the eveningtide of this nineteenth century, " Hide thy face from my sins, and blot out all mine iniquities," for Jesus' sake.

When the condition of these lost ones was first revealed to me by the Spirit, I hastened to tell the fathers and mothers how the children had been swept over the precipice; how they were even now falling over the cataract like drift wood, uttering a piercing cry for help as they *fell*. Yet but few listened to my story, so I fell into hearty sympathy with the silver tongued prophet when he asked, " Who hath believed our report? "

Later down the ages God hath raised up another Isaiah, who, beholding the maelstrom and whirlpool into which thousands of America's best womanhood

MRS. A. L. PRINDLE.

have fallen by the cruel, relentless hand of man, cried out, "Save her! save her!" I refer to dear Brother Charles N. Crittenton, whom to know is to love. He commenced this work in New York City twelve or fifteen years ago, when the devil seemed to have his own way. He went down into Baxter street and one dear girl said to him: "Mr. Crittenton, I would leave this place, but I don't know where to go; you would not have me, nobody cares for me; my own mother has shut the door against me." It was then he decided, after much prayer and thought, that he would undertake to work for the erring girl. How many times he has been called a lunatic, because he has for his great object in life to help the perishing girl!

You would be startled and alarmed by the enormity of this sin if the real facts were revealed, one of which I will give you.

A young man, now well saved, thank God, about two years ago, after hearing me speak upon this subject in the Gospel Tabernacle, came trembling and shaking under the power of God, confessed to me most humbly, tears streaming down his face, "that before his conversion and marriage, in a distant city, he had been instrumental in pushing one hundred mothers' girls over the precipice into the dark waters of woe and despair." He said, "Shall I go to heaven and those girls go to hell? God forbid," said he, as he brought his hand down on the desk. "Mother Prindle, will you go with me to that city and help save them? Will you go with me and establish a Home through which these perishing ones that I have destroyed and ruined may be helped to a better life?"

Careless mothers, arouse yourselves, to save your beautiful daughters from this terrible fate. You may, indeed, hasten the coming of the Lord, who has all power in heaven and earth, by preaching the Gospel to all perishing ones, for then shall the end come. Praise God, He is coming!

This modern Isaiah, our beloved Brother Crittenton, whose tongue is not only silver, but his words gold,
has consecrated every dollar to the uplifting of fallen
humanity.

The twenty-one Florence Crittenton Missions, under
the supervision of our beloved and honored brother,
Charles N. Crittenton, are scattered all through the
United States. They have of late been organized into
a National society. By the payment of one dollar a
year any person can be a member of this organized
body, and so aid in pushing the work. Circles will be
formed in all cities where missions have been established, for the prevention of this terrible sin, as well as
the rescuing of those who have fallen into it.

The Gospel Rescue Car, owned and fitted up by
our dear brother Crittenton, is the latest feature of the
work; he has paid for this car with its furnishings, five
thousand dollars.

Through this channel, our dear young girls are rescued, and cold, dead Christians made alive, Circles
formed and public sentiment created, and money raised
in behalf of this cause, which is so near and dear to the
heart of our coming King.

We are in confident expectation to belt the entire
globe with Florence Crittenton Missions.

When one of these wonderful Missions has been
planted in our own capital, Washington, D. C., the plan
in embryo is, to move across the Atlantic, at our beloved
Lady Henry Somerset's special request, and plant a delightful Home for the poor, ostracized English girls, for
whom my heart aches.

I saw all phases of London life during my trip
abroad, but no scene touched my heart more tenderly
than those nightly witnessed of the hopeless condition
of the once noble, pure English girl. She is indeed,
according to the lines of Whittier, "hunted, outlawed,
held in thrall," whom nobody loves.

Picadilly and Regent's Square are literally thronged at midnight with this class of lost maidenhood.

Brother Coote and I stood upon the steps of Hugh Price Hughes' glorious Mission, and witnessed the wholesale traffic in mothers' girls, and for some reason he is not able to gather in one of those dear ones, and the ground seems to be covered with them. Such a sight I never beheld in New York. I had a wonderful heart-felt feeling with the prophet Jeremiah, as he exclaimed, "Oh, that my head were waters, and mine eyes a fountain of tears, that I might weep day and night for the slain of the daughters of my people."

I remained after my friends had returned to America, to awaken an interest in the hearts of the Saints of God. Had personal interviews with the best Rescue Workers at Lady Henry's request, such as William T. Stead, Hugh Price Hughes, Mrs. Bramwell Booth and many others, so that now a location is selected, and sufficient interest created to establish this much needed work in God's own time.

I was enabled to speak, through an interpreter, to the poor perishing girls in Paris, where Arthur Booth Clibborn and his devoted wife have done such a marvelous work for our risen Christ.

I want to solicit the hearty co-operation of all God's dear consecrated children, for the furtherance of this most Christlike work, and for the ingathering of multitudes of precious young girls, who, through the deceitfulness of sin, and the artfulness of wicked men, fall an easy prey to the wiles of the devil.

After a long and interesting interview with William T. Stead, he said, in parting, "For God's sake, go on with your noble work, Mother Prindle."

I am pained at times by some remarks made by professedly consecrated Christian workers, who have said in the face of our reports that they "did not believe that one out of a hundred was saved in the Florence Mission." On the contrary, I have been nearly six years

CHARLES N. CRITTENTON.
FOUNDER OF THE FLORENCE CRITTENTON MISSIONS.

in this lighthouse, and I know scores and scores of girls who are filling honorable positions to-day, whose dwelling once was in the Tombs, the slums and the dives of our city. Many are at work in the Master's vineyard, and many others give evidence of a bright and glowing future; many of them have made happy mothers.

I want to tell you that I never was prouder than I am now of a class of women who are coming up out of the depths of sin. They were mothers' lost daughters, but they have been washed in the blood of the Lamb.

I will just note one or two instances. One was a Southerner, who came to us. Her father was a Methodist minister. She went down into great wickedness; her health was broken. One day in our Home she gave her heart to God. She was washed in the blood of Jesus Christ, and to-day she is the wife of a noble Christian man, and they have a delightful home and a family altar.

I want to speak of an older one. You say, "These older ones you can do nothing with." Not so. It seemed that nothing would rouse Mary to a sense of her condition at first. I went into the dormitory, where she was lying upon her bed, and said, "Mary, come down; come down to the meeting. Do you know you are on the brink of the precipice of eternal ruin?" She said, "Do you mean I am going to hell?" I said, "That is what I mean, unless you come to Jesus and be saved." She arose and dressed herself and came down and knelt in prayer with us, and she was wonderfully saved. I put these four words on her fingers, "Thou, God, seest me." She has been marching on toward heaven and glory ever since.

I could tell you of a great many missionaries raised up from the Florence Mission. Our dear Belle has gone to glory, and another has been appointed in her place. We have one in Pittsburgh, one in Virginia, another in Gloversville, N. Y. We have several in the Salvation Army, who make bright and beautiful workers, good soldiers for Jesus.

I have been nearly seventeen years in the work, and "have not got weary yet." I want no other or better evidence that Christ is coming soon, than that He is waking up the sleeping churches to a sense of their responsibility for God on this line.

Christian mothers and wives, God help you to enter into this work as never before. God help you and bless you!

Praise God for this Social Purity Congress! Every paper read and every word spoken in its interest are like so many polished stones in the great building, the architect of which is our Maker and our God. While rescuing the perishing and caring for the dying, I most fully realize the value of the old adage, that "an ounce of prevention is worth more than a pound of cure;" and so with tongue and pen I would cheer you on, dear fellow workers, with the encouraging words of our Lord, when He said to His disciples, "Ye shall reap in due time if ye faint not." "The battle is not yours, but the Lord's." Glory to His holy name!

ADDRESS BY MRS. MARY A. LIVERMORE.

Mrs. Mary A. Livermore gave the closing address of the Congress:

Any one who has passed much time in Europe cannot help having noticed the baneful effects of the State regulation of vice. I have seen so much of it and its effects that it seems to me there is nothing more horrible, more to be dreaded than its introduction into America. If a woman walks along the streets of Paris, even if accompanied by her husband, she is insulted by a majority of the eyes of the men that pass her. Their expression is unmistakable.

The reason for such a state of affairs is simply that women are put below par by the universal regulation of prostitution. Dealing in this vice is put on a level with the sale of dry goods, cereals, or other marketable commodities. The law is made in such a way that man, and not woman, gets the advantage. Its aim is to make sin safe for men only. And they feel that, too. They look upon woman as their prey.

Do we want that sort of thing in America, where the women are free and the young girls go in and out unattended and yet in perfect safety? They are safe because they are under the protection of the American man. And there is no other man like the American man. Whatever woman may come to in the future her best protection must always be in the heart of man. Do we want vice regulated here? I cannot think of anything more deplorable for America and I would rather die than see it brought here.

Thus far we have been saved, but this Congress for purity was not called a whit too soon. We have heard the claims of a certain class of men that their morals shall be just where they choose to put them, while they

MRS. MARY A. LIVERMORE.

put the standard of women up so high that angels can scarcely live up to it. That is why I say this Congress is needed. Let decent, chaste, highly moral, God fearing, law abiding people speak out their denunciation of this horrible immorality that is daring to plant its colors on our shores.

I have had an experience of many years in rescuing fallen women, and it is my belief that even if there is reformation in these cases it is not possible to forget the past. Those who have fallen can never regain their pure, white souls. You know what a glorious work John B. Gough did for temperance after he had given up drink. Well, he told me that often when he was speaking from the platform a ribald jest, an oath, a bad story which he had heard in some saloon years before would come to his lips and he would almost cry it out to the crowd listening to him.

What we need most of all to establish is one standard of morality for both sexes. I think women are much to blame for the erection of this double standard which now prevails. Sweet women have said to me, "You can't expect young men to be as careful as young girls." I do expect it. I more than expect it; I demand it. I don't believe boys would be impure if they were properly trained at home by their mothers.

I marvel at the way mothers let their young girls "scoot" about in large cities after dark. I have often seen two or three of them on the street, gaily dressed, laughing and making fun among themselves, but always attracting the attention of the hunters of human souls. I wonder if the mothers are not fools to think that their daughters can run loose without coming to ruin? This subject used to worry Wendell Phillips so that he wanted a law passed forbidding boys and girls below a certain age from being on the streets after a certain hour.

Our boys and girls come into the world with the appeties and passions of humanity, which are meant to be their servants, not their masters. These instincts are full grown before we know it—long before the reason and judgment are mature—and our young people are confronted with outside temptations which have greatly increased of late years. I in my youth never heard of such things as my grandchildren have to meet. My married daughter tells me the same. The forces of evil seem to be far sighted. They see that the temperance and purity movement, starting often in weakness and unwisdom, is destined to grow and threaten their strongholds; and they are preparing their forces to meet it. Petroleum V. Nasby has described to us the insidious and carefully prepared temptations by which, while still a mere boy, he was led into habits of drinking. The same course is pursued in regard to the social evil. I saw in front of my lawn the other day a group of boys ten or eleven years old, intent on some small cards, passing them around, and apparently playing a game with them. I said to my eight year old granddaughter, "What are those boys so interested in?" She answered, "They are playing with cigarette cards, so as to make money out of them." "Cigarette cards!" I said. "What are those?" "Oh, they are very bad, grandma." "Have you seen them, then?" "I have seen them once or twice, but mother told me I must not look at them, nor let Johnny" (her younger brother). Later some of those cards came into my hands, and I was shocked. They were not all of them bad—at least, some had nothing worse on them than the picture of a prize fighter—but others were very bad indeed. Boys make collections of hundreds of these cards, and the seeds of impurity are thus implanted in their minds. A Boston teacher lately wrote me a long letter telling me how the little fellows in the schools were absorbed in these cards and gambled with them, and the teachers saw the evil effects.

Another thing: I am occasionally obliged to go to my home in Melrose by a late train, and I am always made uncomfortable by the number of young girls going home unattended, or attended by some boy of their own age. What are their parents thinking about?

Another difficulty is the backwardness of women in talking of these things. The women's clubs now have a million members. In their meetings they could discuss ways of saving the boys and arousing the parents without any danger of their words appearing in the paper next morning—the great bugbear of women in speaking of these subjects.

It is not safe for a mother to be out of her son's confidence. Let her rear him with the same standard of purity as for his sister, and she will save him from things that in his after life he would give anything to have undone. If the mother is backward and prudish, I can tell her that there are other teachers right across the road, at the drug store, the grocery store, the railroad station, who will give her boy lessons that he will be sorry for later. People talk about sowing wild oats, as if they never came to harvest. "Whatsoever a man soweth, that shall he also reap." As if a young man could smirch his soul and wash it all off as he might wash his hands! Nature never forgives. You cannot jump from the gutter into heaven.

We must lay greater stress on early education. We must not take it for granted that because children are born in good homes they will turn out all right. If we do not look after these matters we shall see our country covered all over with the State regulation of vice. While there is a great International Federation to break down this evil system in Europe, constant attempts are made to introduce it here. I meet things now in America which remind me of Paris or Brussels. We are getting Europeanized, and there is danger that all the old standards will be swept away. A merely material civilization, however superb, will crumble down into rottenness, and nothing can save it.

To women I would say, the policy of reserve and *laissez faire* will not do. The evils about us must be met, and they can be met. We are asked, "What are you going to do about it?" Eliminate it, with the help of God and of the decent people of America; and there are a great host of them. When we join hands with God to work for righteousness, we partake of His almightiness, and we shall win.

THE RESOLUTIONS OF THE CONGRESS.

The following resolutions, read by the President, were unanimously adopted as voicing the sentiment of the Congress:

That chastity, a pure, continent life alike for men and women is consonant with the best condition of physical, mental and moral health.

That prostitution is a fundamental violation of the laws of health; is degrading and destructive to the individual, a menace to the home and to the nation.

That State or municipal regulation of prostitution is morally wrong; is worse than a sanitary failure; is cruel and unjust to woman; creates a shocking traffic in girlhood.

That all possible effort should be made to educate public opinion and maintain a high, equal standard of morals for both men and women.

That facilities should be provided for the treatment of venereal diseases as readily as all other diseases in all hospitals under the control of municipalities or other public bodies, as well as in those supported by voluntary contributions.

That homes should be everywhere established by Municipal and State, as well as voluntary aid, as agencies for the reclamation and rehabilitation of erring girls.

That the State should punish, by imprisonment rather than fine, organized prostitution, procurism, the keepers of houses of prostitution and the rental of houses or other dwellings for such purposes.

That the congratulations of this National Purity Congress are hereby extended to Josephine E. Butler and her European co-workers of the International Federation for the abolition of State regulation of vice, upon the encouraging progress of their crusade for the abolition of the odious system of State sanctioned debauchery and the promotion of public morality.

That the hearty thanks of this National Purity Congress are hereby extended to the Baltimore Meeting of the Religious Society of Friends, Park Avenue, for the use of its Meeting House kindly proffered for its sessions.

That the grateful acknowledgments of this Congress are hereby expressed to the representatives of the press of Baltimore for their excellent reports of the proceedings.

SUPPLEMENTARY.

PERSONAL AND SOCIAL PURITY.

By Rev. Joseph May.

I Cor. vi. 19: "Know ye not that your body is the sanctuary of the Holy Spirit which is in you? Glorify God, therefore, in your body."

Of all the institutions of Providence in nature, doubtless there is none more remarkable, more interesting or more important than that of sex. All through the vegetable and the animal world, above the very lowest biological forms, this law reigns with scarcely any exceptions, that the continuance of every species depends upon the concurrence and co-operation of *two* parental organisms. The flowers that deck the fields are distinguished into types corresponding to the paternal and maternal. The fishes of the sea swim in parental pairs; the nest upon the bough, jewelled with its eggs, is guarded by wedded mates in whom the distinction of office begins to be clearly apparent in the external features of either; and while the mother bird sits closely and diligently at home the father hovers about to supply her with food, to regale her with song, until the shells burst, the helpless little ones appear with their hungry cries and the parent pair unite in ceaseless, self-forgetting care to feed and defend and finally to train their infant brood.

Among the animal tribes the same touching drama is repeated. The mother to bear and to rear, the father, who begets, to maintain and to defend, and as we rise in the scale, higher intelligence manifesting itself in ever

REV. JOSEPH MAY.

increasing assiduity, devotion, self sacrifice and parental joy.

The highest example of this complex law of distributed functions, of union, and of parental co-operation, appears in the intelligent, voluntary association of individuals of our own race in marriage. In man, the characteristics of the sexes become highly differentiated; their particular offices are markedly contrasted; the necessity of the one to complement the other and of the two to form a perfect one is especially obvious. And in the moral relations of the two the necessity of each to the other, the helpfulness of the reaction of each type of character upon the other, the general purpose and design of Providence in the institution of sex, dawn clearly upon us.

That purpose obviously is—as every final aim of the divine mind must be—moral. In the vegetable world we doubtless see it to be so only symbolically; in the animal it is real and unquestionable. Possibly we can distinguish it when we study it in man. The prime condition of moral life is the conquest of self. In this there must be control of what is necessarily the strongest original instinct of every organism—that of self-preservation. This must not be extirpated, and the control must be in the interest of a nobler element of being, in the interest of character, which is only the shape and condition of what we call man's spirit, what we believe to be his eternal part. That this spiritual nature is also to be attributed to what we have hitherto called the brute creation, is the conclusion to-day of an increasing number of serious thinkers. If we are not prepared for that opinion (which makes all self-conscious vitality a sign of spirit) we yet have an example in the animals of the necessity of at least rudimentary moral ideas to even the lowest forms of social life. The preservation of species depends on the fierce traits of parent beasts being controlled and impulses of tenderness and care being developed, at least towards each other and their young. Actually, a genuine moral training is received by even brute natures in their social lives, and for it in them, as in intelligent beings, one principle was indispensable—the principle which should be sufficient to conquer self without destroying it—and that is the principle of love. The first form of such moral development is that which arises in this wonderful relation of sex. The theory of sex is obviously that of two natures complementary to each other, of which the one is needful to the wholeness, the perfectness of the other. Out of this need arises the instinctive longing in which the union of the sexes begins. In their united relation the first demands begin to be made, in every tribe, on the power of the moral nature to assert itself and to dominate the animal. Something of self-sacrifice must characterize the relations of the most brutal pair; and in the care of offspring a new instinct awakes to add itself to the former. Among the human race, the principle of love aroused by sex, developed by the family relation, extends to others of their kind, and so we have the beginnings of society, which is the prime condition of human progress and ultimate civilization. Somewhat thus, at any rate, we may trace the workings of Divine creative thought in the constitution of nature, and that moral purpose which, as it must guide all else which God does, is also present in the institution of sex.

Certainly, in the case of man it is, as I have called it, altogether the most remarkable and important fact in our constitution, and the most influential, whether as regards human happiness and welfare or the moral progress of our race. No relation of human beings approaches in depth and completeness that of the married pair. In none does the essential spirituality of our nature more distinctly reveal itself to consciousness than in this when it is pure and noble. No form of joy approaches this, beginning in the ecstacy of awakening love and continuing in the settled and perfect harmony

which becomes almost an identity of the two individu-
alities.

Since such is the importance of the relation of the
sexes, it is the fact, historically, that there is no
better test of the moral progress of social man
than the institution of marriage furnishes. The position of woman, as the brute possession, as the domestic
slave, as the cherished companion, finally, as the acknowledged moral and social peer of man, marks
accurately the advance of our race from animalism and
the sole sway of brute force, to the ascendency of the
spiritual nature and of moral principle.

And because of this high importance of the relation
of the sexes to earthly happiness and welfare, to moral
health and progress and to the development of the
spiritual nature, how can we adequately express the
sanctity of it, the reverence with which so peculiar
and precious a thought of God ought to be regarded
and the vigilance with which it should be defended in
the facts of social life, in the habits of the individual,
whether in marriage or out of it, and even, as Jesus
warned us, in the secret thoughts of the heart?

It is certain that up to this time society has not attained to a self-consciousness sufficiently noble on this
point. I doubt if the young are so taught as justly to
feel the dignity, the holiness of the married relation.
Too much it is the subject of instinctive rather than
reflective and religious action. I cannot speak strongly
enough in rebuke of the levity with which it is often
treated in conversation, and in publications the only aim
of which is to make unworthy profit by catering to the
lower tastes of the people In all this is genuine sacri-
lege.

And all treatment of the institution of sex and the
relation of marriage which is not dignified and reverent
ministers to distinct and vicious profanation. The
more elevated anything is, the more diligent the care
with which it must be cherished. And as it is of the

mystery of this relation of sex that it involves not only man's higher spiritual nature (which, I repeat, is the essence of it), but co-ordinately his lower, the animal nature, there is ever present the danger that it should become a ministry to base and degrading passions instead of to the noble traits and sentiments it is capable of cultivating. The necessary exigency of the instincts on which depends the perpetuation of the race, lends them a power as subtle as it is great. The spirit of marriage itself may be ignoble and debasing, and the painful ineffectiveness and misdirection of the moral training which, up to this time, society gives to its members, are shown in nothing more glaringly than by the wide persistence in this nineteenth century of those debasing and destructive vices in which the sanctity of the relation of sex is mocked and bestial indulgence both destroys the body and corrupts to its foundations the spiritual nature.

It is a healthful token of the times that these evils, the extent of which has too long been cloaked by false and injurious sentiments, are now being laid open to the light of day; that organized efforts are being made to combat them, and especially to set in motion in society the forces of a moral education which shall elevate in us all conceptions and sentiments regarding the relations of the sexes; which shall defend our youth from the temptations of their own complex natures and from the insidious evils of low standards, gross social maxims and the myriad-fold enginery of vice. This cannot be done too discreetly and delicately, but it must be done effectively. Society has slept far too long in presence of evils, often imperfectly known to those who should be most ready to work for their correction, but the key to which is apt to be rudely thrust into the hands of each rising generation. Alongside the world of respectable society in every Christian, as in the pagan ages, has existed and exists this world of shame and sin, of corruption, of the most cruel slavery, of disease, despair and death. Beneath the orderly and glittering surface of society beams this foul and miry sea in which are forever engulfed successive armies of the more helpless sex, and in which the bodies and souls of the stronger are often befouled beyond purification. It is the fact that the fall of some of the greatest social structures of the past was in very large measure wrought by the vices which sapped the manhood of communities far advanced in civilization. Rome herself fell because she could no longer recruit among her own sons, or even from the nations she had admitted to her citizenship, the armies needed to withstand the remoter barbarians who pressed upon her in all the vigor of a semi-civilization unenervated by luxury and vice. We have not yet, we may trust, reached the point where political corruption, the effeminacy and self-indulgence of wealth, disrespect for the sacredness of marriage, pervading moral indifference, actual vice, shall make the return to social health and safety hopeless; but it is certain that we are already reproducing in the ignobleness and venality of our public men, in the extravagance and luxury of our wealthy class, in the freedom of divorce, not a few of the features which preceded, as efficient causes, the downfall of ancient civilizations.

Certainly we have forces of defence beyond those possessed by any ancient society. The general wholesomeness of American home life is far from impaired. Modern life has vastly more numerous interests than ancient to occupy leisure and employ the vacant energies of men. The moral standards held up in preaching and teaching are largely high and idealistic. Religion has a powerful hold upon our communities. Multitudes, even, who do not associate themselves with the churches yet admit its influence as cherished in their own hearts. Especially the growing influence of women is a saving power among us, the value of which we are only beginning to appreciate.

These forces we ought to utilize and direct to the development of a newly enlightened principle and sentiment of personal and social purity. See exactly what this work consists in. It is to be stated in exactly the words in which you would define the whole work of religion. It is simply the conquest and control of the flesh by the spirit. It is the regulation of physical appetite and the thoughts of the heart by moral principle in obedience to that self-respect which we owe ourselves as beings convinced that we are of nature akin to God himself. Interpret your nature as animal only and you become the servant of its appetites and passions. Convinced that the reality of your being is spiritual, your loyalty goes out to that immortal principle which is the rightful sovereign of this perishable body.

Self-respect is the basis of all virtue, and pre-eminently it is the defense of purity against vice. All yielding to physical appetite is dishonorable, degrading to immortal man, be it that of the glutton, the drunkard or the libertine We call those actions crimes, by which other persons are injured or the peace of society disturbed. Vice is the practice of anything which lowers or defiles our own nature. Vice is simply consent to the animal, the beast within us. It is a condescension to the swine, the tiger, which lurks ever in man's physical part and makes him, when he gives way to it, the most terrible beast of all. The classic legend of Circe was really a myth, full of instruction. When they yielded to the solicitations of vice, incarnate in the temptress, men simply abrogated the empire of their moral part, and became the brutes their lower natures resembled.

I heard lately of a strange disease, the essence of which consists in a return to the features of the primitive man. The brow recedes, the jaws protrude, the hair becomes profuse and coarse, the hands become ape-like, the eyes red-hued, and the whole shape simian rather than human. Such is, morally, the man who gives himself up to vice. It permeates the whole nature, to corrupt each instinct, to thwart all noble aspirations, to pervert every thought of the heart. I have known men, still young, and outwardly attractive, but whose whole natures had been *soiled* throughout ; who could no longer see one object with a cleanly and honest eye. To such the whole world is discolored. *These* are the true penalties of sin, my friends—these, and not fabled, after-death horrors. *To be* debased, vice-stained ; to have all your instincts perverted, your tastes polluted—this is your punishment, none the less heavy and terrible though you do not realize it, but go on delighting in the filth of your life. Yes, and there are others, too, which must reach every soul of man at last: the shame and pain of awakening out of all this; the terrible effort which the soul must make to recover health and sanity. I have heard of a youth who—too late to save a life undermined by debauchery—yet awoke to the sin and shame of it and put it from him; but though recovered in spirit, the now hateful memories of the past, his very dreams, became like the furies who pursued Orestes, an awful scourge, hourly chastising his redeemed soul, and driving him to his earthly grave, exhausted in the contest.

Let us, by the grossness, the uncleanness, the bestiality of all vice, *prejudice* youthful hearts against it; not needlessly revealing the offensive forms it actually takes in the world, but showing them the ignoble quality of any yielding to the lower propensities which beset us all. To the little child this choice may present itself in many ways which are trivial only in form; and a victory in some pettiest struggle between the animal and the spiritual, to which parental care has contributed, may mark the taking for all time of the better path. Purity, moral refinement, the honor of the bodily frame as the tenement of the immortal spirit, as the temple of God, if kept worthy of His presence—let these breed not only fixed principles of character, but also deepseated *taste* for everything which is sweet and pure and good. Cast character early in these moulds and the youth will go out into the world with a triple shield before him.

And, from the first, my friends, every virtue should be taught as absolute in itself; therefore as the need, the law and the grace of all human beings, irrespective of physical distinctions. The moral law, the inevitable needs and qualities of the spirit, are not in any way modified by variety of physical functions, however important. No doubt the peculiar types of the male and the female are ineffably contrasted. Vigor, force, energy may more peculiarly mark the one; grace, delicacy, sensitiveness the other. But while either sex loses something of its own power and beauty if its type is metamorphosed into that of the other, yet, at the same time, each must essentially incarnate the traits of the other, or it will fail of its own perfection. The vigorous man who really lacks delicacy, tenderness, sensitiveness, the graceful woman who lacks self-reliance, courage, energy, is distinctly felt to be a difficient example of the one type or the other. It is a mistake, therefore, in dealing with the young, to emphasize the distinction of sex. Teach every virtue to both, and nature will take care of the types.

Above all, let it be no longer possible in humane, refined, enlightened society to distinguish between the sexes as to the shamefulness of vice. The cruelty of the world, its lingering barbarisms, are shown in nothing more markedly than in the treatment hitherto of the man and the woman who have united in a common sin. Such a distinction is a simple relic of the period in which woman was man's mere possession, when he might do as pleased him, but her act of sin was an infidelity to him as her master and lord. That the descent to vice seems a longer path for the one than for the other is, also, only a token of the false moral education which has involved that distinction between the sexes,

395

against which I have just protested. The boy should have been so taught that the downward step would be as difficult for him as for the girl. But, if a distinction is ever to be drawn, it is vastly more often in favor of the woman, who has fallen, ten times to one, from over-trustful affection, from poverty or from ignorance of the world, where the man has yielded to the temptation of his own passions, as for him almost the sole possible impulse to vice. Nothing still contributes to perpetuate licentious ways so effectively as the subtle influence of a double standard of personal morality. So long as ladies who would deem themselves besmirched by the presence of a sinful sister-woman yet admit to their tables and their firesides men habitually addicted to vice, there is little hope for the moral regeneration of society at this point. No possible influence could be worse for young men than to see guilt tolerated in the one which blasts beyond all hope the other. In the eye of all-pure heaven all sin is one. The guilt, the shame, consists in the submission of the higher nature to the lower, the triumph of the flesh over the spirit; and this is the same whether the moral economy which condescends to vice ·be associated with a masculine frame or a feminine one. Here, most certainly, there is no respect of persons with God. His holy finger writes but one standard for all His children. It is that in the one and in the other the spirit must reign and the flesh must serve. It is that law in which Jesus summed up the whole moral obligation of man, " Be ye perfect, as God himself is perfect." Yes, my friends, yes, young man, young woman, equally, it is "the soul that sinneth, it shall die."

WILLIAM LLOYD GARRISON.

THE RELATION OF POVERTY TO PURITY. *

By William Lloyd Garrison.

The growing scientific consideration of current questions does not impair but strengthens the moral and religious grounds upon which primarily all reforms rest. It makes clearer the causes of evils, and suggests practical methods of cure. It warns reformers against wasting efforts on palliatives, urging them to stop the endless pruning of branches which grow faster than the shears can ply.

The warfare against a universal appetite is not like a crusade to destroy a concrete wrong. Those who put on the armor of temperance and social purity can cherish no hope of seeing a triumph such as the abolition of slavery gave the Abolitionists. The enthronement of individual conscience and self control above the merely sensual nature of man is essential to that reconstructed society which is the dream and aim of all who would leave the world better than they found it. This implies the continued upward struggle of the human soul, marking progress, but reaching no finality.

But the great advances made in civilization cheer us on, and as the world grows wiser it is not unnatural to think that the impetus towards good increases with every generation. Progress goes forward on many lines, all essential, and the reformers' difficulty is to keep the true sense of proportion, the temptation being for each to magnify unduly his special reform. I shall hardly hope to escape the charge of disregarding my

* A paper read at the Boston Conference of the American Purity Alliance.

own warning in treating the question now under discussion, but in the few minutes allowed me I shall present what seems to me the most remedial method of treating the problem of prostitution, which we euphemize as the social evil.

We have been in the habit of ascribing poverty chiefly to intemperance. It is now becoming clear that we have mistaken a partial effect for an original cause. Frances E. Willard, with that progressive wisdom which is her noble characteristic, declares that until the conditions which now breed poverty are changed, the temperance movement cannot fulfill the hopes of its advocates.

As with the temperance agitation, so with the work of social purity. Until we trace effect to cause, and find out the springs of licentiousness, we but beat the air. The misdirected effort and waste of energy spent on attempts to pluck a few brands from the burning is deplorable. Fresh fuel is in ridiculous excess of the brands withdrawn. Whence come the young and innocent, in ever increasing numbers, to feed the fires of the passions? Is it not from poor conditions of living, unnecessary and avoidable, that the majority of the unfortunates are evolved?

It is easy and popular to treat the subject with vagueness. It soothes the sensibilities and lightens individual responsibility when we persuade ourselves that these evils are inevitable in the nature of things, that an overruling power is largely accountable for them, and that the only remedy is education and self control, which means that we wash our hands of the botheration and take our thoughts from unpleasant things.

There are those, however, who see the misery and who believe they see, also, its chief cause, as well as the remedy which is its crying need. With that perception and belief a personal responsibility for the wrong cannot be evaded. Woe is me if, having the light, I do not hasten to spread it! To be silent and satisfied with alleviatives while the perishing classes swell their numbers in steadily progressing ratios with the victims of social wrong and injustice is to be a sharer in the responsibility.

As one of those who are convinced that the so called social evil, like that of drunkenness, is largely the direct product of man's inhumanity to man, I shall try to show that poverty is the chief promoter of prostitution. If the postulate is granted our quest must be for the underlying causes of poverty, especially of that poverty which is not voluntary, and which society distinguishes as enforced poverty, consequent upon scarcity of employment and unhealthy conditions of living.

Wendell Phillips once said, " Open to a man a fair field for his industry, and secure to him its gains, and 999 men out of every 1,000 will disdain to steal. Open to woman a fair field for her industry, let her do anything her hands find to do and enjoy her gains, and 999 women out of every 1,000 will disdain to debase themselves for dress or ease."

Mr. Phillips was then arguing for the political equality of women, and the better state of things was predicted upon the opening of the industrial avenues at that time closed to them. Since then a vast number have been opened to the sex.

Everywhere women invade occupations once held sacred to men, and society is safer and better for the change. But new light has dawned upon the economic world. It is evident that, if women should be granted their unquestionable right of equal suffrage, if every channel of trade or profession should open at their touch, we should still have the ghastly problem of enforced poverty, and its unending procession of recruits to the ranks of women who are forced to make merchandise of themselves. Why? Because something more is needed than the equality of the sexes. The system that makes and perpetuates poverty is in itself sufficient to account for the degradation of both sexes. It closes to both a fair field for industry; it decrees that the gains of labor shall not be secured to the laborer; it sustains conditions where women will continue to debase themselves for dress or ease, yea, for the bare necessities of existence. That system which stubbornly thrusts itself across the path of every present social reform is the legalized ownership and monopoly of land.

In spite of social progress, and notwithstanding the vast increase of national wealth, poverty has kept an equal pace, with its brood of poisonous evils. The millionaire has grown to the multi-millionaire, and the pauper of old days has been succeded by the tramp and the slums, wherein lurk the greatest dangers to our civilization. As Dean Farrar tersely puts it: "When zones of plethoric riches, of selfish luxury, of materializing egotism, are conterminous with zones of squalid wretchedness and practical heathendom, such juxtaposition, as a wise bishop has warned us, tends to produce cyclones."

Wendell Phillips' utterance which I have quoted is susceptible of a broader interpretation than he dreamed. To-day it will be accepted as an admirable statement of the fundamental reform which aims to restore to mankind the heritage of the earth, which has passed into private and exclusive hands. " A fair field for industry, and a security of gains to the owner." That sums up the whole contention, and it can only be realized when the bounty of nature, the source of all wealth, is open on equal terms to every child of humanity. Stated in economic terms, it is " equal access to natural opportunity, and unhampered interchange of products."

I have no time to enlarge upon or explain the Single Tax Reform, but I affirm its pertinency to the discussion of social purity, and shall attempt to make clear my meaning by illustration.

Poverty is the hotbed of impurity. In every city the tenement house, with its crowded occupants and unhealthy ventilation, with the impossibility of individual privacy and delicate reserve, produces its natural fruit.

What makes tenement houses and human hives of misery when there is illimitable space for homes of comfort? Plainly it is the monopoly of land and speculation in that element which no man made and upon which all men must live and work. That the power over men arises from ownership of land as well as from ownership of bodies is growing more and more patent. Go with me to the North End, or to the shady side of Beacon Hill, where the victims of landlordism are in daily and painful evidence. Reckon the enormous percentage of return that such investments yield. If you need assistance consult Father Field, that faithful worker and missionary among the colored poor.

The inevitable question that presents itself to thinking minds is: "How, with two thirds of the area of Boston unoccupied, should it be necessary for human beings to live in such closeness and squalor, for which they are obliged to yield so much of their earnings?" Surely not for the buildings they inhabit, some of which are so vile that they are constantly threatened by the Board of Health. The sole reason for the exorbitant rents exacted is the artificial enhancement of land values, made possible only by withholding from use the idle land and putting it beyond the reach of labor. It is so much opportunity for self employment subtracted from the sum which would be more than enough for all.

Suppose two-thirds of the supply of flour in Boston were locked up for speculative purposes, in order to increase the price of the one-third on sale. How soon this "corner" in an essential article of food would be denounced! But its baneful effect would not be comparable to the constantly existing corner in land which exists in every centre of population. The artificial scarcity of flour would at once cause thousands of barrels to rush in and fill the vacuum. But land cannot rush in to break the land monopoly. It is a fixed quantity, and speculators can hold it with an iron grasp with assured confidence.

THE NATIONAL PURITY CONGRESS.

Given a paradise of a world, with superabundance of opportunity for all the people that should ever inhabit it, but retain the system of land ownership, the permission for the few to monopolize its surface, and compel men to pay for the privilege of living on the planet, and it would need no prophet to foretell that in a certain period, when the earth was privately owned, enforced poverty, with its attendant crime and misery, intemperance and prostitution, must follow as the day the night. If light and air could be as easily appropriated and sold as land, it would be done with equal justice.

Insufficient wages is another mighty factor in the social purity problem. Between the wages of sin and the wages of the sweat shop, the simple wonder is that so many women in need can hold to lives of chastity. In Baltimore, recently, Mrs. Charlton Edholm, of Chicago, a missionary for the rescue of fallen women, attending the Purity Congress, went with others to visit disreputable houses, and pray and sing to the inmates. In one a girl of eighteen said: "I know you mean well by coming here, but I don't know how much good it will do. Instead of coming here you had better go around to some of these factories and shops that grind a poor girl down to $2 a week, and get them to pay better wages. It's no use; a girl can't live on what she gets. You had better put in your efforts there." At another place Mrs. Edholm urged one of the inmates to leave the place. "I would like to," she said, "but I cannot. I have two children that I have to support and pay for their schooling. One is eleven and the other thirteen. They are not in this city. My children are the purest, sweetest things on earth. I wouldn't have them know about me for the world. I want to leave this life, but I cannot. You don't know how it is."

Ask yourselves what makes wages so low that women are forced to lives of shame? Lack of employment, you say. Why should there be a lack of employment in this country of superabundance? Is not all wealth evolved from land by the application of labor, not alone by agriculture but by trade, manufactures and production of all kinds, every one of which is dependent upon access to land? If, therefore, employment is scarce, it implies a scarcity of productive land, for where such land is plenty and accessible, there never has been and can never be enforced idleness. Until all the desirable land of a new country passes into private ownership, such a thing as complaint of lack of work is never heard. The sole complaint is lack of workers.

This great and favored country is as yet a virgin territory, its resources barely touched. It is ready to respond lavishly to labor. It holds in its broad bosom wealth ample to support in comfort and luxury many times the present population. Yet we are here to discuss evils arising out of overcrowding and idleness enforced. Is it not pitiful?

O friends, look beneath the surface, and find the real enemy which you are only fighting in its deceptive and protean forms. Its essence is land monopoly.

> Then waste no time on lesser foes
> In strife unworthy freemen,
> God lifts to-day the veil, and shows
> The features of the demon.

At each end of the social scale your greatest difficulties exist. I have dwelt upon the end of poverty, and desire to affirm that the end which is typified by bloated wealth is likewise a nursery of impurity. Who can compute the numberless maidens sacrificed annually to the market sustained by profligate and gilded patronage? Excess of wealth implies luxurious pleasures and vices, schemes to kill time, to banish ennui, to invent new sensations of bodily excitement. Here extremes meet.

> Strange dance! 'Tis free to Rank and Rags;
> Here no distinction matters;
> Here Riches shakes its money bags,
> And Poverty its tatters.

From the ranks of want come the sacrifices that wealth demands. The human soul is in the market, and for sale with the body.

How comes this excessive opulence in few and dangerous hands? Trace any of the well known fortunes of this country or Great Britain, and you will find that their genesis is in the monopoly of land, or some special and unjust privilege. Land ownership is simply the power of excluding those who must use the earth, except on terms that enrich him who renders no service, at the expense of him who renders it all.

To me the land reform seems most reasonable and fundamental, and I beseech the friends of purity to consider it, if they would put this reform upon a practical and effective basis.

In the establishment of the single tax, to repeat the words of Wendell Phillips, "nine hundred and ninety-nine out of every thousand women will disdain to debase themselves for dress and ease," and he might have added "for necessity," because under justice such necessity cannot exist.

REV. WM. N. M^CVICAR, D. D.
PRESIDENT PHILADELPHIA SOCIAL PURITY ALLIANCE.
LETTER ON PAGE 8.

PUBLIC BATHS AND PUBLIC COMFORT STATIONS AS RELATED TO PUBLIC MORALS.

By Wm. H. Tolman, Ph.D.

The Brooklyn Bridge was built in theory hundreds of years ago, but only in our day has its roadway been one important means of transportation between the two cities. Likewise in the realm of morals, theories have been promulgated all through the ages and some have been realized in fact, because founded on the bedrock of righteousness. The problem of the next century will be that of the city, because the gregarious or social instinct is strong. The city is therefore a storm centre, and heated winds of passion, vice and crime are sweeping in with cyclonic fury, leaving behind a track of ruin and desolation.

The wisest work to-day is performed by those who are studying the causes of social diseases with the same microscopic and scientific care that is used by the physicist in his laboratory, or the physician in his clinic. The more causes are studied, the more pointedly is the conclusion driven home that there is no one solution for the vexed and vexing problems of the day. As a corollary to this proposition, no one problem can be decided individually, it must be viewed in connection with all the others. Social problems are to be solved by a recognition of the conscience, the physiology and the mentality of each individual. If humanity could be tied up in bundles like asparagus, the task of dealing with these problems would be easier, but there is a vast amount of humanity in each personality.

The theorists in Social Purity have been hard at work, but I believe the time is now ready for determining the location, building the piers and stretching the cables of one bridge, which shall afford an escape from a menaced immorality, with its attendant consequences.

The matter of public baths is only now receiving the attention of our American cities. The Continental cities are centuries in advance of us, and were the baths of Europe closed I believe a revolution would follow.

In the selection of your home one of the first rooms to receive your careful attention is the bathroom. You must have those conveniences. The need of a bath for comfort and cleanliness is axiomatic. East of the Bowery and south of Fourteenth street is a population of half a million, for the most part those who live in the tenements. Two hundred and fifty-five thousand of this number came under the personal investigation of the Tenement House Committee of 1894 and it was ascertained that out of the number only 306 have access to bathrooms in houses in which they live! But, you say, they can get a bath at some other place. On general principles if you want a bath you desire it with a certain degree of regularity, and within walking distance of five or six rooms at the outside.

If a man, woman or child living in the district above wants a bath and cannot get it at the home they must go to the Baron de Hirsch baths, Market and Henry streets; The People's Baths, 9 Centre Market Place, under the care of the Association for Improving the Condition of the Poor; the Demilt Dispensary, Twenty-third street and Second avenue; the Cathedral Mission, Stanton street, or the Riverside Association, West Sixty-fifth street. In thousands of cases, to avail oneself of these facilities, a loss of time is involved, and the expense of car fare is a deterrent force, particularly if the family is taken. Surely the city of New York, the Empire City of America, provides public baths for its inhabitants. With the exception of the floating baths in Summer,

WILLIAM H. TOLMAN, PH.D.

there is not a single public bath provided for New York, although it must be stated that his Honor, Mayor Strong, recognizing the necessity and the duty of such provisions, has appointed a Mayor's committee of three, to take the whole matter under advisement.

There is not a single city in America which makes suitable provisions for public baths and there are scores of cities which make absolutely no provision. The Continental cities provide them as a matter of course.

In 1894 the Committee of Seventy felt that it would be recreant to its ante-election pledges if it failed to realize them. Accordingly, sub-committees were appointed to take under advisement the platform pledges regarding baths and lavatories. "We favor the establishment of adequate public baths and lavatories for the promotion of cleanliness and increased public comfort at appropriate places throughout the city," was one plank in their platform.

The Committee were obliged to work up these subjects from the beginning, as nothing has been done in this line. A preliminary report was made to the Committee of Seventy early in 1895. When the Committee of Seventy came to an end in June, 1895, the existence of the sub-committees likewise terminated. A unique but complimentary step was taken by Mayor Strong, in recognition of the public spirit and practical work of this sub-committee, by appointing them in July a Mayor's Committee on Public Baths and Public Comfort Stations. Plans for a public bath have been accepted by the Board of Health. Its cost, including the lot, will be in the neighborhood of $150,000. It will be located in the vicinity of Tompkins Square, a densely populated neighborhood. It will have accommodations daily for 2,500 bathers. This bath house will be the first of a series of seven, located in the congested parts of the city. In connection with the bath should be a wash house, where the laundry work of the family may be done away from the narrow limits of tenement house home. It is calculated that one hour will suffice for the laundry of a family of five. The charge increases for each additional hour for the sake of discouraging professional laundresses from using the wash house.

The following are the recommendations:

1. That the spray or rain water system of baths be adopted, because, primarily, there is no waste of water; and, in the second place, the cost of erection is very moderate; and lastly, it is characterized by cleanliness and simplicity.

2. Bath houses at a moderate cost should be erected in close proximity to those requiring them, rather than the erection of two or three great bathing institutions costing large sums of money.

3. That the bath houses should contain proper and requisite divisions for the use of the cleanly and those not clean; and that each should contain some system for fumigating clothes when necessary.

4. That such public schools, where it may be practicable, should be equipped in the basement with baths similar to those in the Hebrew Sheltering Guardian Asylum, with requisite divisions for women. This can be done at a very small outlay, because the boilers already in use for heating the building will usually suffice to heat the water for an 800-gallon tank. These baths could be used by the women during the school hours and by the school children after school hours and on Saturdays, and would in no way interfere with the usefulness of the school buildings.

5. That the following six sites for public baths be chosen:

   a. The vicinity of Washington and Carlisle streets.
   b. The vicinity of Chatham Square.
   c. The vicinity of Essex Market.
   d. The vicinity of Tompkins Square.
   e. The vicinity of 58th street and 11th avenue.
   f. The vicinity of 110th street and 2nd avenue.

This number of houses will give bathing facilities for hot water baths for at least 15,000 people daily.

6. That in the tenement house districts public wash houses be opened in connection with the baths, thereby relieving many homes of one and two rooms of the unhealthy conditions of laundry work.

By a public comfort station is meant the convenience of a public water closet or urinal. The best types are the underground lavatories, as they are called, although it should be stated that the lavatory really is the provision of towels and soap for washing the hands or face. Attendants keep the conveniences scrupulously clean, and fees nearly defray the operating expenses. The English and the Continental cities provide these public comfort stations as a matter of course, and are increasing the number. The same need exists in New York as in other cities. What provision is made by the metropolitan city of America for these conveniences? Outside of the parks there is not a single public comfort station, and those in the parks are totally inadequate and unsanitary.

HEALTH DEPARTMENT, BOSTON,
March 5, 1894.

I have to say that we have twenty-one public urinals.

DEPARTMENT OF PUBLIC SAFETY, PHILADELPHIA,
February 17, 1894.

Regarding the number of public comfort stations in Philadelphia, I beg to report: There are comfort stations in each of the following squares: Independence, Franklin, Washington, Penn, Treaty and Norris, with accommodations for five or six persons at a time. The largest public retreat is at the City Hall.

DEPARTMENT OF PUBLIC WORKS, CHICAGO,
February 17, 1894.

I have to inform you that the city of Chicago has no public urinals or water closets.

THE NATIONAL PURITY CONGRESS.

MAYOR'S OFFICE, ST. LOUIS,
November 2, 1894.

DEAR SIR:—St. Louis has no public lavatories on the street nor elsewhere except in the parks where the Park Commissioner provides them.

DEPARTMENT OF CITY WORKS,
BUREAU OF LOCAL IMPROVEMENTS, BROOKLYN,
November 21, 1894.

The city has no water closets, urinals or lavatories for the public use except in the parks.

SURVEYOR'S DEPARTMENT, CITY OF BIRMINGHAM,
February 13, 1894.

The total number of urinals in the city is 96 and the number of stalls therein is 437. Seventy-eight of such urinals are cleansed once each day by hand, by water delivered through a flexible hose, and by scrubbing with bass brooms. Fourteen urinals in class 2 are flushed on face of divisions during the Summer season by means of a continuous water supply between the hours of 6 A. M. and 11 P. M. Four urinals in class 3 are flushed by automatic delivery at intervals of forty-five minutes, night and day.

The annual cost of maintenance for each stall, including gas, water, cleansing and painting, is as under:
Class 1, £1 2 10. Class 2, £1 7 8. Class 3, £1 5 10.

LIVERPOOL, January 1, 1894.

The City Engineer concludes that public conveniences are referred to. There are 222 public urinals in the city of Liverpool, with an aggregate number of 595 stalls. There are also three public water closets, and these are provided in every case with an attendant. Just recently three underground conveniences, and a sum of £3,500 has been included in the estimates for the current year for this purpose.

A few public conveniences are supplied by the Department of Public Parks, but in order to ascertain the approximate number the report of the Board of Excise must be consulted, with this caution, that the numbers as there furnished are the result of private enterprise, and are not made possible by the public authorities. From the report of the Board of Excise for the fiscal year ending April 30, 1894, there were licensed 6,710 saloons for the sale of strong and spirituous liquors, and 537 saloons for the sale of ale and beer only, a total of 7,247. That is the approximate number of water closets or urinals. In other words, what the city fails to provide for the convenience of its citizens the saloonist supplies. This is done as a matter of business in order to attract customers, for the liquor offered for sale is the least attraction of the modern saloon. The lavatory accommodations are as ample and as clean as it is possible for them to be built, and many of them will compare very favorably with those in the finest appointed hotels. With a knowledge of these facts it is no surprise that the saloon is a power in politics, and deservedly so, because it provides for the welfare of a large part of the community, and common decency will lead a man to recognize in some way the man or the institution that does him a good turn. The saloonist, however, recoups himself for his outlay in the increasing number of patrons who frequent the place for the lavatory accommodations solely, but in addition patronize the bar, because large numbers of men have a feeling of sneaking meanness in the thought of getting something for nothing, hence a glass of beer, or whiskey, as the case may be, is bought. Illustrating this point by a concrete case, from a letter received January, 1894:

"Being by no means an abstainer or temperance man, but rather one of that vast crowd who do not drink because of the want of the stimulant, but will not say no when in company or at table, these people would, perhaps, never enter a saloon from one end of the week to the other, were it not for a factor far more powerful than the average of good intentions, namely, 'nature's demand,' which will and must be recognized by all. In this great city of ours we no doubt lack good government, rapid transit, and who knows what all; but we certainly do need public closets as much as we need food and air. The writer knows, from personal experience, that the first glass of liquor, drank for no other reason but simply as a means of compensating the saloonkeeper for the use of his closet, has been the direct cause of subsequent humiliation and misery, not to mention the expenditure of money which would have done much good elsewhere."

There is, therefore, no reason why the municipality should not make ample provisions for water closets, particularly in the tenement house district. This is a matter which should be brought to the attention of thoughtful people, in order that the action of such legitimate demands should be backed up by such an impact of public opinion in its favor, that the question should be not "when," but "how and where."

What, accordingly, are the conveniences of water closets and urinals in the tenement house district, where there is the greatest density of population? From a recent study made by the Church Temperance Society, in forty-seven blocks in Houston, Stanton, Rivington, Delancey and Broome streets, 55,357 persons lived in 589 houses. According to a recent sanitary census the tenement house population is eighty-seven per cent. of the district. In these forty-seven blocks, 213 families lived in homes of one room, and 3,685 in homes of two rooms. Of the total number of dwellers in the district studied, 25,539 were children or young people. In this district most of the houses are old-timers, and the sanitary accommodations correspond. In very few dwellings are there water closets on each floor. The usual accommodations are a row of water closets in the courtyards and a urinal in one corner. The conditions are again complicated by the fact that the courtyard is also the passage way for the occupants of a rear tenement. Under the very best conditions such arrangements are unsanitary, especially when used by ignorant or careless people. But apart from any considerations like these, such accommodations are a constant obstacle to modesty and refinement. All through the tenement house district are shoals of children; hence the more reason why the community should interest itself in insisting that every precaution conducive to morality and purity should be taken in behalf of its growing citizenship. All through this district the only conveniences are those provided by the saloons.

If it be unquestioned that a lavatory offers a convenience which is demanded by the needs of the entire body of the citizens, absolutely without exception, a nineteenth century municipality is culpable in not itself making suitable provisions for such accommodations, and allowing a small part of the community to do so, thereby deriving a revenue from the same, as is the case of the saloonist. He exploits communal need for private gain.

Regarding Public Comfort Stations, the Mayor's Committee recommends:

1. The duplication of the conveniences in the parks and the enlargement of those already built. The enlargement can be done at a comparatively small expense, as the extension of the plumbing will be a moderate item.

2. The ample provision of conveniences for women as well as for men, the former provision to be secured by "ladies' châlets," that is, a convenience divided into two parts—one for the sale of millinery or small notions, and the other for the lavatory, the entrance of which will be through the shop.

3. The opening of a sufficient number of underground water closets at the entrance to the parks, for example, at Fifty-ninth street and Eighth avenue and Fifty-ninth street and Fifth avenue, and also near the crowded thoroughfares, as Madison Square Park, Cooper Union Park and Chatham Square.

4. The provision of a sufficient number of surface water closets, in the front of which may be a barber shop and bootblacking stands, with the lavatory in the rear.

5. That all public buildings, as far as practicable, which are the property of the city, should be provided with lavatory accommodations on a generous scale, for the use of the public.

Regarding both baths and public comfort stations, the Committee would recommend:

1. That a certain part of each bath and convenience should be free, in order that necessitous cases may be relieved; for the remaining part, a fee should be charged, which sum will contribute towards the operating expenses, and will enable the patrons of the establishment to retain their self respect.

2. That the baths and water closets shall be in charge of a sufficient number of paid attendants.

3. That the baths and water closets should be under the jurisdiction of the Health Department, under a department to be known as the Bureau of Public Comfort.

The new social spirit is not commercial, but is humanistic, believing that the claims of life precede those of property. The city is the civic home of all its inhabitants, and you should not rest content till New York City affords the essentials of a well ordered home to all the component parts of its citizenship. If the city homes are so small that some of the essentials cannot be there provided, they must be furnished outside. Two of the essentials are public baths and public comfort stations, which should not be furnished free, but should be paid for by those who use them.

The Mayor's Committee is devoting thought and energy to providing the city with these two essentials of right living, and it looks to you for that co-operation which will form part of an enlightened public opinion demanding these provisions immediately and in sufficient numbers.

DEMORALIZING LITERATURE.*

By Anthony Comstock.

For every effect there is first a cause. Before each harvest a seed sowing or planting.

The carnage of battle makes the ambulance corps a necessity. The ravages of intemperance makes imperative the efforts of temperance reforms. Hospitals and asylums are forced into existence by the inroads of disease, wounds and physical pain upon the human race. The degradation of men and women has called into existence Rescue Bands, Magdalen Homes, Midnight Missions, Christian League Industrial Clubs and the American Purity Alliance.

In like manner the systematic corruption ot the youth of this nation by means of demoralizing publications and articles for immoral use has made absolutely necessary the work of the New York Society for the Suppression of Vice, which society I have the honor to represent here this afternoon.

The scattering over the land of a corrupt literature, in thousands and millions of instances, has been the seed sowing from which has come the harvest of crime, squalor, misery and death which this Alliance is considering to-day.

An army in the field of active service is divided into departments, divisions, corps, brigades, regiments, companies, squads and details. Each soldier has an individual assignment either in the ranks or on detail service.

---

* Abstract of a Paper read at the New York American Purity Alliance Conference.

ANTHONY COMSTOCK.

All march under one leader and fight for one object. Upon the march the advance guard, pioneers, sappers or miners go in advance, the rear guard and ambulance corps follow behind.

The American Purity Alliance to-day combines the advance guard, pioneer and ambulance corps. The latter in the army cares for the wounded and dying. So the Magdalen Homes, Rescue Bands, Midnight Missions, Christian League Industrial Clubs and kindred organizations—the ambulance corps of the American Purity Alliance—are seeking to rescue and save those who have been wounded and degraded. They are dealing with the effects of the devil's seed sowing of intemperance and demoralizing books and pictures.

The Society for the Suppression of Vice and that noble band of White Ribbon women—the National Woman's Christian Temperance Union—represent a work similar to the advance guard and the pioneer or sappers and miners corps of the army. We are locating worse than masked batteries, sunken mines and ambuscades. We are contending against dangers and foes worse, a thousand fold worse, than any foe that simply destroys life or blows the body into fragments. We are assailing foes more to be dreaded and shunned than any contagion that ever arose from sewer pipe or stagnant pool. We are camped upon the trail of an insidious and deadly foe; one that not only wrecks the physical but infects the moral nature, opening the door to spiritual degradation and death. Corrupt publications are pestilential blasts from the infernal region that wither and sere holy aspirations in the soul. They are precursors of evil, and only evil. They are practically the devil's kindling wood with which he lights the fires of remorseless hell in the soul.

Once admitted into the chamber of imagery in the heart of the child—into memory's storehouse—they are employed by imagination and fancy, the re-imaging faculties of the mind, as material from which seductive entertainment is furnished to lure the soul away from God. The mind runs riot with sin. Once the re-imaging faculties of the mind are linked to the sensual nature by an unclean thought the forces for evil are set in motion which rend assunder every safeguard to virtue and truth.

A perpetual assault is made upon the citadel of thought. Secret hours are spent dreaming over the story of vice and crime. The receptive mind of youth drinks in sensational, foul and criminal story with an avidity that is fearful to contemplate.

To those who have seen the results of these worse than the sting of asps, no surprise is felt, when in after years is heard the moan of the aged person praying to be delivered from the sins of his youth.

The degrading of the youth of this nation by the sickening details of loathsome crimes, the horrors of blood and thunder stories, the dime and half dime novel and paper, and the foul oozings of defiled minds in many of the weekly papers, to say nothing of the nameless books and papers, is one of the highest crimes that can be committed against the future of this nation.

These brutal assaults upon the native innocence of youth and children is laying burdens upon the rising generation which will be grevious to their future welfare and heavy to be borne.

Alas! that the greed for gain should turn the mighty press of this land into engines of corruption. The degrading of our youth is a crying evil to day. It is a seed sowing from which brothels, dives, prisons, penitentiaries, asylums and early graves are fast being recruited.

The report of the New York Society for the Suppression of Vice, which is about completed for 1895, while it shows gratifying results shows also cause for alarm.

The matters destroyed are one thing. But the matters which are to-day at large (worse than ravenous beasts or poisonous serpents), prowling about the country and trailing their slimy and venomous form among the youth in our institutions of learning, is an entirely different thing.

That report contains the arrest of 2,044 persons, and the seizure of 63,139 pounds of books, 27,424 pounds of stereotype plates for printing books, 836,096 obscene pictures and 5,895 negatives for making the same. Also 96,680 articles for immoral use, 1,577,441 circulars, catalogues, songs and leaflets, 32, 883 newspapers, 1,102,620 names and post office addresses seized in hands of dealers to which circulars were being sent.

Henry B Blackwell

EQUAL SUFFRAGE VS. PROSTITUTION.*

By Henry B. Blackwell.

Among the underlying causes of prostitution and of the double standard of morals for men and women out of which prostitution grows, the political disfranchisement of women is the greatest of all. The only cure for the social evil is by developing self reliance and self respect among women, and respect for women among men. But so long as a woman's opinion is not considered worth counting in the great consensus of public opinion, the annual election, so long men will hold an exaggerated estimate of their own superiority, and a contempt for the personality of women; while women themselves will be depreciated in their own estimation. A bright, intelligent woman said to me recently: "There never was a woman who would not prefer to be a man, and never a man who would prefer to be a woman." If that be so, it is because women have not a fair chance under existing social conditions.

Prostitution is the direct result of the exclusion of women from public affairs. Nine-tenths of the outcast women, we are assured, were corrupted and ruined by some man before they reached the age of mental maturity. In no single case have these men ever been punished for their crime, while their partner in guilt has been branded with lifelong infamy. Year after year the suffragists have petitioned their State Legislatures to raise the age of consent, as it is called—the age of protection, as it should be called, so that no girl shall be capable of giving her legal consent to her own degradation until she is capable of contracting to buy or sell

* A Paper read at the Boston American Purity Alliance Conference.

property or to make any other legal contract. That age, in the case alike of men and women, is twenty-one years. If any man having improper relations with a girl not yet of age were, by our statutes, liable to the penalty of rape, that single act of legislation, properly enforced, would almost put an end to prostitution, and would encourage honorable marriage. But it is almost hopeless to secure such legislation by the votes of men alone.

Next in importance as a cure for prostitution to the establishment of legal majority, twenty-one years, as the limit of the age of protection, is the suppression of the dram shops. These establishments are potent allies to sexual vice. They stimulate the passions of men; they separate men from the society of respectable and self respecting women. But without the united votes of women and men the dram shops cannot be suppressed, and if drinking is to be, as the Boston *Herald* asserted editorially last week, the permanent habit of society, then we should adopt the German custom of having the women and children go with the men to the beer gardens and drink with them. To separate the sexes in their social habits—to give the men a monopoly of drinking and smoking, while making these enjoyments discreditable in the case of women—is a violation of the law of nature which decrees that "it is not good for man to be alone." But woman suffrage will be not only a preventive of sexual vice, it will be its cure. By arousing women to self respect and a public duty, it will organize women as a class for self protection. Sexual vice is the deadliest foe of the home. The outcast woman is a direct menace to the virtuous woman as maiden, as wife and as mother. Women, when once accustomed to exercise the rights and duties of citizenship, will unite, in every town and in every ward of a city, to reform, to protect, to redeem fallen women.

Women as voters will put an end to the useless and cruel raids of the police, who spasmodically arrest and make public, and degrade unfortunate women, often without any evidence of criminality, while they conceal and exempt from arrest and punishment the male associates of these women. When good women, who are more than ninety-five per cent. of their sex, become aware that God has made them responsible for their frail and erring sisters, they will find means of giving every woman an opportunity of living an honorable and respected life. In short, suffrage will mean for women precisely what it has meant for men. It will give women position, power, freedom, incentive, opportunity. It will open to them all useful and lucrative employments. It will remove from them the temptations to mercenary marriages, which are the source of so much lifelong misery to all concerned. It will give men added respect for women, since power always commands respect. As Col. Higginson has well said, it will mean for women as a sex, self respect and self protection.

If I did not know from the political experience of the human race the value of equal suffrage to every class that has attained it, and resultant benefit to society which has always followed every extension of political power, I should despair of the Republic. The great twin evils of licentiousness and intemperance can never be extirpated by a political society of men alone. One part of the woman's work in politics will be the extirpation of these curses.

PROTECTION FOR YOUNG WOMEN IN STORES, FACTORIES, AND OTHER PLACES OF BUSINESS.*

——— —

BY ISAAC H. CLOTHIER, PHILADELPHIA.

Because I have been an employer on a considerable scale, of both men and women, for over a quarter of a century, I have been asked to present some views to this Conference regarding practical measures looking toward increased safety for young women employed in large mercantile and manufacturing establishments and in other exposed business positions.

That my experience has been almost exclusively of an administrative and executive character, and not in the line of addressing public assemblies, is, perhaps, the very reason I have been asked to treat the practical subject which has been assigned me.

Let me preface the expression of the few thoughts I have to offer on the present occasion, by frankly admitting that I have heretofore shared the general feeling, that the less said on such a delicate subject as the relation of the sexes the better.

It has been generally assumed that because of the nature of the subject it should be avoided, and not even mentioned in mixed assemblies of men and women, on the ground that there was danger therein, and that true manliness and womanliness held themselves above the suspicion of dwelling in thought on such subjects, or on any subject unworthy of the true manly and true womanly nature.

The whole matter is admittedly one of great delicacy, and most difficult to deal with satisfactorily. So delicate is it that those who have been first stirred to

———
* A Paper read at the Philadelphia American Purity Alliance Conference.

call attention to the subject have sometimes been char-
terized by most worthy people as morbid or unhealthy
in their imaginings or oversensitive in their feelings.
While the extent of the evil is conceded, it has been believed that there was more or less danger in discussing
impurity or social evils, and the good to be secured
would not offset the demoralization incurred by dealing
openly with such unsavory themes. Sharing this view
heretofore and measurably now, I have been led to believe that it is in some respects erroneous, and that the
great and terrible evil of impurity stalks abroad in this
professedly Christian land, secretly revelling in the fact
of its security, partly because Christian men and women,
whose skirts individually are clean, hesitate to discuss
and denounce it, because of the peculiar character of its
wickedness and wantonness.

For the reason that it is a delicate subject, it would
seem to be all the more obligatory that it be met as its
nature and importance demand, and especially with
regard to its far reaching consequences. But it should
be constantly remembered that the whole matter needs
to be treated with the greatest care, delicacy and tact,
without undue zeal or unnecessary expression. The
Purity Congress of Baltimore, the proceedings of which
I read with interest, has led in the movement toward
awakening and influencing the public mind on this important subject, and in arousing the sleeping consciences
of the men and women of the nation to their deficiencies, in thus practically ignoring a subject which is one
of the most important that this age has before it for consideration, and which cannot be ignored without danger
to the community and to future generations. And the
poison does not descend only, but must inevitably widen
on either side, corrupting the community in ever increasing measure, unless the fierce light of public
reprobation is turned upon it.

Believing as I do that the work indicated by the
Baltimore Congress should grow and increase with wide

and beneficent effect, I felt willing to aid, in ever so small a measure, by complying with the request made of me, not because I have any specially practical measures to recommend to my brother merchants, whose ranks I have only just left, but that as one of them for almost a generation I have at least the right to commend the subject to their considerate judgment. While I trust I have been interested in all measures tending to the general comfort and well being of employees, both men and women—and for the latter more than the former, because of their greater need—I cannot claim to have given this particular subject the close personal attention which its nature and importance demand, nor to have had, during the years of close absorption in business cares and responsibilities, the real concern which should have led me to adopt every safeguard which could possibly be adopted to further the object desired. The firm of which I was an active member up to the beginning of the present year, employed, perhaps, a thousand women in the various capacities of saleswomen, cashiers, typewriters, sewing women, etc., etc., and an approximate number of men. It has always been our aim to employ the better class of young women rather than those which could be had at the lowest rate of wages, believing it to be good business policy to possess service of the best and most intelligent character. It is believed that success attended our efforts in this respect, and one reason therefor, and for the comparatively high *morale* of the force, is the fact that the engagement of the help has always been done either by a member of the firm, or by those in whom we had the fullest confidence as respects moral character and their treatment of those with whom they were brought into contact, especially young women. There can be no doubt that wrong has been done to young and innocent girls by unprincipled men to whom has been entrusted the engagement of the force of employees in large establishments. By this I do not refer to actual or direct ruin, but to a loose and coarse disregard of the respect due from all men to all women, and especially from those in authority to young women forced by the pressure of circumstances to place themselves in positions almost of supplication and dependence, from which their natures often shrink, but which they are compelled to assume in obedience to the necessity which knows no law. From the rude stare, the coarse remark, the lewd joke, perhaps the familiar and at first repulsive touch, they have absolutely no appeal, except to throw up their means of livelihood, and the first step is often thereby quite involuntarily and unconsciously taken toward a lowering of self respect, and of that fine instinct of womanhood which more or less dwells in every woman, and is at once the charm and preservation of the sex.

The great body of women who have succeeded to an inheritance of purity and refinement, and who from infancy have been tenderly matured and guarded from every unworthy influence, can scarcely realize or believe possible the conditions under which their less fortunate sisters are forced to exist and battle for a bare subsistence. With a natural feeling of horror they would shrink from any treatment which in the slightest savors of disrespect or familiarity, and even regard with aversion those who had been subjected thereto, with the belief, natural in their cases, that every woman should be surrounded with an atmosphere of purity, which unconsciously to herself preserves her from all contaminating influences, innocently, but surely repelling the first intimation of familiarity. This we know, of course, to be the case with the women with whom we mingle in our daily lives.

I would here bear cordial testimony that the women whom I have met on a business plane for many years, the great body of employees of our house, were as refined in feeling, as self-respecting, and as far above all unworthy influences as any class of women in the community. And I would add that many of these women have personally exemplified in their characters and lives the dignity, the strengthening effect, I might say the refining influence of labor, which is God's great boon alike to man and woman.

The community of women to whom I have referred as lacking business experience and as being entire strangers to many actual and sad phases of life, can scarcely conceive the defencelessness of their young sisters under circumstances such as I have briefly indicated, in quest of employment, scarce because of the over-demand, and therefore hard to obtain, and dispensed sometimes by unprincipled men with little or no respect for all that is fine and best in womanhood. Under such harrowing circumstances, with actual necessity compelling them to remain and receive the miserable pittance of wages which stands between them and utter destitution, is it strange that the finer instincts of many inexperienced girls are liable to become callous, their tastes vitiated, and the way prepared in many cases for absolute ruin? That instances such as I have referred to are comparatively rare is to be sincerely hoped, but that they do exist can, I believe, be easily attested. I have been assured on good authority that an employment representative of a mercantile establishment, when told by young girls that they could not possibly exist on the small wages offered, was in the habit of asking in reply whether they had not gentlemen friends who would help, and that nothing was easier than thus to have their wages amply enlarged.

For the sake of human nature let us trust that such cases are rare, but while one such instance exists let us not shut our eyes to the terrible possibilities involved. What is needed, perhaps, is not so much to dwell on extreme cases as to call the attention of employers and of the great community which stands back of and influences employers, to the exposed condition of young women, even under the most favorable circumstances, and to urge them to adopt every measure that may be practicable for their protection, not alone from absolute ruin, but from a deterioration of the moral sense and pure womanly nature which low and coarse surroundings inevitably induce.

I wish it were in my power to suggest some more practical measures for increased protection. From the nature of the case the suggestions must be general, not specific. Let the employing agents be most carefully selected, as well as all men in authority over young women, and let it be well understood that any proven breach of propriety or undue familiarity will be visited by swift and ignominious discharge. Of course injustice must never be done on the other side, but what is needed is the prevalence of a moral sentiment crystallized into law-upholding respect for womanhood, and asserting that any familiarity is indeed the unpardonable sin

In a city like Philadelphia, with the high personal character of its leading merchants, it is certain that every reasonable precaution would be by them most cordially approved and adopted if brought to their attention. But the keen competition of the times and the cares and responsibilities of business lead to everything being placed upon a business basis, and, without a pronounced and increasing public sentiment upon the subject, it is not unlikely that the care and precautions which should be adopted might be overlooked or postponed by the best-intentioned employer. I do not at this time venture to suggest to those who are as well informed as myself regarding the subject any other practical measures of reform than those which will commend themselves to every employer when the subject is considered. I would however suggest that not only measurably to remove temptation should reasonably good wages be paid to young women, but that as a measure of sound business policy it at least pays its way in the sure betterment of the service, an important step toward financial success. But I would place the subject on higher ground.

I ask employers to consider their peculiar and solemn responsibility toward these defenseless children entrusted to their charge. In this age of wondrous strides in material advancement shall not Christian enlightenment prevail and increase, in humane methods of transacting business and in the care of those who perform, each her humble but important part of the service which animates these great hives of human industry? Perfected organization seems almost to have reached its limit. The next step should certainly be the humane care and safety of the force, especially those who need it most. And public sentiment now being gradually awakened will powerfully aid in the blessed consummation of this Christian hope.

———

Since this paper was prepared I have been asked by a leading woman and housekeeper of this city to introduce into it that which is somewhat germane to the subject—a plea to young American women to engage in household service instead of store or factory work.

I wish it were in my power to aid in so desirable a consummation, and that a sentiment could be awakened among the young women of the nation leading them to seek positions where there is to-day so great a need for intelligent service, where they would be safe from danger, where their surroundings might be elevating and congenial, and their occupation not only unobjectionable but desirable in every sense. There are tens of thousands of comfortable homes scattered all over our land, thousands of them refined and cultured homes, needing intelligent, competent service, that tens of thousands of young women could render with great reciprocal advantage, who are now overcrowding the labor market with danger, discomfort, and almost starvation to themselves and their competitors, in the fierce race for subsistence.

There is no more honorable or self-respecting service than that of the household. The science of cookery for instance, as taught to-day by the Drexel and other kindred institutes, is as elevating in the acquirement and practice as any other art or industry. The same may be said of other duties of the household properly performed. I know the reputation of the service suffers from the ignorant and inferior character of too many of those who have engaged therein. I know, too, the difficulties of the situation, and that the responsibility of the present position lies not alone on one side. Employer as well as employed, mistress and maid alike need to be educated to an appreciation of those difficulties and the remedy. Let the character, dignity, and independence of household service be recognized by the housekeepers of the land, and then properly set before our young women, and a vast, new avenue of self-respecting, useful, and well paid occupation lies before them.

With some comparative knowledge of the subject and distinct convictions thereon, I simply present the matter and invoke in its behalf that enlightened public sentiment which, once fully aroused, is all powerful.

Laura Ormiston Chant.

LETTER FROM MRS. LAURA ORMISTON CHANT.

Mrs. Laura Ormiston Chant, who had recently arrived in Boston from London, was invited to address the Congress, but prevented by prior engagements. The following letter was read by the President :

BOSTON, Mass., Oct. 11, 1895.

MY DEAR MR. POWELL:

I am indeed grieved that engagements here prevent my being able to be present at the National Purity Congress, in Baltimore.

There is tough work on hand in Massachusetts in view of the referendum on municipal suffrage for women, and I am glad to be able to help a little. If only the comfortable women of the United States knew how awful a shadow of legalized vice hangs over and menaces the future of their country, they would compel men to give them at least the same power of protecting their sex against unequal and unholy legislation, as men possess.

The right to express their convictions through the orderly but effectual medium of the ballot may one day be the only barrier between the women of America and the supreme, unutterable degradation of continental Europe. Anyhow registration for the vote on the referendum ends on October 16th, and on that day I start for Baltimore—only to miss the National Purity Congress. I am, as I said, very sorry, but will do my best to atone on the 18th. Affectionate wishes for your success. Yours sincerely,

L. ORMISTON CHANT.

436

THE CANADIAN LAW FOR THE PROTECTION OF WOMEN AND GIRLS, WITH SUGGESTIONS FOR ITS AMENDMENT AND FOR A GENERAL CODE.

By D. A. Watt.

What modicum of truth formerly pertained to the ancient adage, that the ballads of a people were more important factors in the formation of national character than their laws,* has long ago ceased. The rule now is that the public conscience is, for the most part, created and maintained by statute law, and by scarcely anything else. The slave trade may be quoted by way of illustration. So long as that infamy remained a legal and lucrative occupation, persons presumably reputable and Christian engaged in it with the approval of the world and even of the church, but so soon as it was stigmatized by law as felony, it speedily became odious. Hence the importance of having laws which make for righteousness, and not, actively or passively, for vice and crime.

At the outset we may enquire what are the limits within which the law may reasonably enforce righteousness and protect rights, in connection with what is somewhat loosely termed social morality? As defined by the late William Shaen, an eminent English jurist, these are, at their minimum, (1) the protection of minors absolutely; (2) the protection of majors from force or fraud or falsehood, or intimidation of any kind; and (3) the protection of the community from public scandal.

It goes without saying that the law should rebuke the double standard of morals currently held, and should

---

* " Let me make the ballads, and who will may make the laws."

deal impartially with all persons, be they men or women, rich or poor.

Legal provisions protecting the rights of women and girls may be civil or criminal, either or both. In Canada matters civil belong chiefly to the Provincial legislatures, and matters criminal to the parliament of the Dominion.

THE CIVIL CODE OF QUEBEC.

The civil code of this Province is, in effect, the Code Napoleon, amended from time to time by the legislature, and subject to further amendment by the same authority. In theory the rights of minors, widows, and other dependent persons, are carefully conserved by its provisions, but in practice we have found much to be desired. Mr. Shaen's requirements in substance are: (1) The father and the mother of a child are jointly and respectively liable to each other, to the child and to the State, for the suitable mainten- ance and education of said child; (2) if the parents are married they are jointly and severally guardians of such child; (3) if the parents are not married the guardian- ship remains with the mother alone; (4) all minor chil- dren without guardians (or having such are out of their possession) are ipso facto wards of the State; (5) breaches of trust, slanders, libels and such like, as well as all crimes, to be subjects of a civil action for ex- emplary damages in favor of the victim, as well as of criminal indictment ; (6) to which I would add that every child should be legitimate of its mother.

The code's estimate of the crime of adultery may be judged from two of the articles dealing with causes of action for " Separation de corps " (sic):

> "187. A husband may demand the separa- tion on the ground of his wife's adultery.

> "188. A wife may demand the separation on the ground of her husband's adultery, if he keeps his concubine in their common habita- tion."

Legislation respecting marriage and divorce have, however, been reserved for the Dominion Parliament.

THE CRIMINAL CODE OF THE DOMINION.

The criminal law of the Dominion is the common law added to and amended by British and Canadian legislation and by "case" law, so called. The statutory provisions have recently been gathered together into one bill entitled "The Criminal Law Act of 1892," and the references below are to the sections of this enactment. The titles under which the crimes under consideration have been grouped are—(1) Offences against morals, and (2) against parental and conjugal rights; (3) Nuisances; (4) Vagrancy; (5) Assaults; (6) Rape* and Abortion; (7) Bigamy, and (8) Abduction. For convenience sake I range them under somewhat different headings, confining myself within the limits assigned to me, to wit, the protection of women, and especially of girls.

Following Mr. Shaen's dicta more or less closely, it is assumed that the criminal law of all countries ought to protect—

(1) minors from incitement to vice or immorality absolutely, that is, the age of so called consent for both sexes† should be the age of majority, whatever that may be; and

---

* In respect of this crime Canada has, for the first time, I believe, in British legislation, enacted into statute law the revolting dictum that a husband may force his wife without being punishable. Stephen is much less emphatic. He says of England (Digest, 1894, p. 208): "A husband, it is said, cannot commit a rape upon his wife * * * (Hale P. C., 629). Hale's reason is that the wife's consent at marriage is irrevocable. It may be doubted, however, whether the consent is not confined to the decent and proper use of marital rights. If a man used violence to his wife under circumstances in which decency or her own health or safety required or justified her refusing her consent, I think he might be convicted at least of an indecent assault." In Canada, however, a man may use violence upon his wife irrespective of her condition and of his, and may injure and infect her and her unborn child, and be within his rights as here defined. In a recent case in India a husband did to death his child wife, and was punished with twelve months imprisonment.

† See Article 334 of the French Criminal Code, which reads as follows:

"Quiconque aura attenté aux mœurs en excitant, favorisant, ou facilitant habituellement, la débauche ou la corruption de la jeunesse de l'un ou de l'autre sexe au-dessous de l'âge *vingt-et-un ans*, sera puni d'un enprisonnement de six mois à deux ans, et d'une amende de cinquante francs à cinq cents francs."

(2) majors from such incitement by means of false-hood or fraud or intimidation, of any kind; and

(3) majors and minors alike and especially, from their relations, and from persons in authority over them, or who are in positions of any form of trust or responsibility towards them or towards the public; and also

(4) from procurors or other infamous traffickers in vice, whether for the home trade or for exportation. All these propositions are in general accord with the laws respecting property. To this I would add a fifth:

(5) That the crime of adultery be constituted a felony, punishable as perjury now is, to which crime it is akin.

That the Canadian law comes very far short of these reasonable requirements is shown by the following synopsis:

ABDUCTION

This crime is commonly named in extradition treatises and, as defined in our code, is as follows:

281. "Every one who * * with intent * * takes away or detains any woman of any age against her will " or

282A. In event of such woman being an heiress or " presumptive next of kin, from motives of lucre "; or

282B. In event of such heiress being a minor (i. e., under 21 years of age) then " out of the possession and against the will " of her parent or guardian: is subject to fourteen years' imprisonment; and

283. If the girl be under 16 years and be not an heiress the mere taking of her "out of the possession," etc., is punishable with five years' imprisonment; and

284. If the girl be under 14 years and the intent be to steal her or her clothing the punishment is seven years' imprisonment.

It will be seen that the already protected minor heiress is further well protected up to the full age of 21 years; that the non-heiress is less well protected and up to the age of only 16 years; and that, if she be a non-heiress, the child's clothing is deemed more worthy of mention than her chastity. In this respect the British and Canadian laws are alike. In no other code that has come under my notice, is the protection given to girl-hood, between the ages of consent and majority, made to depend on the wealth of the victim, although this factor might very properly be taken into account when awarding punishments. A reasonable provision res-pecting abduction might read somewhat as follows:

Every one who, without lawful authority or excuse, takes, harbors or detains a woman or girl

(1) Being a major, by force or otherwise than with her consent, free-will and conscious permission; or

(2) Being a minor under 21 years of age

(*a*) For an unlawful purpose consummated or attempted or with unlawful intent, or

(*b*) For a lawful purpose without the consent of her parent or guardian

—is guilty of abduction.

It is of course assumed that the general provisions of the law will otherwise provide that certain women, lunatics and others, are incapable of giving consent; that consent procured by falsehood or fraud is no con-sent at all; that attempts are punishable as well as the completed offence; and aiders and abbettors as well as principals. Also that punishment is graduated accord-ing to the degree of guilt, and the power or authority of the criminal over the victim, and also according to her youthfulness and helplessness.

One peculiarly foul example of this crime that goes all unpunished in Canada, is the common instance of the criminal who elopes with a girl from an adjoining

State, and who escapes punishment on the plea that both the abduction and the seduction were compassed outside the Dominion. Under Article 355 those who "bring stolen property into or have it in possession in Canada" are liable to seven years' imprisonment, while those who bring stolen girls are unpunishable by her laws.

THE TRAFFIC IN VICE.

The import and export traffic in women to replenish brothels is fairly well met in Section 185 of the law, which is in part copied from the British Act of 1885 of notable memory. The procuration clauses have, however, proved ineffective, inasmuch as intent of prostitution has to be proved, whereas intent of defilement ought to suffice, at least until the crime of abduction is more stringently defined. But within our own country the traffic goes on all unchecked. The spasmodic arresting, fining and again letting loose on society of brothel-keepers, brothel-owners, and brothel-mongers generally, serves merely as an advertisement of their infamous resorts; and as a license fee, good until the time comes round to make the next raid. Those vile trafficers in vice, with their equally atrocious touts, bullies, placeurs, and souteneurs, all living for the most part on the avails of prostitution, ought to be universally dealt with as felons, and as the common enemies of mankind. Their occupation is akin to piracy and the slave trade. Meanwhile they are all too leniently dealt with everywhere. Recently in India a placeur was prosecuted for selling one of his imports, an Austrian girl, to a rich lecher, but the English judge (Mr. Pigott) acquitted the criminal on the ground that the girl was sold for concubinage, which was no offence, and not for prostitution, a sale for which would have been an offence.

Girls over 14 and under 16 are, under section 187, forbidden to be harbored in a brothel on pain of two years' imprisonment, but when of or over 16 they are without this protection unless they be heiresses, in which case the harboring keeper (282) is liable to fourteen years' imprisonment if the girl be under 21 years old. We do not complain of the protection thus given to the rich and guarded heiress; all that we have asked, and hitherto in vain, is that equally effective protection be given to her poor and friendless sisters.

BREACH OF TRUST.

This crime is universally recognized as heinous in matters relating to property, but scarcely at all recognized in dealing with offences against the person. For long years we have been seeking to remedy this effect, but until the late Sir John Thompson took charge of the Department of Justice, little progress was made. In 1890 he introduced to Parliament a bill, one section of which was to protect dependent women against their relations and another against their employers. In both cases the clauses were so "amended" in their passage through Parliament as to greatly minimize their scope, leaving them almost valueless for protective purposes.

The clause respecting relations (176) as introduced, protected a woman from defilement by persons more nearly related to her, by consanguinity or affinity, than the fourth degree of civil law.* As passed it applies only to the grandfather, father and brother, and to marriage as well as defilement.

The clause respecting employers is as follows, the interpolations being printed in italics: "183. Every one is guilty of an indictable offence and liable to two years' imprisonment, who, being a guardian, seduces or has illicit connection with his ward, and every one who seduces or has illicit connection with any woman or girl of previously chaste character (*and under the age of twenty-one years*) who is in his employment (*in a factory, mill or workshop*), or who, being in a common employment with him (*in such factory, mill or workshop*), is

---

* In New York a judge may not sit on a case when either litigant is related to him " within the sixth degree of affinity or consanguinity."

under or in any way subject to his control or direction." Instead of covering all dependent women, the protection is now limited to factory operatives who are chaste minors.

By another clause (186) the parent or guardian who procures or is party to the defilement of a woman is punishable; but the husband, brother, uncle, or other relation is not punishable; in doing so they are within their legal rights. Clause (185) punishes the *giver* of "any drug, intoxicating liquor, matter or thing with intent," but if the defiler be another person he is free under the clause.

Another class of breaches of trust which the Dominion leaves untouched has been dealt with by an act of the Ontario Legislature, passed in 1887, "for the protection of women in certain cases." It enacts that "no person shall at any time or place within the limits of any institution to which *the prison and asylum* act applies, unlawfully know any female, who is capable in law of giving her consent, while she is a patient or is confined in such institution." The benefits of this law are applicable only to the gaols, prisons, etc., of that province, and we have no equivalent law for this province, the legislation is probably as *ultra vires*, the provincial legislature. The only persons who are judged to be incapable of giving consent are (189) "a female idiot or imbecile, and an insane or deaf-and-dumb woman or girl;" also conditionally an heiress under twenty-one and a non-heiress under sixteen; and absolutely any girl under fourteen, as noted herein.

These provisions come very far short of the third requirement mentioned above, but they are all that most persistent efforts have hitherto obtained from the Dominion Parliament.

DEFILEMENT.

The age of consent in Canada (sec. 269) is 14 years, of and over which the unguarded non-heiress may be

said to be an open prey. Nevertheless she may not
(181) be "seduced," if "of previously chaste character,"
nor (187) harbored in a brothel, if she be under 16; and
(182) if seduction be compassed by a promise of marriage, and the criminal be himself *over* 21, then she is
protected *up to* 21. By (184) "illicit connection with
any female passenger" is forbidden to any "person employed on board of any vessel" on pain of fine and imprisonment for one year. A conspiracy (188) "to induce any woman to commit adultery or fornication" is
criminal provided that false pretences be used, the pro-
viso being a change for the worse in the common law.

What is usually termed "ordinary immorality,"
that is, unlawful relations, whether permanent or casual,
between a man and a woman, being majors, with no
element on either side of relationship, incest, adultery,
or bigamy, or of fraud, falsehood, public scandal, or
what not, is meanwhile assumed to be without the scope
of criminal law.

INDECENT ASSAULTS.

The low or high tone of public morals, especially
among the governing classes of a community, may be
accurately gauged by the legal procedure respecting the
odious crimes against girlhood commonly ranged under
this head. Two recent cases occur to me from the high
court of this city. In one an uncle, a family man of
mature years, assaulted and foully diseased his own
child-niece of tender years; his punishment was eighteen
months' imprisonment. In the other, a burly ruffian,
who waylaid and assaulted a little girl on her way from
school under circumstances of exceptional brutality, was
similarly punished. In England matters are much worse.
Judging from the proceedings of the courts presided
over by Judges Granthan, Hawkins and others, the crime
of rape has been abolished there when the victim is a
child. These judges award three and six months'
imprisonment to criminals like the foregoing, while

445

sending others to years of penal servitude whose offence is trivial thieving. In all this they doubtless adequately reflect the sentiments of the community within which they live and move and have their being.* If stripes are proper anywhere it is in cases of revolting crimes such as these. There is, however, but one adequate and proper penal consequence, and that is the castration of the habitual criminal, as well in his own interests as in the interests of the community and of posterity.

ADULTERY.

Edward Livingston, the eminent American jurist, in his work, "A System of Penal Law for Louisiana," at page 173, says of adultery: "As far as I am informed it figures in the penal law of all nations, except the English, and some of their most celebrated lawyers have considered the omission as a defect. Neither the immorality of the act nor its injurious consequences on the happiness of women, and very often on the peace of society and the lives of its members, can be denied. The reason then why it should go unpunished does not seem very clear. . . . Where the law refuses to punish this offence the injured party will do it for him-

---

* Indecent assaults on little girls and aggravated assaults on wives and children are, perhaps, the most rampant forms of crime in English life. In Scotland they are less so, and scarcely at all in Ireland. Moreover the supine indifference to these phases of crime on the part of the community is phenomenal. At a large congress of religious and temperance women held last Summer in London, a principal subject of debate was the casual outbreak of lynching in the Southern United States, while these infamous and brutal offences, being continually committed under their own eyes, were not even mentioned. Nor did the good people see anything incongruous in this action; the parable of the mote and the beam did not even occur to them.

Here is a clipping from a weekly English newspaper, "Truth": William Rolfe, an elderly man, who had been in court for the same offences before, was convicted of assaulting two little girls of seven and eight years old, and sent to prison for one month. Isaiah Burron, 65 years old, was convicted of assaulting a little girl of five years old, having first taken her to a public house and dosed her with rum. He also got one month. George Holland's victim was also five years old, and he also got one month.

The editor, one of the very few who notice such travesties of justice at all, comments thus:—"It is of course something that the judges imposed any imprisonment for, as I show every week, it is quite a common practice to allow offenders convicted of the most ruffianly assaults or the grossest cruelty to escape with a mere fine."

self; he will break the public peace and commit the greatest of all crimes, and he is rarely or never punished."

The stigma still rests on English law, and on the laws of most of her colonies, as well as of those communities (including the State of New York) who have taken their jurisprudence from England. To this day the crimes of incest and adultery are in that country mere eclesiastical offences, unpunishable at common law. The tendency of all English speaking communities to square themselves in respect of their morals down to or below the level of their statute law is well exemplified in England, where, among no inconsiderable section of the people, adultery is scarcely esteemed to be a crime at all.

Apart altogether from moral considerations, adulterous connections are, perhaps, the most fruitful source of ruined homes, brutality to children, and even of child murders.

GENERAL.

The sections of the code which relate to Bigamy, Marriage, Mock Marriage, Vagrancy, and so forth, do not call for special mention, save that in vagrancy cases the girls and women are commonly punished with vindictive ferocity, six or twelve months in gaol, and sometimes four or five years in a so called reformative prison, while the male criminals are as commonly let off with a trivial fine. The double standard of guilt, with its accompanying low standard of public morality, holds full sway in this community.

The sections respecting polygamy have been phrased so as to include every form of that offence as formerly practiced in Utah and elsewhere abroad, and to exclude, with a dexterity that is Satanic, the forms practiced at home.

The Dominion is without divorce laws and divorce courts. An aggrieved innocent spouse may, however, petition the Dominion Parliament. A committee of the

447

Senate inquires into the case, and, if satisfactory proof be forthcoming, reports a bill for the applicant's relief, which Parliament usually passes. Speaking broadly, the woman and the man are dealt with equally.

THE CHILD'S CHARTER.

The Imperial Parliament, first during the session of 1889, and subsequently in 1894, passed legislation that has been fittingly termed *The Child's Charter*, under which cruel treatment will be more easily prevented than hitherto, and the unhappy lot of the " child of the English savage" greatly mitigated.

The law is in two divisions, the first dealing with the ill treatment of children, and second with their employment and labor. The age has been assimilated to the age of control, to wit: sixteen years for both girls and boys. To ill treat or neglect a child or youth under sixteen is now a direct offence, and if the ill treated child's life was insured, or if any money would come to its guardian at its death, the punishments are doubled. Any one who has the care or custody of a child is required to see that it is well treated, and is himself responsible for its ill treatment by others. When a child " is found wandering," it is no longer the child who will be arrested and sent to gaol, but the unfaithful guardian. Moreover, those who cause or procure a child to be ill treated or neglected are equally culpable with those who do the evil deeds.

So far as the act deals with child labor it may be esteemed an extension of the Factory Acts. As regards such offences as begging, it is not the child beggar who is arrested and gaoled, but the person who sends it out. Street hawking is left to be dealt with by the local authorities; but here, too, it is not the child hawker that can be punished, but the person who profits by its work. The law does not in express terms recognize the great heinousness of cruelty when committed by persons in power and authority over the suffering victims, but it is a step in that direction, although in England ruffians continue successfully to plead their "ownership" of the victims in instigation of punishment. We have not yet obtained similar legislation for the Dominion, but the Province of Ontario has a somewhat similar law, the enactment of which is probably beyond its constitutional powers.

Baby farming, with its fearful mortality, is a more passive form of cruelty somewhat rampant in Canada, especially in our cities. What appears to be wanting is a more stringent law to induce, and, if need be, compel the mother to care for and nurse her child, whenever she is physically capable of doing so.

THE C. D. ACTS.

These unmentionable acts are nominally upon the Canadian Statute book. Shortly after their enactment in Britain, at the time when brotheldom held sway in the governing circles of that country, some of the governmental departments entered upon a propaganda to procure similar enactments throughout the colonies and dependencies of the Empire. These missionary efforts for the propagation of vice were remarkably successful, over twenty different colonial governments having yielded to the imperial solicitations.

The Canadian Act was passed in 1865. A final clause, inserted by the Canadian Prime Minister, read— (23) "This Act shall continue in force for five years from the passing thereof and no longer." No steps were taken to put the act in force, and in the year 1870 it expired by efflux of time and disappeared from the Canadian Statute book.

In 1886 the Imperial Parliament repealed all the acts in force in the mother country, and since that time many of the colonies have done likewise. During recent years the principle of the acts is everywhere more or less discredited. It is no longer held that state medical inspection can by any possibility make vice innoxious. As a mere matter of fact it has been proved to a demon-

449

stration that the system increases vice, stimulates lust, and multiplies and intensifies disease, so that apart altogether from moral considerations its hygienic failure suffices to condemn it.

GOVERNMENT BY POLICE.

The most serious blot on the common methods of enforcing the laws for the protection of girlhood and the conservation of public morals is the holding aloof therefrom of the reputable and law-abiding sections of the community, and the devolution of the duty on the police. The only duties proper to a police force are to protect the public in person and property, to pursue criminals and bring them to justice, to maintain public order, and to execute warrants. The Magna Charta provided that no freeman was to be "put to his law" on the uncorroborated testimony of the police, but in respect of morals we have changed all that. Now-a-days the police trepan, arrest on view, complain and witness; whereupon a police justice judges, and condemns. It is the police and nothing but the police all through. A police-ridden community does not live under law, but under mere police discretion. Whom they will they prosecute, whom they will they refrain from prosecuting and the motives in both cases are sufficiently notorious to leave unmentioned. If the duty be laid on the police "to detect crime" they will justify their existence by the easier process of manufacturing crime. Those periodic raids and woman-hunts with which we are so familiar are akin to the slave-hunts of former days, and like them serve but to degrade the victims, to corrupt the agents, and to demoralize the body politic. A truth which of all others moral reformers should keep continually before them is the unalterably inherent vileness of government by police.

CONCLUSION.

The stock objections which are constantly urged against legislation of this character may be summed up in the word "blackmail." When the British age of consent was raised from 10 to 13 years, and again from 13 to 16 years, brotheldom shouted "blackmail." And so also in many of the States. In 1887 New York raised the age from 10 to 16 years, and more recently to 18 years, in the face of similar opposition. But even were the objections valid they are inconclusive seeing it is not a proper function of law to afford men protection in the commission of vice and crime. Experience however has shown the objections to be baseless. The existing laws of all civilized countries bristle with opportunities for the bringing of false accusations, and yet such are of rare occurence. Moreover should the feared results follow they may easily be counteracted by other penal enactments.

While unprepared to assert that too much philanthropic attention is being given to reclamation, certain it is that too little has heretofore been given to prevention. Of all preventable agencies nothing can equal a decent, reputable and moral criminal code, not so much in its punitive character as in its deterrent, and especially in its educative character. Now, as in Apostolic days, the law is a most effective schoolmaster in morals, for evil or for good.

I suggest that a committee of Jurists be named by the Alliance to formulate a code of law, and thereafter to press its acceptance on all legislative bodies within its sphere.

THE REGULATION OF VICE.

Miss HARRIET A. SHINN, representing the Civic Federation of Chicago, asked a series of questions at the close of one session of the Congress, and brief, informal answers were given by several delegates. These were summarized by Miss Shinn as follows:

1. What is the result of the license system in the United States, and is it to be recommended for a city like Chicago ?

A. There is no formal avowedly license system in the United States. There was one experiment, that was St. Louis; it was a failure in sanitary, restrictive, and in every possible sense. In Berlin, where the license system is and has been in practice it is shown by actual figures that in five years prostitution increased 50 per cent.; the numbers licensed increased, and disease increased to an alarming extent; that the examinations were practically worthless, as the naked eye can detect only about one in five cases ; that even if an examination were made every day—and the law called for examination twice a week—it would still be impossible to detect disease, as it is as likely to manifest itself first in the deep recesses of the body as elsewhere; that upon a bacteriological examination 40 per cent. of those pronounced healthy were found to be diseased; and that one out of every ten of the male population of Berlin was found to be infected. Paris showed a larger per cent. The result of license is always bad, and *safety from infection cannot be had by medical examination.*

2. Is it practicable to suppress prostitution ?

A. There must first be the foundation laid by the right training before it can be totally suppressed. Investigations made in Paris, as well as Berlin and other cities, have shown that while large numbers of prostitutes have been driven from the streets by attempts to regulate vice, yet the effect has been to largely increase clandestine prostitution. That it can probably never be wholly suppressed, but it can by wise laws well enforced be reduced to a minimum, just as thievery and murder are reduced to a minimum.

3. What is the practical way to deal with it?

A. The aid of the police must be secured, and such men *only* must be put in office as will conscientiously and faithfully perform their duty; for it is useless to attempt the enforcement of law by officers who are themselves in sympathy with and friends of the inmates of such houses. That politics enters into this question, and without political aid the subject cannot be properly dealt with. That the ballot in the hands of women would do much toward its practical solution.

4. Would it be advisable to enforce existing ordinances, and throw inmates of such houses into the street?

A. If any one commits murder the question is not asked, " Shall we enforce the ordinance?" And neither should we hesitate to enforce ordinances against prostitution. That while there should be no interference with private personal freedom, yet the official recognition of such vice is no more to be permitted than murder and theft. That some provision should be made by the city to put these inmates into rescue or other homes, and that harshness towards them should be avoided.

5. Is it better to confine such houses to certain districts in a city?

A. No; emphatically no. It is bad enough to have tolerated vice, but it is infinitely worse to have vice legalized, sanctioned and encouraged by municipal authority. As far back as in Rome the experiment was tried, and it was an utter failure.

ALLIANCE MEMBERSHIP AND AUXILIARIES

The objects of the AMERICAN PURITY ALLIANCE are stated in its constitution as follows:

ARTICLE II. The objects of this Alliance are the repression of vice, the prevention of its regulation by the State, the better protection of the young, the rescue of the fallen, the extension of the White Cross among men, and to maintain the law of purity as equally binding upon men and women.

The conditions of membership in the ALLIANCE are as follows:

ARTICLE III. Any person who consents to the principles of this constitution, and who contributes annually one dollar or more to its funds, may be a member of this Alliance, and shall be entitled to a vote at the meetings.

Provisions are made for auxiliaries as follows:

ARTICLE VIII. Any Purity or White Cross association founded on the same principles may become auxiliary to this Alliance, by contributing annually the sum of five dollars to its treasury. The officers of each auxiliary association shall be ex-officio members of this organization, and shall be entitled to deliberate and vote in the transactions of its concerns.

Any one consenting to the principles of the ALLIANCE may become a member by the payment of one dollar or more annually to its treasury, and be entitled to vote at its meetings. and receive a copy of its Annual Report.

The necessary legal requirements of corporation, to enable the ALLIANCE to receive bequests, having been complied with, we give herewith the following as a suitable form to be incorporated in the will of anyone desiring thus to aid and perpetuate its important work for the promotion of purity, and the better protection of the young of both sexes:

FORM OF BEQUEST.

I give and bequeath to "THE AMERICAN PURITY ALLIANCE, ncorporated in the year 1895, under the Laws of the State of New York, the sum of..Dollars, to be used for the purposes of said ALLIANCE, and under its direction.

SOCIAL PROBLEMS
AND
SOCIAL POLICY:
The American Experience

An Arno Press Collection

Bachman, George W. and Lewis Meriam. **The Issue of Compulsory Health Insurance.** 1948

Bishop, Ernest S. **The Narcotic Drug Problem.** 1920

Bosworth, Louise Marion. **The Living Wage of Women Workers.** 1911

[Brace, Emma, editor]. **The Life of Charles Loring Brace.** 1894

Brown, Esther Lucile. **Social Work as a Profession.** 4th Edition. 1942

Brown, Roy M. **Public Poor Relief in North Carolina.** 1928

Browning, Grace. **Rural Public Welfare.** 1941

Bruce, Isabel Campbell and Edith Eickhoff. **The Michigan Poor Law.** 1936

Burns, Eveline M. **Social Security and Public Policy.** 1956

Cahn, Frances and Valeska Bary. **Welfare Activities of Federal, State, and Local Governments in California, 1850-1934.** 1936

Campbell, Persia. **The Consumer Interest.** 1949

Davies, Stanley Powell. **Social Control of the Mentally Deficient.** 1930

Devine, Edward T. **The Spirit of Social Work.** 1911

Douglas, Paul H. and Aaron Director. **The Problem of Unemployment.** 1931

Eaton, Allen in Collaboration with Shelby M. Harrison. **A Bibliography of Social Surveys.** 1930

Epstein, Abraham. **The Challenge of the Aged.** 1928

Falk, I[sidore] S., Margaret C. Klem, and Nathan Sinai. **The Incidence of Illness and the Receipt and Costs of Medical Care Among Representative Families.** 1933

Fisher, Irving. **National Vitality, its Wastes and Conservation.** 1909

Freund, Ernst. **The Police Power:** Public Policy and Constitutional Rights. 1904

Gladden, Washington. **Applied Christianity:** Moral Aspects of Social Questions. 1886

Hartley, Isaac Smithson, editor. **Memorial of Robert Milham Hartley.** 1882

Hollander, Jacob H. **The Abolition of Poverty.** 1914

Kane, H[arry] H[ubbell]. **Opium-Smoking in America and China.** 1882

Klebaner, Benjamin Joseph. **Public Poor Relief in America, 1790-1860.** 1951

Knapp, Samuel L. **The Life of Thomas Eddy.** 1834

Lawrence, Charles. **History of the Philadelphia Almshouses and Hospitals from the Beginning of the Eighteenth to the Ending of the Nineteenth Centuries.** 1905

[Massachusetts Commission on the Cost of Living]. **Report of the Commission on the Cost of Living.** 1910

[Massachusetts Commission on Old Age Pensions, Annuities and Insurance]. **Report of the Commission on Old Age Pensions, Annuities and Insurance.** 1910

[New York State Commission to Investigate Provision for the Mentally Deficient]. **Report of the State Commission to Investigate Provision for the Mentally Deficient.** 1915

[Parker, Florence E., Estelle M. Stewart, and Mary Conymgton, compilers]. **Care of Aged Persons in the United States.** 1929

Pollock, Horatio M., editor. **Family Care of Mental Patients.** 1936

Pollock, Horatio M. **Mental Disease and Social Welfare.** 1941

Powell, Aaron M., editor. **The National Purity Congress;** Its Papers, Addresses, Portraits. 1896

The President's Commission on the Health Needs of the Nation. **Building America's Health.** [1952]. Five vols. in two

Prostitution in America: Three Investigations, 1902-1914. 1975

Rubinow, I[saac] M. **The Quest for Security.** 1934

Shaffer, Alice, Mary Wysor Keefer, and Sophonisba P. Breckinridge. **The Indiana Poor Law.** 1936

Shattuck, Lemuel. **Report to the Committee of the City Council Appointed to Obtain the Census of Boston for the Year 1845.** 1846

The State and Public Welfare in Nineteenth-Century America: Five Investigations, 1833-1877. 1975

Stewart, Estelle M. **The Cost of American Almshouses.** 1925

Taylor, Graham. **Pioneering on Social Frontiers.** 1930

[United States Senate Committee on Education and Labor]. **Report of the Committee of the Senate Upon the Relations Between Labor and Capital.** 1885. Four vols.

Walton, Robert P. **Marihuana, America's New Drug Problem.** 1938

Williams, Edward Huntington. **Opiate Addiction.** 1922

Williams, Pierce assisted by Isabel C. Chamberlain. **The Purchase of Medical Care Through Fixed Periodic Payment.** 1932

Willoughby, W[estal] W[oodbury]. **Opium as an International Problem.** 1925

Wisner, Elizabeth. **Public Welfare Administration in Louisiana.** 1930

DATE DUE